the dahlia
bakery
cookbook

dahlia
bakery

the dahlia bakery cookbook

SWEETNESS IN SEATTLE

TOM DOUGLAS
and SHELLEY LANCE
Photography by Ed Anderson

WILLIAM MORROW
An Imprint of HarperCollins*Publishers*

THE DAHLIA BAKERY COOKBOOK. Copyright © 2012 by Tom Douglas. All rights reserved. Printed in China. No part of this book may be used or reproduced in any manner whatsoever without written permission except in the case of brief quotations embodied in critical articles and reviews. For information address HarperCollins Publishers, 195 Broadway, New York, NY 10007.

HarperCollins books may be purchased for educational, business, or sales promotional use. For information please e-mail the Special Markets Department at SPsales@harpercollins.com.

FIRST EDITION

Designed by Lorie Pagnozzi

Photography by Ed Anderson, photo assistant Sarah Flotard, except for page 18 by Sarah Flotard

Library of Congress Cataloging-in-Publication Data

Douglas, Tom, 1958–
    The Dahlia Bakery cookbook : sweetness in Seattle / Tom Douglas and Shelley Lance. — 1st ed.
        p.   cm.
    Includes index.
    ISBN 978-0-06-218374-3
    1. Baking.   2. Dahlia Bakery.   3. Bakeries—Washington (state)—Seattle.
    I. Lance, Shelley.   II. Title.
    TX763.D69 2012
    641.81'5—dc23
                                                                    2012018047

20   21   22   23   SCP   10   9   8   7

To all the bakers who get up soooo early . . . ya'll crazy!

the dahlia bakery team

contents

introduction

BAKERS ARE CRAZY

THE DAHLIA BAKERY COOKBOOK blends two parts of the cooking world often at odds with each other—savory chefs and pastry chefs. No one can mistake me for a baker. In fact, I'm far from it. What's the difference? you might ask. Hmm . . . indulge me for a moment. Bakers are crazy, bakers are irrational; bakers are perfectionist; bakers need to know mathematics; bakers are chemists. Need I go on? They're just smarter than the average bear and thus by nature are difficult to get on with. I don't say these things to be mean or subversive—absolutely not. I state these cold hard truths out loud as a form of recognition and . . . ah . . . respect.

It has long been insider's knowledge that cooks and bakers generally don't get along. Bakers are lonely melancholy sorts (okay, I jest) who usually start work in the wee hours of the morning, alone with their thoughts. Most are free of the chaos of the hot line and are quite happy about that.

Cooks are a scrappy lot, often feeling a bit of sting from the prior late night. When they return to work the next day, they're aggravated by the sight of the bakers, who are finishing their shifts with a knowing glance that suggests, "You naughty boys and girls stayed out a little too late, didn't you?" Cooks "throw" recipes and menus together and scramble for virtuosity, while bakers carefully measure their way to deliciousness.

There are, of course, some inescapable similarities. Ten hours on the 110-degree hot line doesn't faze a seasoned line cook in the same way cumulus clouds of flour and thousands of pounds of wet sticky bread dough don't make a serious bread baker flinch. Loading a wedding cake into a van to travel across city streets at rush hour takes a pastry chef's steely determination, as does facing down ten waiters and a ticket machine printing orders faster than the savory chefs can call them out to their brigade.

Many of these judgments of each other's profession seem to be falling by the wayside. The line between fine dining, casual café, and down-home bakery has blurred tremendously over the last twenty-five years. I for one am happy about it.

THE DAHLIA BAKERY

The Dahlia Bakery Cookbook gets you behind the scenes and into the heat of the kitchen. Our recipes run the gamut from easy to tough, but you can be assured we have tested and retested every one, so if you put in the energy and indulge yourself with the time needed, you'll be rewarded with a most delicious and, dare I say, memory-making taste.

After all, that's the fun part of writing this book—watching you, the consumer, enjoy the final product that years of effort, joy, experience, and a lifetime of trial and error have brought to these recipes.

We see it every day at the Dahlia Bakery and at our other restaurants and catering events. We hear the oohs and aahs when folks spot the silky

cream-clouded triple coconut cream pie draped with ribbons of shaved white chocolate and fat shards of flame-toasted coconut chips. We see faces, lots of faces, transformed into expressive bliss after sampling a bite, realizing that beneath the creamy coconut custard is a perfectly golden crispy shredded coconut crust. Some eyes close immediately as customers enjoy the taste of real ingredients instead of factory-made fake whipped cream and laboratory-designed distinctly unnatural flavors. Other eyes bulge open, and we can tell this just might be the best bite of pie they've had in ages.

While the coconut cream pie is what gave this little bakery its life, other Dahlia Bakery treats have inspired raw emotion as well. Peanut butter cream–filled peanut butter cookies were known to make screenwriter and novelist Nora Ephron dizzy with delight. The food website seriouseats.com says production chef Gwen LeBlanc's English muffins crafted into tasty griddled egg and ham sandwiches, spread with a touch of spicy mustard and dressed with arugula, may be the best ever. My mother even says that our savory, slightly creamy tomato soup, redolent with herbs, a touch piquant from cayenne pepper, and served with a butter-grilled Beecher's Flagship cheese and basil sandwich on "house loaf," might be as good as hers. Now that's a real compliment!

Every single pastry and savory chef who's worked with us over the years has left a mark on the Dahlia Bakery racks and in the recipe file. Chef

Shelley Lance, my coauthor and inspiration for this book, has married both sets of these skills, which are the foundation of the Dahlia Bakery to this day. When we started working together close to thirty years ago, we were immediately simpatico when it came to the dessert menu: simple, seasonal, delicious—Betty Crocker on steroids! I would say there's no finer set of taste buds in our entire company than Shelley's, and as a matter of fact she uses them many times a week as the quality control chef for all of our businesses. Shelley literally tastes her way through each menu every week to ensure that our good intentions are reflected on every single plate.

LIFE IS TOO SHORT:
EAT AN ÉCLAIR

Ever have one of those "indulgence" moments that stop you dead in your tracks? The exact definition of the word is "the act of gratifying or yielding to a wish," according to *Webster's*. Perhaps it was this morning, when you added an extra-thick layer of last spring's homemade strawberry jam to your toast. You remembered every detail of that dewy morning in June when the berries were perfectly ripe, hanging so heavy and fat with sugar they practically begged you to eat them. You could see the proud look on the farmer's face upon weighing and checkout, yet he must have noticed your lips stained the color of his crop. Not all the strawberries made it into the wooden basket, but they certainly didn't go to waste, did they? Just one bite into your ruby red jammy toast is enough to make you set aside a weekend this June to stock the larder all over again.

My particular Dahlia Bakery indulgence is a maple éclair, an almost daily treat I afford myself right at that blood sugar crash hour between 4:00 and 5:00 P.M., when lunch begins to wear off and dinner is too far away to wait. My preference is for the pâte au choux to be baked to a golden brown toast color and left to cure for a few hours. A well-made pastry cream sweetened with sticky brown maple syrup and cooked thick enough to bite through—not squirt through—comes next. To finish the éclair, heavy with the piped-in custard, it's held upside down and the top is dredged through glossy maple fondant and set to rest for an hour or so to get to a slightly crystallized finish. A shot of espresso is the perfect complement to this snack, and I'm now ready for the rest of my day.

Desserts are often classified as indulgences— more so than a 16-ounce T-bone or a nice bottle of wine. This is oddly an American phenomenon in comparison to other Western cultures. Dessert is a course, not an indulgence; it is a fitting finish, planned in accordance with the balance of the meal. To skip this is a deprivation for you and your guests. Maybe you or they are just not worth the effort? Somehow you or they don't deserve dessert? I think you do!

MIGHTY TASTY MEMORIES

Tasty memories stand in for the real thing when the desire is there but the reality is not. In a split second, your mind can transport you back to Paris and the achingly good macarons at Pierre Hermé or Ladurée or the irresistible cup of *chocolat chaud* at Angelina on rue de Rivoli. Could be you've never been to Paris. Maybe your memory bank senses a fire from your youth for the simple yet indelible Toll House cookie studded with semisweet chocolate chips, baked with brown crispy edges and a softish, chewy center, always waiting to be scooped off the cooling rack when you arrived home from school.

Of course, when the yen is too great, you must satisfy it physically. You slip a stray crumb snatched from a trimmed cake edge or take a deliberate swipe straight from the "these are for dinner so DO NOT TOUCH" pile and pop it secretly into your mouth. When it comes to actually tasting memories, nothing escapes your senses. Every nuance is important. From the audible snap of a thinly covered chocolate-dipped truffle filled with a well-aged Armagnac ganache to the sensual, honey-smooth creaminess on your tongue of a heavily yolked crème caramel. Wow . . . it's even

better than you could have imagined! You close your eyes and lapse into an ethereal *mmmm*.

A simple taste or smell easily evokes a past time or place. It's almost like a rope around your neck, a leash that yanks your back to how you became you and why the hell it matters where and how you grew up. I am absolutely the end product of years watching and helping my grandma Florence make her schnecken on the kitchen table when visiting her home on the south side of Chicago, and in later

years when she moved in with our family in Newark, Delaware. I would wake up in the morning to the smell of yeast dough as she rolled it thin with her favorite red-handled rolling pin. By the time I got downstairs, half the kitchen table was covered and ready for the next step—a thin spread of "real" butter over the entire sheet of silky dough. Then on go the brown sugar, cinnamon, and nuts and/or raisins, if desired, and it's finished with a careful roll-up of the entire lot into a squishy log of 2 feet or more. Slices of an inch or so were placed snugly into pans that were buttered, sugared, and generously dotted with pecans to make a nutty caramel when turned out hot from the oven. The coolest part of reflecting on these tasty memories, especially ones that go back to such a young age, is sitting with my mom and yakking about them, kibitzing about what I remember and what she remembers, sorting fact from hazy, sweet-laced, nostalgic recollection. My essence of self and my joie de vivre are mingled with these tastes and traditions collected from my family tree, my travels, and my relationships.

DIAMONDS AND MIXERS ARE FOREVER

When my wife, Jackie, and I were newly married and had plenty of other places to spend our money (like rent), we dedicated the cash we would normally have spent on birthday and Christmas presents for each other to buying a KitchenAid stand mixer for our ill-equipped abode. The ones we used at the restaurants beat boiled potatoes into a smooth-as-silk mash, whipped cream by the quarts, and kneaded bread dough effortlessly. We certainly had to have one at home, didn't we? We must have eyeballed them at ten different stores before we settled on the white C5 with a 5-quart bowl that came with a free sausage stuffer if we bought it that day. So romantic, right? I could have bought Jackie a diamond necklace and she wouldn't have been any happier than she was with that shiny white mixer sitting on our counter. To think how many times we've used that thing, how many Thanksgivings, Christmases, and family Sunday suppers it has been a part of, and it's there to this day, twenty-nine years later.

My mom's kitchen is anchored by a 1954 Wedgewood gas stove, certainly an indulgence when my father made the deal for it with his employer, the Rheem Co. What a '57 Chevy is to car history, Wedgewoods and O'Keefes and Merritts are to the annals of gas stoves. Ours has a white porcelain exterior with chrome top and handles. A flexible back shelf, handy for warming plates or to stow hot food until the entire dinner is ready, sits right below the clock/timer with matching salt and pepper shakers. Six gas burners are framed with cast-iron grates, and the two ovens each have a pullout broiler below them. All systems are controlled by "Robert Shaw" thermostats, top-quality thermostats still used on some of the best stoves today. Each part is easily removed for cleaning, polishing, and reassembly. Growing up, one of my jobs in the kitchen was to do just that after each meal.

What were my parents thinking by spending $260 (with my father's employee discount) on a stove when they had a mortgage, three kids, and plans for more? It's not as if they were rich. Far from it. Recently I asked my mom how they came to justify such an indulgence when there were many cheaper stoves to be had. With a wry smile she said she was smitten by its chrome detail, six burners for her fast-growing family, and especially the two ovens, so that she could bake and roast at the same time. "We needed a stove, and we knew it would last a long time because of how well it was built, so we bit the bullet, saved the money, and bought it—plain and simple." It probably was my father's commission check for the whole year, but priorities are priorities. I've been pestering my folks for the last thirty years about who's going to get this beauty in their will . . . it better be me!

If you want to be all the baker you can be, don't skimp on your equipment—board scrapers, bowl scrapers, firm rubber spatulas, a balloon whisk for whipped cream, Silpats, thick-bottomed pans, sturdy cookie sheets, parchment, stainless-steel bowls, a calibrated scale, heavy-duty measuring spoons and measuring cups (both liquid and dry), solid rolling pins that fit well in your hands. Baking is a sport in which every detail counts. Just as the right tools help make a carpenter, a well-equipped kitchen can help make the baker.

INDULGE YOURSELF

Thanks for indulging in the purchase of this book. Your passion for food, how it's made, where it came from, who grew it, and, most of all, the traditions and lore of why it's on your table can be infectious. Pass it on to your friends and family. Don't be the one who loses the recipe card file for lack of effort. Be the one who shows up on Christmas morning with home-canned brandied cherries for gifts rather than the manufactured crap. Be the one at the office water cooler telling your coworkers about the new hot bakery or restaurant down the street that is kicking serious ass. Turn your three meals a day from "I don't have time to cook" to "I can't wait for dinner!" Indulge yourself.

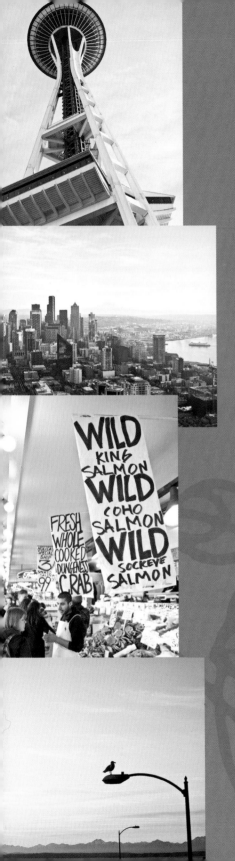

1. Dahlia Bakery—Pick up a couple coco pie bites and a cup of coffee and sit at a table outside. Get a loaf of pecan flaxseed bread and take it to eat in your hotel or throw it in your suitcase.

2. Sur La Table—The original store is in the Pike Place Market and is still the greatest place to fill any holes in your baking arsenal, from pans to parchment to pastry tips.

3. Le Panier in the Pike Place Market—One of the oldest French-style bakeries in the city. Buy a couple friande cookies and sit at the counter overlooking the market.

4. Fran Bigelow is Seattle's Queen of Chocolate. Her posh new showplace is the Fran's Chocolate next to the Four Seasons Hotel on 1st Avenue. Purchase a few of her justly famous salted caramels or a jar of intensely rich chocolate sauce.

5. Take a bus to Ballard and check out Theo Chocolate for "bean to bar" fair trade, organic chocolates.

6. While you're in Ballard, stand in line for a perfect croissant or a custardy slice of quiche at Besalu.

7. Also in Ballard, try a molten chocolate cake at Autumn Martin's new shop, Hot Cakes.

8. Take a cab to Eastlake Ave. E to my favorite of the Grand Central stores. If the crusty-edged coconut layer cake is on offer, grab a slice.

9. Take light rail to Columbia City and stop by Columbia City Bakery. The seeded baguettes are killer!

10. Need a cuppa with that pastry? You're in Seattle! Pick up a few bags of coffee beans to take home and compare. My favorite is still Starbucks (the original store is in the Pike Place Market), but also try Vivace, Vita, Zoka, and Lighthouse Roasters, to name a few other coffee bean companies that got their start in the Emerald City.

essential baking knowledge

This section gives you information for pastry-making success based on the experience of the bakers in our professional bakery facility, the Dahlia Workshop.

Read "Equipment" (page 25) to get a sense of a basic kitchen arsenal of tools.

Before you start a recipe, always read it all the way through.

Next, set up your mise en place by measuring out all your ingredients and organizing your equipment. Read "How to Measure Ingredients by Weight or Volume" (page 11) and measure carefully.

Read "How to Bring Ingredients to Room Temperature" (page 12), because room temperature can be important to a recipe's success, especially when emphasized in the headnote.

Read "Salt" (page 22) before you substitute table salt for kosher salt in any recipe calling for more than a teaspoon of salt.

Buy a timer and use it. If a recipe says, "cream the butter and sugar for 3 minutes," it doesn't hurt to turn your timer on. Always use your timer when baking.

Buy a ruler. If your dough should be rolled ¼ inch thick, check with the ruler before you roll it out too thin.

Do you know that your oven is accurate? Buy an oven thermometer and use it.

Read "How to Bake" (page 16) and rotate your baking pans in the oven as needed.

ABOUT WEIGHING INGREDIENTS

Professional pastry bakers measure ingredients by weight (ounces or grams), but most home bakers measure by volume (measuring cups and spoons). Because weighing is more accurate and there's a movement among home bakers to use weights, in this book we give both options. (Note that ounces, when they're listed next to grams in the ingredient list, are ounces by weight.)

Measuring by weight is especially useful for dry ingredients, such as flour. If you measure a cup of flour three times in a row, then put it on the scale each time, the weight will probably vary slightly each time due to discrepancies in the exact way you filled the cup.

In addition, measuring cups and spoons are not calibrated to a universal standard, so those made by different manufacturers will give you slightly different measurements. We found as much as a 1½-ounce difference in weight using 1-cup measures from different sets.

Though weights are more accurate for pastry baking, most American home cooks do still measure by volume using measuring cups and spoons, so we prioritized volume when we measured ingredients for our recipes. (In other words, we wanted to be able to say a recipe calls for "1 cup flour," not "1 cup plus 2 teaspoons flour," which might happen if we weighed out the flour first.) So, for example, we measured flour into a cup, to get the volume measurement, then we weighed that cup of flour to get the grams and ounces, rounding up or down as needed. Because volume measurements are somewhat variable (especially for flour), and because we measured by volume first and by weight second, there may be small discrepancies in the grams and ounces for an ingredient from recipe to recipe (1 cup of all-purpose flour may range in weight from 4.2 ounces to 5.2 ounces, for example), but these slight fluctuations will not affect the success of your recipe.

On the savory side of the professional kitchen, scales are not used, or needed, for measuring ingredients the way they are in the pastry kitchen. So for the savory recipes in this book, such as egg muffin sandwiches and eggs Benedicts, grilled cheese sandwiches, and stratas, we generally do not give weights (unless the ingredient is purchased by weight in the supermarket, such as a pound of potatoes). When a savory recipe includes a pastry, we give weights for the pastry but not for the savory filling.

We considered a large egg to be a measurement, since every large egg should be about the same size, so did not give weights for eggs.

Also, we did not weigh amounts of 2 tablespoons or less, since it's more trouble than it's worth. It's easiest just to use a teaspoon or a tablespoon and be done with it.

HOW TO MEASURE INGREDIENTS BY WEIGHT OR VOLUME

If you would like to weigh ingredients, purchase a good-quality battery-operated digital kitchen scale.

To measure flour and other dry ingredients by weight (grams or ounces), first set your scale to zero. Then place a lightweight bowl or other container on the scale and use the tare function to set the scale back to zero. Use a scoop to add the flour, sugar, or other ingredient until the digital readout shows the number of grams or ounces you need for the recipe.

To weigh liquids, set the scale to zero, put a volume measuring cup on the scale, and tare back to zero again. Pour liquid into the measuring cup until the digital readout shows the number of grams or ounces you need for the recipe.

To measure flour and other dry ingredients by volume (cups, tablespoons, or teaspoons), put your measuring cup or measuring spoon into the container and scoop up more than enough to fill the cup or spoon. Use a metal icing spatula set on its edge or the dull side of a knife to cut through the mound of flour a few times to allow the dry ingredients to settle into the cup. Then sweep off the excess mound of flour with the edge of the spatula or knife. As an alternative, you can scoop the ingredient into a measuring cup and follow the same procedure. You may get slightly varying weights by whether you spoon flour into the cup or scoop flour up with the cup, but the amount should not be large enough to affect your recipe.

If using a measuring spoon, use the same technique: scoop or fill the spoon to overflowing, then sweep it flat with the straight metal edge of an icing spatula or the back of a small knife.

Do not pack ingredients into the measuring cup or spoon, except when instructed to pack, as for brown sugar.

To measure liquids by volume, pour the liquid into a liquid measuring cup up to the line but not over the line, checking at eye level.

HOW TO BRING INGREDIENTS TO ROOM TEMPERATURE

For the best emulsification and aeration of a batter, it's important to have ingredients at room temperature. Cold ingredients just won't trap and hold air as well as room-temperature ingredients will, and trapped air is what makes your cakes, cupcakes, and muffins beautifully light in texture. Also, many of our recipes require softened butter, such as when butter and sugar are creamed together, and eggs and egg whites will whip to the best volume when using room-temperature eggs.

Some recipes don't really require room-temperature ingredients—for example, if you're making a batter that must rest in the refrigerator or if you're making something that doesn't have a light, delicate texture. Whenever room-temperature ingredients are especially important, we emphasize it in the headnote to the recipe.

Take butter out of the refrigerator and let it set at room temperature for a few or several hours. Or you can put butter in a microwave and carefully zap it a few seconds at a time, up to 30 seconds if necessary. Softened butter should be soft enough to offer only a little resistance when pressed with a finger but should not be so soft that it is melting.

For food safety, you don't want to leave eggs out at room temperature for too long, so the best way to bring refrigerated eggs (whether you need whole eggs, yolks, or whites) to room temperature is to put the whole eggs in a bowl of hot tap water for 3 to 4 minutes. Then, when they've warmed up, remove them from the water and break the eggs.

You can zap sour cream in the microwave a few seconds at a time to warm it up to room temperature. Milk, cream, or buttermilk can be warmed very slightly in a saucepan over low heat.

If room temperature is especially important for a particular recipe and your kitchen is cold, you may want to warm mixing bowls, especially the metal bowl for the electric mixer, with hot water, then empty and dry them before using.

HOW TO CHOP CHOCOLATE

Most top-quality chocolates will be sold as a bar, chunk, or block. For chopping chocolate, a serrated knife works best.

HOW TO SHAVE CHOCOLATE

If you have a 10-pound block of chocolate the way pastry chefs do, you can set it on your work surface and scrape across it horizontally with a large knife to make chocolate shavings. But most likely you'll buy a much smaller chunk of chocolate that's been cut from a 10-pound block. Buy a chunk that weighs at least ½ pound. The best way to shave it is to hold it vertically on your work surface (with the longest side vertical) and scrape a small sharp knife downward to produce thin shavings of chocolate.

HOW TO MAKE CHOCOLATE CURLS

You need a block of chocolate that weighs at least ½ pound; closer to a pound is even better.

The chocolate must be room temperature, not cold.

Grip a chef's knife by both the handle and the top of the blade to hold it straight and steady. Slowly pull it toward you across the chocolate in long strokes, scraping with the edge of the knife to form curls. Another method is to pull them off the block of chocolate using a vegetable peeler, but your block of chocolate must be at the perfect warm but not melty temperature. If your chocolate is too cold, you can zap the block in a microwave for a few seconds.

HOW TO TOAST AND CHOP NUTS

For the best flavor and fragrance, nuts are usually toasted before being used in a recipe. If you have only a small quantity of nuts to toast, you can place them in a heavy skillet over medium heat for a few minutes until they're lightly browned and aromatic. But for the most even toasting, place the nuts on a baking sheet in a preheated 350° to 375°F oven for 5 to 10 minutes or longer. Whether you are toasting nuts on the stove or in the oven, stir the nuts occasionally while they're toasting and watch them carefully so they don't burn. Pine nuts brown quickly, while bigger nuts such as pecan halves and hazelnuts take longer.

For some recipes, such as the Piedmontese Hazelnut Cake (page 298) and the Toasted Pine Nut Amaretti (page 139), we prefer a longer, slower toasting time for the nuts so they're toasted all the way through and not just browned on the outsides. For example, for Toasted Pine Nut Amaretti (given above), we like to toast the pine nuts for 20 minutes at 300°F. Whenever a long, slow toasting of the nuts is preferred, this is stated in the headnote to the recipe.

If the recipe calls for toasted and chopped nuts, toast them first, allow them to cool to room temperature, then chop them using a chef's knife or a food processor. When chopping nuts in a food processor or electric nut grinder, it's especially important to cool them first; then, when they're in the machine, pulse on and off briefly, taking care not to turn them into a paste. A more specialized piece of electric equipment, such as a Cuisinart electric nut grinder (see Sources), does a good job when nuts must be finely ground.

Nuts and seeds are high in oil and turn rancid quickly. For longer storage, freeze them in sealed plastic bags.

HOW TO SIFT

It's fine to use a traditional sifter with a crank handle for sifting. Traditional sifters are too small and slow for the professional kitchen, so the Dahlia Workshop bakers instead use sieves for sifting. If you would like to use sieves, you'll need a large one and a small one, depending on the quantity of dry ingredients. It's not efficient to sift a moderately large quantity of flour, for example, though a small sieve.

When sifting, shake the sieve; it helps to tap against the sieve with a metal icing spatula or some other tool. If there are lumps that don't go through the sieve, press them through with a rubber spatula or a plastic dough scraper. When sifting thicker dry ingredients, such as brown sugar or almond meal, you will probably need to use a spatula to force them through the sieve.

Kosher salt doesn't go through a sieve, so we add the salt somewhere in the process after we sift.

You can sift into a bowl, or you can sift onto a sheet of parchment paper. Dry ingredients sifted onto a sheet of parchment paper can be picked up by grasping the corners of the papers and pulling them up to create something like a tote bag for the dry ingredients; then you can pour from the parchment into a bowl. Also, you can pick up a piece of parchment and angle it so that you can pour directly into the mixer bowl of an electric mixer while the machine is running.

Sometimes you're directed to sift dry ingredients two or three times. You can sift the dry ingredients back and forth between a bowl and a piece of parchment paper, or you can use a couple of bowls.

HOW TO WHIP EGG WHITES

Make sure your bowl and whisk are clean and dry with no trace of grease.

Separate your eggs carefully so there's no trace of yolk in the whites.

You'll get the most volume if you whip room-temperature egg whites (see "How to Bring Ingredients to Room Temperature," page 12), but it's a little easier to separate eggs without getting any yolk in the whites when they're cold. If you find it difficult to separate the yolk and the white from a room-temperature egg, use a cold egg instead and let the whites sit at room temperature for a little while to warm up before beating them.

As you whip the egg whites, add the sugar gradually to get the best volume.

Egg whites whipped to stiff peaks should be smooth and glossy. Do not overwhip whites to the point where they may become broken and weepy.

HOW TO FOLD WITH A WHISK

Folding is a technique used when combining light airy ingredients, such as beaten eggs or egg whites, with heavier ingredients, such as flour, in a way that avoids taking the air out of the mixture. When folding, you combine the ingredients gently, turning the mixture over and over on itself using a flexible (rubber or silicone) spatula.

To fold with a whisk, use the same folding motion you would use with a flexible spatula, but use a balloon whisk instead. This way you work out the lumps in a muffin or cake batter at the same time you fold the ingredients together. Also, you may be able to fold everything together with a whisk using fewer motions than if you were using a flexible spatula, so you won't overwork the gluten in the flour and make the baked goods tough.

When directed by a recipe to "fold using a whisk," just be sure you use a gentle folding motion—don't beat or whip the mixture with the whisk.

HOW TO MIX BATTERS IN THE ELECTRIC MIXER

Here are some tips for using an electric mixer to mix batter. Most of this advice applies to cakes, muffins, quick breads, and even cookie doughs.

Often the recipe will specify that you beat on low, medium, medium-high, or high speed. Many electric stand mixers (such as KitchenAid) have 10 speeds. If your mixer has 10 speeds, 2 is low, 4 is medium, 6 to 8 is medium-high, and 10 is high speed.

One of the keys to beautifully textured baked goods is emulsification. To emulsify means to combine liquids that are not easily blended together. When ingredients are well emulsified, air bubbles are trapped, which lightens the finished product.

The batter will emulsify best at room temperature, so first bring the refrigerated ingredients to room temperature (see page 12). If you have heated an ingredient, like melted butter or chocolate or toasted nuts, allow that ingredient to cool to room temperature before adding it.

Often you begin a batter by creaming butter and sugar together. Start with softened butter and beat the butter/sugar mixture until it's fluffy and lighter in color, which means air has been trapped.

Break your eggs into ramekins before adding them to the mixer; don't break them directly into the mixer bowl. This way, if there are any bits of shell, you can remove them easily. If you're adding both whole eggs and egg yolks, you can break all the whole eggs into one small bowl and all the egg yolks into another small bowl; then, when directed by the recipe, tip them out one by one, carefully letting them slip out of the small bowl into the mixer bowl.

Scraping down the mixer bowl and the paddle as needed is important. Be sure to scrape thoroughly when you're creaming the butter and sugar and adding the eggs. When you add the dry ingredients, you want to be able to mix quickly and deftly with less scraping so you don't have to worry about overworking the gluten in the flour.

Before adding the dry ingredients, you can transfer them (sifted first, if specified) to a relatively narrow container, such as a 6-inch-tall plastic storage container. Then you can pour from this container directly into the mixer bowl while the mixer is running. If you've sifted dry ingredients onto a piece of parchment or wax paper, you can carefully pick up the parchment by the corners, like a tote bag, and transfer the dry ingredients from the paper to the mixer bowl.

When a recipe calls for you to alternate adding dry ingredients to wet ingredients, always end with dry ingredients.

Also, when incorporating the dry ingredients,

you don't have to completely incorporate one addition of dry into your batter before adding the next addition of wet. Incorporating the dry ingredients three-quarters of the way before the next wet addition is fine and will help prevent overmixing. Of course when you make the final addition of dry, completely incorporate it into the batter so everything is mixed together lightly but well.

After you've gone to a lot of trouble to make a beautifully aerated cake batter, don't bang the pan on the counter to level the batter in the pan or you'll lose all the air. Instead, twirl the pan or use a spatula to smooth the top. (The exception is a very thick cake batter that may need a few hard taps to get potential air pockets out of the batter before it is baked. The recipe will direct you to do this when needed.)

HOW TO ADJUST FOR THE HEAT ON AN ELECTRIC COIL BURNER

Sometimes a recipe requires changing a burner from high to medium or low. If you have a gas stove, the burner temperature will change as soon as you turn the knob. But if you have an electric stove with coil burners, the burner retains the residual heat of the coil for several minutes even after you have switched the dial. With some cooking procedures, such as for pastry creams or jellies, leaving your pot on too-high heat for even a few extra minutes can ruin the finished product.

If you have an electric stove with coil burners, we suggest you turn another electric burner coil on to the low or medium setting ahead of time so that, when needed, you can switch the pot immediately from a higher temperature to a lower one.

HOW TO BAKE

All of these recipes were tested in a conventional oven, not a convection oven. Be sure your oven temperature is accurate. The best way to do that is to buy an oven thermometer and use it every time you bake. Also, buy a timer and use it. Baking a cookie or a cake only a few minutes too long can make the difference between a perfect pastry and a mediocre one.

Whenever possible, bake in the middle of the oven, because the heat will be most accurate there. Generally, you should rotate your pan about halfway through the baking time, because most ovens are not perfectly even in temperature. But for some recipes, we advise you not to open the oven door for a certain amount of time, so don't rotate the pan until the time is up.

We tested recipes with one rack in the middle of the oven to get the most accurate temperature, but for recipes such as cookies you will probably want to put two baking sheets in the oven at the same time. The heat in the top and bottom of the oven will not be the same, so if you have two baking sheets in the oven, when you open the oven door to rotate the pans, it's important to switch them between the two racks as well. Also, if you have two baking sheets in the oven at the same time, your baking time may be slightly different from the time given in the recipe, and it may take longer to bake one of the pans than the other, so check carefully to determine when your pastries are done.

Rustic pies, because of their longer baking time in a moderate oven, were tested with two baking sheets in the oven at the same time. (So, if you cut one of these recipes in half and have only one baking sheet in the oven, your baking time may be a little shorter.)

When asked how long it takes to cook or bake something, a typical chef or pastry chef will say, "Until it's done." That means the responsibility is on you, as the baker, to make the final judgment call that something is done before you take it out of the oven.

We've given a baking time as accurately as we can for every recipe, but always look at the visual cues, not just the time. We may say "the cookies should be evenly golden brown," or we may say "a skewer inserted into the cake will come out with a few moist crumbs clinging but no batter." Always use these cues to determine when your pastry is finished baking and use the baking time as a guideline. Ovens bake differently, and there are other factors that will affect baking time—for example, the exact thickness of a cookie, or the temperature of the dough when it went into the oven, or the type and thickness of your baking pan. Of course, if you didn't check the temperature of your oven with a thermometer, and your oven is not accurate, you'll certainly need a different baking time from what the recipe directs.

If you're making a big batch of cookies and baking in batches, always be sure to cool the baking sheets before using them again. If the weather is cold (if you're baking Christmas cookies, for example), you can put the baking sheets on top of something heatproof outside the kitchen door to cool them down quickly.

Also, whenever we tell you how many cookies, éclairs, or rustic pies will fit on a baking sheet, we are assuming the size of a professional half sheet pan, which is 13 inches by 18 inches. If you're using a different-size baking sheet, you may not be able to fit the same number of pastries on it.

HOW TO TEST FOR DONENESS WITH A SKEWER

If your toothpick or wooden skewer comes out completely dry, your cake (or muffin or quick bread) may also be dry. There should be a few moist crumbs clinging to your skewer, but no wet batter.

ingredients

Almond flour: Almond flour, also called almond meal, is made of very finely ground almonds and can be found at well-stocked supermarkets and health food stores. Both Bob's Red Mill and King Arthur Flour sell almond flour in supermarkets or online (see Sources).

Almond paste: Almond paste is made from ground blanched almonds and sugar in a ratio of about 50/50, plus a little corn syrup or glycerin. You can find almond paste at well-stocked supermarkets, where it is usually sold in a can or a plastic-wrapped tube. Almond paste is not the same as marzipan, which contains more sugar.

Barley malt: Barley malt, made from sprouted barley, has a malty flavor similar to but not as strong as molasses and is available at health food stores and well-stocked supermarkets such as Whole Foods (which carries Eden's Organic

brand). If you don't have barley malt, you can substitute honey.

Butter: We prefer unsalted butter. The only recipe in this book that recommends the use of a higher-fat lower-moisture European butter such as Plugra is the "Worth the Effort" Puff Pastry recipe (page 226).

Cherries, dried: Dried cherries can be found at supermarkets, often in the bulk section, or online. We like dried cherries from Chukar Cherries, a local Pacific Northwest company (see Sources).

Chocolate: See "Our Favorite Chocolates," page 21.

Citric acid: See "About Jams and Jellies," page 352.

Cornmeal: For the cornmeal muffins, we like the slightly rustic texture of Bob's Red Mill cornmeal, but for the cornmeal tart dough, use a regular medium-grind cornmeal and do not use a stone-ground type with a rustic or coarse grind.

Eggs: We use large eggs and consider that to be a measurement, so be sure to buy eggs graded "large."

Flour: See "About Flour" (page 22).

Mascarpone: Mascarpone is an Italian triple cream cheese, available at cheese stores and supermarkets with well-stocked cheese departments.

Pectin: See "About Jams and Jellies" (page 352).

Salt: See "Salt" (page 22).

Semolina: Semolina, available at well-stocked supermarkets, is coarsely ground durum wheat. It adds texture, flavor, and golden color to cakes when used in combination with regular wheat flour.

Sugar, crystal: This is a coarse decorating sugar that can be sprinkled on the tops of muffins before baking or used to decorate frosted cupcakes or sugar cookies.

Sugar, maple: Maple sugar is made by boiling the sap of maple trees long enough to boil off all the water so that only the hardened sugar is left. It's available at well-stocked supermarkets such as Whole Foods, and it can be ordered online (see Sources).

Sugar, raw: Raw sugar, or turbinado sugar, is made by steaming unrefined raw sugar. It has a pale brown color and light molasses flavor, and it's coarser than granulated sugar.

Sugar, superfine: Superfine sugar, also known as *baker's sugar*, dissolves more quickly than regular granulated sugar, which is why we recommend using superfine in some recipes such as meringue, buttercream, delicate cakes, and jams and jellies. The Dahlia Workshop pastry bakers always use superfine sugar, so if you prefer, you can use superfine sugar instead of granulated sugar in all of our recipes calling for granulated sugar, substituting it in equal amounts.

Thyme and lemon thyme: We particularly like to use lemon thyme in desserts and pastry for the lemony fragrance and taste (and it's easy to grow in the garden or in a pot on the patio), but if you can't find lemon thyme you can substitute regular thyme. In either case, use fresh thyme, not dried.

Vanilla beans: See "How to Make Vanilla Bean Sugar" (page 64).

Vegetable oil: Use a neutral-tasting vegetable oil such as canola oil. The Dahlia Workshop bakers often use rice oil, which has a mild, light flavor but may be more difficult to find than canola oil.

Vegetable shortening: We prefer a no-trans-fat solid vegetable shortening such as no-trans-fat Crisco.

OUR FAVORITE CHOCOLATES

Chocolate pies, cookies, and cakes will be only as delicious as the chocolate you put in them, so always buy the best-quality chocolates for baking, and that includes chocolate chunks, cocoa, milk chocolate, unsweetened chocolate, and white chocolate.

For dark chocolate, referred to in this book as *bittersweet,* use a chocolate that's about 70% cacao solids (though a chocolate with at least 60% cacao solids, often called *semisweet,* will also work.) A good-quality milk chocolate should have 35 to 40% cacao solids. Unsweetened chocolate, which contains no sugar and should be 100% cacao solids, tends to be used in old-fashioned recipes, like our brownies. For the white chocolate curls on the coconut cream pie, be sure to buy real white chocolate that contains cocoa butter, not white chocolate "coating."

Theo, a Seattle chocolate maker producing premium organic and fair trade chocolate, is one of our favorites. Theo's small-batch production takes chocolate through the entire process "from bean to bar" at its factory in the Fremont neighborhood. Our pastry bakers sometimes use Theo's 74% Madagascar dark chocolate, which can be used in any recipe in this book calling for bittersweet chocolate. Theo also makes chocolate bars for eating out of hand in fun flavors like chai tea, chocolate curry, and spicy chile.

The Dahlia Workshop bakers also use a French brand, Valrhona, for dark chocolate (70%), milk chocolate (40%), and cocoa. Valrhona cocoa is Dutch processed or alkalized, which neutralizes some of the acidity and gives a darker color to the finished baked goods.

For dark, milk, and white chocolates, the fine Belgian brand Callebaut is also used in our bakery. You may find Callebaut, when sold in a supermarket, as a plastic-wrapped chunk of chocolate that was cut from a 10-pound block rather than as a bar.

Scharffen Berger, an American brand, is also an excellent chocolate. The company sells dark chocolate, milk chocolate, chocolate chunks, and cocoa.

Guittard is another fine brand of chocolate. Bittersweet and milk chocolates, white chocolate, and cocoa powder are available.

Valrhona, Callebaut, Scharffen Berger, Guittard, and Theo chocolates are available at well-stocked supermarkets such as Whole Foods and also online (see Sources).

ABOUT FLOUR

The Dahlia Workshop bakers use Shepherd's Grain flour, purchased from a local wheat cooperative. Since Shepherd's Grain is not available in retail stores, we tested the recipes in this book with King Arthur flours because they're high-quality and available nationwide at many supermarkets and online (see Sources).

For all-purpose flour, we used King Arthur Unbleached All-Purpose Flour, which has a protein content of 11.7%. The all-purpose flour is made from a blend of hard and soft wheat flours, has a 10 to 12% protein content, and is available bleached or unbleached.

For cake flour, we used Queen Guinevere Cake Flour (made by King Arthur Flour), which is a bleached cake flour with a 7% protein content. Cake flour is made from soft wheat flour and is often chlorinated, or bleached, to further break down the strength of the flour. It has a protein content of 6 to 8% and is used when a delicate and tender texture is desired in baked goods. It's possible to buy unbleached cake flour—King Arthur makes one— but we prefer bleached cake flour.

For pastry flour, we used King Arthur Unbleached Pastry Flour, which has a protein content of 8%. Pastry flour is similar to cake flour but is usually not chlorinated or bleached. It is made from soft wheat flour and has a protein content of 8 to 10%. If you prefer, you can substitute cake flour whenever a recipe in this book calls for pastry flour.

For bread flour, we used King Arthur Unbleached Bread Flour, which is high-gluten flour with a 12.7% protein content. Bread flour has a 12 to 14% protein content and is made from hard wheat flour. The high gluten content helps breads rise and gives structure.

For whole wheat flour, we used King Arthur 100% Organic Whole Wheat Flour, which is unbleached, made from red whole wheat, and has a 14.2% protein content.

You can substitute other brands of flour for the King Arthur Flour, but be sure to use the same type of flour with a similar protein content and hard or soft wheat composition. For example, instead of Queen Guinevere Cake Flour, you could use Pillsbury Softasilk Cake Flour, which has a protein content of 6.6%.

SALT

Salt is a necessary element of pastries and baked goods. It is part of the chemistry of baking.

Some of our recipes, such as the biscuits, some of the pastry doughs, and some of the chocolate desserts, may have more salt than you're used to seeing in a recipe. There are times when we season with salt a little more intensely to balance flavors. We like the way a bit of extra salt in a pecan crust balances the lush creaminess of a banana cream pie, for example, or the way a little extra salt balances the deep chocolate flavor in our brownies.

Like many chefs in professional kitchens, we

use kosher salt as our basic everyday salt, even in the pastry kitchen, so the recipes in this book call for kosher salt. Chefs do much of their seasoning by hand, and they often prefer kosher salt for the way it feels in the hand. Because kosher salt is coarser in texture than table salt, a measured tablespoon of kosher salt contains less salt than a measured tablespoon of a fine salt like table salt.

If you are using a small amount of salt, such as a teaspoon or less, it doesn't matter much if you substitute table salt for the kosher salt called for in the recipe. But if a recipe calls for a few teaspoons or more of salt, be sure to use kosher salt or, if you substitute table salt, reduce the amount by about half.

We also use sea salt in the restaurants and the bakery, but most often as a finishing salt, for example by sprinkling a few grains of sea salt on top of a biscuit. Can you substitute sea salt for the kosher salt called for in our recipes? You can if the sea salt has approximately the same coarseness as kosher salt. The most accurate way to know whether you can substitute the same amount of another salt for the kosher salt called for in a recipe is to weigh the salts and compare. If a tablespoon of your particular sea salt weighs about the same as a tablespoon of kosher salt, then you can substitute the sea salt without making adjustments. Here are some salt weights (and you can see that a tablespoon of fine table salt is twice as much salt by weight as a tablespoon of kosher salt):

1 tablespoon kosher salt = 8 grams
1 tablespoon (Morton's Iodized) table salt =
    17 grams
1 tablespoon fleur de sel = 11 grams

So if 1 tablespoon of the type of sea salt you are using weighs close to 8 grams, you can substitute it for the kosher salt called for in our recipes without making adjustments. If it weighs more than 8 grams, reduce the amount of sea salt somewhat.

equipment

Though we do note a few pieces of special equipment in the headnote to many recipes, we don't spell out every piece of kitchen equipment you'll need. The following is not an exhaustive list—you'll also need general kitchenware like bowls, cutting boards, and knives—but read it through to get a sense of what we consider a basic arsenal of tools for baking. For help finding tools, see the Sources at the back of the book.

BAKING PANS, PARCHMENT PAPER, NONSTICK MATS, AND PAPER LINERS

Baking sheets (or cookie sheets): Since a few of our cookies and pastries must be double-panned (which means setting 1 baking sheet inside another to provide more protection from the heat), you need at least 2 baking sheets; 4 baking sheets would be better. Even so, you will sometimes need to bake in batches. We use commercial-weight rimmed baking sheets measuring 18 × 13 inches, called *half sheet pans* in the industry. Another advantage of this type of baking sheet is that two pans nest together perfectly when double-panning is called for. Similar pans are available at kitchenware stores and online such as at Sur La Table and Williams-Sonoma.

Bundt pans: We use a 10-inch Bundt pan. Get one with a good nonstick coating. There are many beautiful Bundt pans, but a pan with a simple scalloped design will be easier to unmold than one with a very elaborate design.

Cake pans: We use cake pans that are 9 inches in diameter and 2 inches deep for all cakes except the Intense Chocolate Cake (page 288), which requires an 8 × 2-inch cake pan.

Loaf pans: We use a medium loaf pan measuring 8½ × 4½ × 2½ inches for the quick breads. Measure your loaf pan first; if you use a loaf pan of a different size, the baking time may differ from that specified in the recipe. A loaf pan with a nonstick coating is a plus.

Muffin pan: We use a standard 12-well muffin pan. Since we line the pan with paper muffin liners, it doesn't matter whether or not the pan has a nonstick coating.

Parchment paper and nonstick liners: We line baking sheets with parchment paper and cut circles from parchment paper to line cake pans. You can buy parchment paper at supermarkets or kitchenware stores, usually as a boxed roll of paper, but you may find better deals online. We found a package of 100 sheets of parchment paper for only $11 at Amazon.com, and you can also find precut 9-inch cake circles there. If you own a nonstick silicone mat (such as a Silpat), you can use it to line a baking sheet instead of using parchment paper. Silicone mats may seem a little pricey, but they can be used over and over.

Pie pans: We use 9-inch glass (e.g., Pyrex) or metal pie pans, about 1½ inches deep, for all of the pies in this book, except the Old-Fashioned Pumpkin Pie (page 181) and the Kentucky Bourbon Pecan Pie (page 197), which require 9½-inch pie pans, also about 1½ inches deep. You can use either metal or glass for any of the pies, but since pies in metal pans bake a little faster than pies in glass pans, your baking times may vary a bit.

Tart pans: We use two-piece metal tart pans with removable bottoms. Most of the tart recipes call for a 10-inch tart pan, except for the Toasted Pine Nut Marzipan Tart (page 245), which requires a 9-inch tart pan.

Tulip papers: The monkey bread recipe requires tulip papers for lining a muffin pan. Tulip papers are larger than standard paper muffin liners. They can be found at some kitchenware stores or online such as at kingarthurflour.com.

Cake cardboards: When you unmold a cake onto a round cake cardboard, you can move the cake to a rack for glazing, or to a cake turntable for frosting, then back to a cake plate for presentation, without disturbing the cake. If the cardboard is the same diameter as the cake, glaze or frosting will not pool on the rim, and also the cardboard won't be visible when you set the cake on a cake plate. Cake cardboards can be found at some kitchenware stores and online stores such as Sur La Table.

Cake turntable: A cake turntable consists of a large plate that revolves on top of a stand, so, as you frost a cake you can keep turning the plate as you work. A good professional-quality cake turntable isn't cheap, and it's not essential, but if you frost layer cakes frequently, it's very nice to have one.

Cooling racks: Buy a few wire racks for cooling cakes, cookies, and pastries.

ELECTRICAL EQUIPMENT

Blender: A food processor and a blender can sometimes be used interchangeably, but a blender is better for wetter, more liquid mixtures.

Deep fryer: For making the Dahlia Doughnuts (page 58) we recommend an electrostat-controlled tabletop deep fryer with a fryer basket, such as Waring Pro. Deep fryers can be expensive, but a one-basket mini deep fryer runs only $40 to $60 and can be found at kitchenware stores or online such as chefscatalog.com.

Food mill: A food mill is great for mashing cooked potatoes without overworking them and can be used to puree berries and other foods.

Food processor: A food processor is useful for many chores in the pastry kitchen, such as chopping nuts or pureeing fruits or vegetables. Also, some types of pastry dough can be made in a food processor. At times, we use the food processor to make a creamy filling perfectly smooth, as for our pastry cream, lemon curd, and chocolate cream pie recipes.

Grinders: An electric nut grinder, such as the one made by Cuisinart, is a specialized piece of equipment, but it can grind nuts beautifully without turning them into paste. Cuisinart's nut grinder will also grind spices, but you can instead use a clean electric coffee bean grinder to grind spices.

Heat diffuser: This is a metal plate or disk, possibly made of perforated steel or coated cast iron, that is placed directly over a burner before a pan is set on top. Because it spreads the heat of the burner evenly and eliminates hot spots, a heat diffuser is useful for long, slow cooking over low heat, especially if it is difficult to modulate the heat of your burner to a low setting. Heat diffusers may be found at kitchenware stores and online such as Sur La Table, Williams-Sonoma, and Amazon.

Ice cream maker: Ice cream makers are available in all price ranges from a state-of-the-art machine with a self-enclosed freezer (a dream to use, but pricey) to a motorized ice cream maker with a removable bowl or canister that must be prechilled in your freezer (such as a Cuisinart ice cream maker, easy to use and affordable) to the old-fashioned bucket and churn chilled with rock salt and ice (fun but more work and messy!).

Pizzelle iron: A pizzelle iron, which cooks batter to produce Italian-style wafer cookies, is similar to a small waffle iron. The size and pattern of the pizzelle will vary depending on the manufacturer of the machine. Buy a pizzelle iron with a nonstick coating.

Stand mixer: If you're a serious home baker, invest in an electric stand mixer. It's an expensive piece of equipment, but a good model will last just about forever in the home kitchen. An electric stand mixer comes with a wire whip, a paddle, and a dough hook. If you purchase an extra bowl, you will save time washing the bowl between uses. KitchenAid sets the bar for electric stand mixers. We also like Viking.

HAND TOOLS

Cherry pitter: You'll find that a cherry pitter is well worth the small investment when you have a pound or more of cherries to pit. You can also use it to pit olives. OXO makes a good cherry pitter.

Graters: A fine grater with a handle, such as a fine Microplane grater, is perfect for grating zest. A box grater is useful for grating cheese or raw carrots.

Kitchen spoons: A couple of large metal spoons, a solid one and a slotted one, will come in handy for a multitude of jobs, such as skimming foam from jam (solid spoon) or lifting ingredients from boiling water or oil (slotted spoon).

Pastry blender, also called *pastry cutter*: This tool, consisting of several thick parallel wires attached on both ends to a wooden or metal handle, is useful for cutting butter into flour.

Pastry brushes: Pastry brushes are useful for many tasks, such as dusting flour from rolled dough,

applying egg wash or starch water to dough, and applying syrups and glazes to cakes. You can butter a pan by using a pastry brush dipped in very soft butter.

Pastry scrapers: A metal bench knife has a rectangular stainless-steel blade and a metal or wooden handle. It's used for many tasks such as cutting or dividing a batch of dough or for scraping and cleaning your work surface. A plastic pastry scraper, which is a flexible piece of plastic shaped like a half-moon, is perfect for scraping out a mixing bowl or filling a pastry bag with buttercream. Both types of scraper can be used to lift dough as it is being rolled, to prevent the dough from sticking.

Pastry wheel cutter, also called *pizza wheel*: A sharp pastry wheel cutter can help you make clean, straight cuts in rolled-out dough.

Potato masher: An inexpensive potato masher is useful for mashing bananas and other ingredients; of course, you can mash potatoes too!

Ricer: Pushing cooked potatoes through a ricer results in a perfect "mashed" consistency without overworking the potatoes or making them gluey.

Rolling pins: Get a large wooden rolling pin that feels comfortable in your hands—whether you buy one with handles or no handles is up to you.

Scoops: Ice cream scoops give you a quick and consistent way to portion cookies, muffins, and cupcakes. If you do much baking, it makes sense to invest in a few different sizes of ice cream scoops. (See "How to Scoop Muffins, Cookies, and Cupcakes," page 74.) You can heap a scoop or underfill it if you don't have all the correct sizes. If you have a scale, you can weigh one scoop to make sure you have filled the scoop to the correct amount (if you are underfilling a 3-ounce scoop to make 2½-ounce cookie dough portions, for example). Buy ice cream scoops that have a release mechanism. You should be able to release the scoop either by squeezing the handle or squeezing a trigger. Scoops are sold by ounce size, or they may have a number. The number tells you how many level scoops you can get from a quart. So a #100 scoop (⅓ ounce or 2 teaspoons) means you could get 100 level scoops from 1 quart. A good assortment of scoops to have for making the recipes in this book: 4 ounce, 3 ounce, 2½ ounce, 1 ounce (or #50), and ⅓ ounce (or #100). This assortment works if you don't mind sometimes overfilling or underfilling a scoop (underfilling the 2½-ounce scoop to get 2 ounces for example). In addition, a ½-ounce scoop (#70) is good for making pizzelle.

Sieves: You'll need a few fine-mesh sieves, both large and small, for sifting and straining. A small fine-mesh sieve can be used for dusting cakes and pastries with powdered sugar.

Spatulas, flexible: For mixing and transferring ingredients, rubber or silicone spatulas (which are heatproof) in an assortment of small and large sizes are essential in the pastry kitchen.

Spatulas, metal: For icing cakes and smoothing batter, buy an assortment of straight and offset metal spatulas in small and large sizes.

Torch, propane or butane: A small handheld torch, used for browning the meringue on a lemon meringue tart and caramelizing the sugar crust on top of a crème brûleé, is available at kitchenware stores, hardware stores, and online. (A kitchen torch will probably be fueled by butane, and a hardware store torch by propane.)

Whisks: Buy a few whisks, both large and small. A large round balloon whisk is the whisk to use when you want to incorporate air into egg whites or to fold ingredients together to incorporate air and smooth out lumps. A straight whisk is useful for whisking ingredients together in a saucepan.

MEASURING AND WEIGHING
Kitchen scale: To weigh ingredients, use a battery-operated food scale with a digital readout. We like OXO's kitchen scale because it's easy to read (the display has an optional backlight) and comes apart so it can be cleaned.

Measuring cups and spoons: For dry measuring you need a nested set of measuring cups (we prefer stainless steel) in graduated sizes including 1/4, 1/3, 1/2, and 1 cup. Dry measuring cups have a level rim so you can sweep off excess dry ingredients with a straight-edged tool. You need a set of graduated measuring spoons ranging from 1/4 teaspoon to 1 tablespoon, and again, we prefer stainless steel. You also need liquid measuring cups in a few sizes, such as 1 cup, 2 cups, and 1 quart. Liquid measuring cups have spouts, like pitchers. Pyrex measuring cups are convenient because you can pour hot liquids into them.

Ruler: Do you really know what 1/2 inch, 1/4 inch, or 1/8 inch looks like? It's not a bad idea to double-check the thickness of your dough or the size of your dice with a ruler. A long ruler or yardstick is essential for puff pastry.

Timer: Whether a timer is built into your stove or you buy a wind-up or digital timer, be sure to use it whenever you bake.

PASTRY BAGS AND TIPS

Plastic-coated canvas pastry bags are available at kitchenware stores or online. The Dahlia Workshop bakers use disposable plastic pastry bags, which spare you the washing and drying of reusable bags. You can find them online (see Sources).

Buy a variety of metal pastry tips, both plain and star tips, in both small and large sizes. (If you use a disposable pastry bag, don't forget to cut off the part containing the metal pastry tip so you can slip out the tip before you throw away the bag!)

Sometimes a small plastic freezer bag with a bit of one corner cut off works perfectly well as a pastry bag, for piping the chocolate into our stracciatella ice cream or for piping royal icing onto cookies, for example.

POTS AND PANS

For cooking smooth, thick pastry creams, caramelizing sugar, simmering jams, and many other tasks in the pastry kitchen, good-quality heavy-bottomed pans that conduct heat well are essential. Avoid aluminum pans, which react with acids in foods, and avoid thin, flimsy pans, which may scorch the food before it is cooked.

Our favorite pans, and the favorite of many chefs, are All-Clad pans. All-Clad pans have a thick aluminum core that runs up the sides and is clad with stainless steel. This means the pans are nonreactive and conduct heat evenly, which gives you the best control. Quality cookware is an investment. These are expensive pans, but they will last forever.

THERMOMETERS

Candy thermometer, also called a *jelly* and/or *deep-fry thermometer*: A typical glass and metal thermometer usually reads in the range of 100° to 400°F. We prefer a battery-operated probe thermometer with a digital readout. It's a little more expensive, but the ease of reading the temperature is well worth it. Polder and CDN both make this type of thermometer, which you can find online, such as at Amazon.com, or at kitchenware stores and well-stocked supermarkets. If you shell out $25 for a probe thermometer with digital readout, we don't think you'll go back to an easy-to-break, bulky glass thermometer that is difficult to clip to the side of the pot and often difficult to read. Also, the range of a probe thermometer is longer than the range of a glass and metal candy thermometer and will cover temperatures from about 20° to almost 400°F, so if you have one of these, you won't need in addition an instant-read thermometer to read temperatures lower than 100°F.

Instant-read thermometer with a digital readout: This type of meat thermometer usually reads in the range of 0° to 220°F, so it's useful when checking that your English muffin dough is 80°F, for example, but the range is not high enough for cooking sugar. We prefer one with a digital readout.

Oven thermometer: This is an inexpensive purchase, but essential for knowing whether your oven is accurate.

english muffin love

ENGLISH MUFFINS AND BREAKFAST SANDWICHES

the "classic" sandwich with smoked pork loin

MAKES **4** SERVINGS

The finished "Classic" sandwich

English muffin sammies are the most popular breakfast at Dahlia Bakery. They fly out the door every morning. I was honored when Serious Eats, the website founded by my friend the food writer Ed Levine, called my Dahlia Bakery egg sandwiches one of the best breakfast sandwiches in the country.

Be sure to get the English muffins well toasted so they get crisp and crunchy. To make a great, drippy, luscious breakfast sandwich with all that soft ooze of egg yolk and cheese, you need good crunch for balance.

When the Dahlia line cooks fry eggs for breakfast sandwiches at the Bakery, they cook them over medium and even stab the yolks to get them more thoroughly cooked because customers take the sandwiches to eat on the run, and we don't want egg yolk dripping on their clothing. But at home you can cook the eggs any way you like. Over-easy eggs will give you deliciously runny yolks to add "sauce" to your sandwich!

Dahlia cooks use thinly sliced hand-cured and hand-smoked pork loin, which tastes very much like good quality ham, on the Dahlia Bakery breakfast sandwiches. Since you probably won't be able to find this product unless you make it yourself, we just call for thinly sliced ham in the recipe below.

Make Dahlia Bakery English Muffins (page 51) or just use store-bought English muffins.

2 teaspoons unsalted butter, plus more as needed for cooking the eggs

8 ounces thinly sliced good-quality ham, such as Vande Rose Duroc ham

4 English muffins, split, toasted, and buttered

About 4 teaspoons Dijon mustard

Four 1-ounce slices Gruyère or Swiss cheese

4 large eggs

Kosher salt and freshly ground black pepper

1. Preheat the oven to 450°F.

2. Put 2 teaspoons of butter in a skillet over medium heat. Divide the ham into 4 equal piles and place them in the sauté pan. Warm the ham gently, turning each pile with a spatula to warm both sides, 3 to 4 minutes. Remove from the heat.

3. Put the bottom halves of the toasted muffins on a baking sheet, buttered sides up, spread with about a teaspoon of mustard, and put a pile of ham on top. Top the ham with a slice of cheese. Put the baking sheet in the oven for a couple minutes until the cheese is melted. (If the top halves of the toasted muffins have cooled, you can place them in the oven as well.) Remove the pan from the oven.

4. Meanwhile, in a large nonstick skillet, using butter as needed, cook the eggs over easy or over medium to your liking. Season the eggs with salt and pepper to taste.

5. Place the ham-and-cheese-topped muffins halves on 4 plates. Top each one with a cooked egg, then put the other muffin half on top, buttered side down, to make a sandwich. Repeat with the remaining muffins to make 4 sandwiches and serve hot.

top: Cooking an egg on the flat top

middle: Putting a slice of cheese on top of the ham (or smoked pork loin)

bottom: Putting egg, ham (or smoked pork loin), and cheese on the bottom half of an English muffin

english muffin sandwich variations

"CLASSIC" SANDWICH WITH SAUSAGE, EGG, AND CHEDDAR

Omit the ham and the instructions for warming the ham. Use 12 ounces breakfast sausage links or 4 breakfast sausage patties. Cook the sausage and drain off the fat. If using links, cut them in half lengthwise and place 2 or 3 sausage halves (depending on the size of your links) or 1 sausage patty on the bottom half of each toasted and buttered muffin. Instead of Gruyère, top the sausage on each muffin half with a 1-ounce slice of cheddar. Put the muffin halves on a baking sheet, melt the cheese in the oven, cook the eggs, and finish the sandwiches as in the master recipe.

"CLASSIC" SANDWICH WITH BACON, EGG, AND CHEDDAR

Proceed as for the sausage egg sandwich variation, using 8 strips of cooked and drained bacon, or 2 slices per sandwich, instead of the sausage. Top the egg with a small mound of arugula before placing the top half of the muffin on the sandwich.

the "prosser farm" sandwich with perfectly ripe tomatoes

MAKES 4 SERVINGS

Make this sandwich when ripe, delicious tomatoes are in season. We use tomatoes from our Prosser Farm in eastern Washington. Your own garden tomatoes or tomatoes purchased from the farmers' market will be perfect here, whether they are heirloom varieties or not. If your tomatoes are small, use a couple slices for each sandwich instead of just one. Instead of parsley, tarragon, and chives, you can use any combination of fresh herbs that you like.

All of our breakfast sandwiches can be varied to suit your taste and mood. For example, add some arugula leaves on top of the egg before sandwiching the muffin together. Or, for a super-deluxe sandwich, make the mashed avocado from the Grilled Cheese with Bacon and Avocado Sandwich (page 344) and spread the avocado on the top halves of the muffins before sandwiching the tops and bottoms together.

Make Dahlia Bakery English Muffins (page 51) or just use store-bought English muffins.

SPECIAL EQUIPMENT: ELECTRIC MIXER OR FOOD PROCESSOR (OPTIONAL)

4 ounces soft fresh goat cheese (chèvre) (about ½ cup)

3 tablespoons heavy cream

2 teaspoons finely chopped fresh flat-leaf parsley

1 teaspoon finely chopped fresh tarragon leaves

1 teaspoon thinly sliced fresh chives

Kosher salt and freshly ground black pepper

4 English muffins, split, toasted, and buttered

4 large slices tomato (1 or 2 ripe, flavorful tomatoes)

Unsalted butter as needed for cooking the eggs

4 large eggs

1. Put the goat cheese and cream in the bowl of an electric mixer with the paddle attachment and beat until the cheese is softened. (Or you can use a food processor, or you can beat the cheese by hand.) Add the herbs and mix to combine. Season to taste with salt and pepper.

2. Put the toasted muffins on 4 plates, buttered sides up. Spread some herbed goat cheese on the bottom half of each muffin on each plate, dividing it evenly. Then top the cheese with a slice of tomato.

3. Meanwhile, in a large nonstick skillet, using butter as needed, cook the eggs over easy or over medium to your liking. Season the eggs with salt and pepper to taste.

4. Top the tomato on each sandwich with a cooked egg. Put the other muffin half on top, buttered side down, to make a sandwich. Repeat with the remaining muffins to make 4 sandwiches and serve hot.

Prosser is a small town, 160 miles east of our Seattle restaurants, in Washington State's high desert country. If it weren't for the swollen Yakima River filled with snowmelt from the volcanic Cascade Mountains, virtually nothing would grow in this area but tumbleweeds and jackrabbits. With the river's flow, Prosser is teeming with apples, cherries, grapes, hops, onions, potatoes, pears, apricots, alfalfa, and livestock. Wineries sprout up on the grassy plateaus of the Horse Heaven Hills and in strip malls in town faster than I can keep track.

My wife, Jackie, is farmer in chief along with "Grandma Sharon," my mother-in-law, and "Pop Pop" Jim Cross, who does all the carpentry on the farm. I'm not sure we realized just how much work farming is, but we also completely underestimated the satisfaction of bringing in the crop. Each year we've expanded the acreage under till with just under six acres planted now. Because we're organic, there's the inevitable battle of wills against the aphids that love the broccoli, the rabbits that munch the lettuce and beans, the mice that always seem to know when the cantaloupes are ripe before we do, the starlings who have an inner refractometer set for the sweetness of our gorgeous apricots and cherries, and the neighbor's bull, who will knock the fence down and munch anything and everything in his path.

The natural hot-weather crops (or should I say "sun" crops, because, unlike Seattle, Prosser gets more sunshine than any place else in Washington) do the best. Most folks just don't realize how big the rain shadow of the 14,500-foot Mt. Rainier is and its powerful effect on both the Seattle weather, with 40 inches of rain west of it, and the Prosser weather (5 inches of rain) east of it. This year we reaped 20,000 pounds of tomatoes from 2,400 plants. That's 83 pounds per plant—wow. Five kinds of eggplants, from the aubergine fat globes to the pristine purple elongated Japanese finger eggplants, made their way to Lola's baba ghanoush and Etta's teriyaki. Peppers, neon colored like you can't believe, ripen with ease and find themselves mixed with chanterelles for an earthy peperonata at the Dahlia and pickled for the porchetta sandwich at the Rub Shack. A special few plants of spicy Thai red chiles are reserved for me to crush the pinky-finger-size wrinkled pepper into a mix of fragrant garlic and fermented black mung beans, producing a musky condiment that's perfect with my favorite brunch dish, Dungeness crab foo yung (You can find the recipe in *I Love Crab Cakes*.)

Sugar Pie pumpkins reign in the squash section of the garden. It's fun to think of their eventual destination while they're just blossoming in July. Our pastry chef, Stacy Fortner, will slice and roast them; then they are pureed and added to a custard to fill her fabulous pumpkin pies. Sugared cranberries and maple-roasted pecans finish the top before they grace some 300 Thanksgiving tables every year.

Each season Jackie works with the chefs of our joints to refine her production down to the tastiest varieties as voted on by the team. We collect compostable scrap from our restaurants year-round and send it off to Cedar Grove, a family-owned Pacific Northwest organic recycling company, to be churned into moist, crumbly, beautiful black compost. In winter it's returned to the fields and spread over the naturally sandy soil for enrichment. From there the rows and quadrants get planted according to sun and rotation patterns. During the annual plant the first week of May it's quite a treat to watch the kitchen and front-of-the-house teams poking seeds into the soil, sowing a crop that they will in turn cook and serve in a few short weeks or months. This is the ultimate in knowing where your food comes from, don't you think?

the "seattle" sandwich with cured wild salmon

Here's an English muffin sandwich with moist, salty lox, mellow herbed cream cheese, and the sweet-spicy kick of pickled onions.

You won't need all the pickled onions, but the leftover onions can be covered and refrigerated for several days. Drain and add them to salads or sandwiches. Try them on a tuna fish salad sandwich.

Make Dahlia Bakery English Muffins (page 51) or use store-bought English muffins. You can make your own cured wild salmon or just buy lox or lox-style smoked salmon.

NOTE: CARDAMOM IS AVAILABLE AS PODS OR SEEDS. IF YOU BUY THE PODS (WHICH STAY FRESH A VERY LONG TIME), YOU WILL HAVE TO SMASH THEM WITH A SMALL HEAVY PAN OR THE SIDE OF A HEAVY KNIFE AND EXTRACT THE TINY BLACK SEEDS.

SPECIAL EQUIPMENT: ELECTRIC MIXER OR FOOD PROCESSOR

pickled onions

1 small to medium red onion (about 7 ounces), thinly sliced

½ cup red wine vinegar

½ cup water

⅓ cup sugar

2 bay leaves

1 teaspoon black peppercorns

1 teaspoon cardamom seeds (see Note)

1 teaspoon kosher salt

dilled cream cheese

4 ounces (½ cup) cream cheese

2 tablespoons heavy cream

1 tablespoon minced fresh dill

Kosher salt and freshly ground black pepper

sandwiches

4 English muffins, split, toasted, and buttered on top halves only

6 to 8 ounces thinly sliced Wild Salmon Gravlax (page 42), lox, or lox-style smoked salmon (about 12 slices)

Unsalted butter as needed for cooking the eggs

4 large eggs

Kosher salt and freshly ground black pepper

1. To make the pickled onions, put the onion in a heatproof bowl and place a fine strainer over the bowl. Put the vinegar, water, sugar, spices, and salt in a small saucepan over medium heat and heat to a gentle simmer, stirring occasionally to dissolve the sugar. Pour the pickling liquid through the strainer and over the onions, discarding the spices in the strainer. Allow the onions to sit at room temperature until cool. When the onions are cool, use a slotted spoon to remove as many as you like for your sandwiches and drain them on paper towels. Cover the remaining onions with plastic wrap and reserve them, refrigerated, for another use. They will last for about a week.

2. To make the dilled cream cheese, put the cream cheese and cream in the bowl of an electric mixer with the paddle attachment and beat until the cream cheese is softened. (Or you can use a food processor.) Add the dill and mix to combine. Season to taste with salt and pepper, but use a light hand with the salt because the lox is salty.

3. Put the muffins on 4 plates, cut sides up. Spread a fourth of the dill cream cheese on the bottom (unbuttered) half of each muffin on each plate and top the cream cheese with 3 slices of lox.

4. Meanwhile, in a large nonstick skillet, using butter as needed, cook the eggs over easy or over medium to your liking. Season the eggs with salt and pepper to taste.

5. Top the lox on each sandwich with a cooked egg and top the egg with some of the drained pickled onions. Put the other muffin half on top, buttered side down, to make a sandwich. Repeat with the remaining muffins to make 4 sandwiches and serve immediately.

left: Putting dilled cream cheese on the bottom half of an English muffin

middle: Slices of wild salmon gravlax placed on top of the cream cheese on the muffin

right: After the egg is placed over the gravlax, the pickled red onions are put on.

wild salmon gravlax

Gravlax is not difficult to make, but curing is a 2- or 3-day process, so plan accordingly.

It's best to use a piece of salmon that is no more than an inch or two thick. A thicker piece will take longer to cure. A salmon fillet with the skin on will help you slice the gravlax paper-thin after it is cured.

SPECIAL EQUIPMENT: ELECTRIC COFFEE GRINDER OR SPICE GRINDER, TWEEZERS OR NEEDLENOSE PLIERS

cure

⅔ cup kosher salt

⅔ cup granulated sugar

¼ cup packed brown sugar

1½ teaspoons paprika

1 teaspoon ground juniper berries (see page 43)

1 teaspoon ground fennel seeds (see page 43)

¼ teaspoon cayenne

salmon

1¼ pounds salmon fillet, preferably wild, preferably skin on, pin bones removed (see page 43)

1. Combine the cure ingredients in a small bowl. Sprinkle the bottom of a nonreactive pan, such as a glass baking dish, with about ½ inch of the cure and place the fish in the pan, skin side down. Blanket the fish with the remaining cure, which should form a layer about 1½ inches thick.

2. Cover the salmon with a piece of wax paper and another smaller pan, then weight it with a few cans. Refrigerate for 2 to 3 days, until the salmon is quite firm to the touch; the exact amount of time will depend on how thick your piece of salmon is. Remove the wax paper and the cans, then use a rubber spatula to scrape the cure from the salmon. Remove the salmon from the pan and briefly rinse it, then pat it dry with paper towels. Slice the gravlax very thinly on the bias.

3. The gravlax will last for up to a week, tightly wrapped in plastic wrap and refrigerated.

how to grind spices

For the best flavor, buy whole spices and grind them yourself. Buy two electric coffee grinders so that you can use one for grinding coffee beans and set one aside just for grinding spices. You can also grind spices with a mortar and pestle, which is fun to use though it takes more muscle.

how to bone salmon

Salmon has rows of pin bones in its flesh. Run your fingers along the surface of the fillet to locate them. Pull them out one by one with tweezers or needlenose pliers.

green eggs and ham bennies with scallion hollandaise

In the immortal words of Dr. Seuss, "I do not like green eggs and ham"—except at the Dahlia Lounge, where they're pretty damn delicious!

Though the Dahlia cooks make hollandaise the classic way, whisking by hand, this recipe employs a blender method, which is an easy and almost foolproof way to make hollandaise at home. Keep in mind that the melted butter should be as hot as possible when you start adding it to the blender. Pour it from the saucepan into a Pyrex measuring cup while it's still almost bubbling hot and start adding it as soon as possible to the yolks in the blender to get the thickest, creamiest texture. Because the scallions add a distinctly green tint to the hollandaise, you can call this "green eggs and ham"!

Make the hollandaise first and keep it warm while you poach the eggs. You can keep a bowl of hollandaise warm over a saucepan of hot, but not simmering, water, but don't let your hollandaise get too hot or it will break. A great way to keep hollandaise warm without worrying about breaking it is to pour it into a Thermos container.

Dahlia cooks hand-cure and smoke pork loin, which they thinly slice for the eggs Benedict. You can use any good-quality thinly sliced ham. You can also use, per muffin half, a single thicker slice of ham or a slice of Canadian bacon. Sauté the thicker slice of ham or Canadian bacon on each side until lightly browned and warmed through.

Make Dahlia Bakery English Muffins (page 51) or just buy English muffins.

SPECIAL EQUIPMENT: BLENDER

scallion hollandaise

½ cup thinly sliced scallions, green parts only

3 large egg yolks

2 tablespoons hot water

1 cup (2 sticks/8 ounces) unsalted butter

2½ teaspoons freshly squeezed lemon juice

Kosher salt and freshly ground black pepper

eggs benedict

2 teaspoons unsalted butter

12 ounces thinly sliced good-quality ham, such as Vande Rose Duroc ham

4 English muffins, split, toasted, and buttered

2 ounces arugula (about 4 cups very loosely packed leaves)

8 eggs, poached (see page 46)

1. Bring a saucepan of salted water to a simmer and have a bowl of ice water ready. Add the scallions to the simmering water, cook for 15 seconds, then drain. Plunge the scallions into the bowl of ice water, then drain again. Using your hands, squeeze out as much moisture as possible. Put the scallions into the container of a blender and blend for a few seconds. Add the egg yolks and blend for a few seconds more. Add the hot water and again blend for a few seconds. (Don't worry if the scallions still seem pretty chunky at this point; they will continue to puree later when you add the butter.)

2. Meanwhile, put the butter into a small saucepan over medium-high heat and cook until melted. When the butter is melted and very hot—bubbling hot is best—immediately pour it into a Pyrex liquid measuring cup. Remove the knob from the blender lid and immediately start pouring the hot butter through the hole in the lid, gradually and steadily. Draping a kitchen towel over the hole and the measuring cup will help cut down on splatters. When all the butter has been incorporated into the hollandaise, add the lemon juice and season to taste with salt and pepper. Transfer the hollandaise to a container and keep warm while you finish the Eggs Benedict.

3. To finish the Eggs Benedict, put the 2 teaspoons of butter in a large sauté pan over medium heat. Make 8 equal piles of the sliced ham and place them in the sauté pan. Warm the ham gently, turning each pile with a spatula to warm both sides, 3 to 4 minutes. Remove from the heat.

4. Put the split, toasted, and buttered English muffins on 4 warm plates. Top each muffin half with a pile of sliced ham. Top the ham with a pile of arugula, then top each muffin half with a poached egg. Ladle hollandaise over each egg, dividing it evenly, and serve immediately.

This technique uses a higher ratio of vinegar to water than you usually see in egg-poaching instructions. But the vinegar, which coagulates protein, helps keep the poached eggs from forming a lot of strands and strings, so they look nice and tidy. Don't worry; your finished poached eggs won't taste like vinegar.

It's important to keep the poaching liquid at a gentle simmer. You don't need to do a lot of swirling or other energetic activity with your eggs—if you practice a few minutes of patience they will poach themselves!

For this recipe we used a heavy 4-quart pan about 10½ inches in diameter that could easily hold at least 4 eggs at a time. If your pan is a bit smaller, you can use less water, but keep the proportions of water, vinegar, and salt the same. You should have a depth of at least an inch of poaching liquid in your pan.

1. Put 2 quarts water, 1 cup distilled white vinegar (or other colorless vinegar), and 2 tablespoons kosher salt in a large wide pan over medium-high heat. Bring the water to a simmer, then reduce the heat to a very gentle simmer.

2. Break the eggs into ramekins. Tip the eggs into the water, poaching them in batches if necessary. Don't stir; give the egg a few seconds to set up. Then, using a slotted spoon, nudge them up off the bottom of the pan to be sure they don't stick. Continue to cook the eggs at a very gentle simmer, lifting them occasionally with the slotted spoon. To check that an egg is done, lift it out of the water and touch it gently with your finger. The white should be set and the yolk should bounce back a little.

3. When the eggs are done (about 4 minutes for runny yolks, but you can cook them to your liking), remove them from the water with a slotted spoon. Set the spoon on a clean, dry kitchen towel for a moment to drain before placing the egg on your English muffin.

4. You can place the poached eggs in a bowl of hot water for a few minutes to keep them warm if you are poaching in batches and not quite ready to plate them. Then lift them out, drain on paper towels, and serve.

how to poach eggs

etta's dungeness crab eggs bennies
with lemon dill hollandaise

MAKES **4** SERVINGS

Etta's, our seafood restaurant in the Pike Place Market, often changes up the flavor of hollandaise by adding ingredients like chipotle or crab "butter." But this simple, classic combo of lemon and dill never fails to satisfy.

This hollandaise recipe is made the classic way, by hand with a whisk. But if you prefer an easier method, you can make it in a blender instead, following the method for scallion hollandaise (page 44). Make the shallot reduction first. Blend the yolks and hot water in the blender. Add the shallot reduction to the blender, then start adding the hot melted butter as in the scallion hollandaise recipe.

Make the hollandaise first and keep it warm while you poach the eggs. You can keep a bowl of hollandaise warm over a saucepan of hot, but not simmering, water. (Don't let your hollandaise get too hot or it will break.) A great way to keep hollandaise warm without worrying about breaking it is to pour it into a Thermos container.

For a vegetarian Eggs Benedict, omit the crab and add some sautéed wild mushrooms to each muffin half, on top of the wilted spinach.

Make the Dahlia Bakery English Muffins (page 51) or just buy English muffins.

lemon dill hollandaise

1 tablespoon finely chopped shallot

3 tablespoons champagne vinegar or other mild vinegar

3 large egg yolks

2 tablespoons hot water

1 cup (2 sticks/8 ounces) unsalted butter

2 teaspoons finely chopped fresh dill, plus a little more for garnish

1½ teaspoons freshly squeezed lemon juice

Kosher salt and freshly ground black pepper

eggs benedict

2 tablespoons unsalted butter

6 ounces fresh spinach leaves, washed, dried, and stems trimmed (about 12 cups loosely packed leaves)

8 ounces fresh Dungeness crabmeat, picked over for bits of shell, or substitute other fresh local crabmeat such as blue crab

4 English muffins, split, toasted, and buttered

8 eggs, poached (see page 46)

1. To make the hollandaise, first make the shallot reduction. Put the shallot in a very small pan or skillet and cover with the vinegar. Cook over medium-high heat, adjusting the heat as needed, until all the liquid is cooked away, 5 to 6 minutes. Remove the pan from the heat and set the shallot reduction aside.

2. Set up a saucepan with 2 or 3 inches of water and bring it to just under a simmer over medium heat. Choose a saucepan that will be large and wide enough to hold a metal bowl and function as a "water bath."

3. In the metal bowl that you have chosen for your water bath (but not over the heat), using a whisk, whisk the egg yolks lightly together. Lightly whisk in the hot water (you can measure it out from the water in the saucepan), then set the bowl over the saucepan of barely simmering water. (The hot water should not be touching the bottom of the bowl.) Use your whisk to whisk the yolks in a back-and-forth motion. Don't whisk in any air and don't get the eggs up the sides of the bowl, where they will scramble and cook. Be sure the water in the saucepan is hot but barely at a simmer. Turn the heat down or turn it off if you think the yolks are in danger of curdling. Keep steadily whisking the yolks back and forth until very thick (but not scrambled or curdled), 3 to 4 minutes.

4. Remove the bowl from the heat and whisk in the shallot reduction. Meanwhile, melt the butter in a small saucepan over medium heat. Transfer the butter to a Pyrex liquid measuring cup to make pouring easier. Add the hot butter to the eggs *very* gradually, whisking constantly (you don't have to do the careful back-and-forth whisking here; just whisk vigorously and steadily) until all the butter is added. (Here are some tips for whisking in the butter: Make a cradle with a kitchen towel to steady your bowl as you add the melted butter. Even better, find someone to help you. One person can hold the bowl and the other can whisk, and you can trade off so your arms don't get so tired!)

5. When you are finished adding the butter, if your hollandaise is thicker than you like it, whisk in a tablespoon or more of hot water. Add the dill and lemon juice and season to taste with salt and pepper. Keep the hollandaise warm while you finish the Eggs Benedict.

6. To finish the Eggs Benedict, put the 2 tablespoons butter in a large sauté pan over medium heat. Add the spinach leaves and cook gently for a few minutes, just until they

begin to wilt. Push the spinach to one side of the pan and add the crab. Heat the crab very gently for a moment, then remove the pan from the heat.

7. Put the split, toasted, and buttered English muffins on 4 warm plates. Top each muffin half with some of the spinach, then with the warm crabmeat. Then top each muffin half with a poached egg. Ladle hollandaise over each egg, dividing it evenly, garnish with chopped dill, and serve immediately.

dahlia bakery english muffins

As with most everything in our restaurants, if we serve it, we make it. Chef Gwen LeBlanc, our inspiring head baker, created this English muffin recipe years ago and has been astounded that every day she has to make more and more because of their popularity. Even though this is an exacting recipe that takes some time, the reward is a feather-light muffin, nice and yeasty with excellent nooks and crannies, that crisps up beautifully when toasted— the perfect marriage with Orange Marmalade (page 356) or as a cradle for Etta's Dungeness Crab Eggs Bennies (page 47).

The details, such as the temperature of the water and dough and accurate measurements of all the ingredients, are very important. Because adding water to the dough is a crucial step, we use the bread baker's lingo of "first portion of water" and "second portion of water."

A thermometer is essential because your water must be 68°F, and your dough, after mixing, must be between 75° and 80°F. If you use your thermometer to make sure that your water is at the correct temperature, your dough, after mixing, will most likely also be at the correct temperature.

The English-muffin-making process involves several hours of resting and proofing. You can finish the process in one long session or, if you prefer, you can break it up into a two-day project by refrigerating the dough overnight at the point where it is ready to be shaped into individual muffins.

English muffins freeze well. Cool the muffins completely and place them in resealable plastic freezer bags. For the best texture, freeze them whole, not sliced. The day before you're ready to eat them, pull as many muffins as you need from the freezer and thaw them overnight on the kitchen counter or in the refrigerator. The next morning, slice the muffins in half and pop them into the toaster.

SPECIAL EQUIPMENT: ELECTRIC MIXER, INSTANT-READ OR DIGITAL PROBE THERMOMETER, POTATO MASHER (OPTIONAL), METAL BENCH SCRAPER (OPTIONAL)

top: Turning the English muffin dough

bottom: The English muffin dough after it has been turned

dough

1 medium Yukon Gold or other waxy potato (5 to 6 ounces/140 to 170 grams)

First portion of water: 1⅓ cups (11 ounces/310 grams) water, at 68°F (cool tap water)

3 cups (14¾ ounces/418 grams) bread flour

¼ cup (1 ounce/28 grams) whole wheat flour

1 tablespoon honey

2½ teaspoons kosher salt

1¼ teaspoons active dry yeast

Second portion of water: ⅓ cup (2½ ounces/70 grams) water, at 68°F

Olive or vegetable oil for oiling your hands and the bowl

for dusting the pans

2 tablespoons all-purpose flour, plus more for dusting the work counter

2 tablespoons cornmeal

1. Cut the potato into 1-inch chunks, leaving the skin on. Put the potato into a small saucepan and cover with cold water. Bring the water to a boil, reduce to a simmer, and cook until the potato is tender, 8 to 10 minutes after the water is simmering. Drain the potato, transfer to a bowl, and, using a potato masher or a fork, mash the potato with the skins on. Measure the mashed potato. You should have a well-packed ½ cup (4 ounces/120 grams) of mashed potato. Discard any excess potato and place the ½ cup of mashed potato in the refrigerator to cool. When the potato is completely cool, start your dough.

2. Pour the first portion (1⅓ cups) of water (the water must be at or close to 68°F; use your thermometer to check) into the bowl of an electric mixer fitted with the paddle attachment. Add both flours, the cooled potato, the honey, salt, and yeast. Mix on low speed for 10 minutes. You should have a soft dough that is sticky, stretchy, and wraps around the paddle. Scrape down the dough. Turn off the mixer and allow the dough to rest in the bowl for 5 minutes.

3. After the dough has rested, turn the mixer to medium speed and mix the dough for another 1 or 2 minutes. At this point the dough should be wound around the paddle and will be stronger, tighter, and stretchier. With the machine running, start adding the second portion (⅓ cup) of water (the water must be at or close to 68°F) about 2 tablespoons at a time. Wait until an addition of water is absorbed before adding more

water. (It is very important to add the water gradually, in about 3 additions.) When all the water has been added, allow the dough to mix for another 2 minutes, until a smooth and shiny dough is formed. Use your thermometer to take the temperature of the dough. The dough must be between 75° and 80°F.

4. (If the temperature of your water was 68°F, the temperature of your dough should be in this range. But if the dough is cooler than 75°F, you can place the dough in a warm place for a little while and check the temperature again. If the dough is more than 80°F, you can place the dough in a cool spot for a little while.)

5. Oil a large bowl. Place the dough in the bowl and roll and flip over into a ball, then cover the bowl with plastic wrap. Place the bowl in a slightly warm place and allow it to rest for 30 minutes. (Slightly warm means warm room temperature. If your kitchen is 68° to 70°F or so, just letting the dough sit on the counter is fine. If your kitchen is cooler than this, find a slightly warm spot, such as near the stove. You do not, however, want to put the dough in a place that is too warm.) After the 30-minute rest, uncover the bowl so you can "turn" the dough. Rub some oil on your hands before turning the dough, because the dough is sticky. Use your hands to reach over to the side of the bowl farthest from you and pull straight up on the dough on that side, stretching it upward. (Stretch it up as far as you can without pulling it so far that the length of dough will break.) Then drop the dough as you fold it over toward the side of the bowl closest to you. Give the bowl a quarter turn and repeat, pulling the dough on the side of the bowl farthest from you, stretching it straight up, then folding the dough over toward the side of the bowl closest to you. Continue giving the bowl a quarter turn, and stretching and turning the dough, until you have gone around the circumference of the ball of dough a total of 4 turns.

6. Then turn the dough over, cover it again with plastic wrap, and return it to the slightly warm (68° to 70°F) place to rest for another 30 minutes. Again,

left: Rolling and shaping English muffins using both hands on work surface

middle: Rolling and shaping an English muffin using one hand on work surface

right: Rolling and shaping an English muffin between your hands

"turn" the dough with oiled hands as described on page 53, working your way around the circumference of the ball of dough a total of 4 times. Then cover the bowl, return it to the slightly warm (68° to 70°F) place, and allow the dough to rest for an hour (which adds up to 2 hours total resting time of the dough). The dough should be sticky, bubbly, and active.

7. At this point you can either finish the English-muffin-making process in a single day and continue to shape, proof, and bake the English muffins or cover the bowl of dough with plastic wrap and put it in the refrigerator overnight. (If you plan to finish in one day but need a stopping point, you can also refrigerate the dough at this point for an hour or more.)

8. When you are ready to shape and bake the English muffins, combine the 2 tablespoons flour and 2 tablespoons cornmeal (for dusting the pans) in a small bowl. Line 2 baking sheets with parchment paper and dust them with the flour-cornmeal mixture. Set the pans aside.

9. Generously flour a work surface (because the dough is sticky), then dump the dough out onto it (removing it from the refrigerator if the dough has been refrigerated). Using a floured metal bench scraper or a floured knife, cut the dough into 12 equal pieces. To shape each muffin, place a portion of dough on the floured work surface and pull the dough up and over itself (in other words, try to fold the dough roughly in half), flipping the portion of dough over so the floured side is now facing up. Scoot the dough to an unfloured or only lightly floured part of the work surface and roll the portion of dough with the palm of your hand cupped over it, using a rolling motion and rolling the dough firmly between the palm of your hand and the work surface, to shape each muffin into a round shape. Ideally, the top part of the dough, which is under your palm, is floured, and the stickier bottom side of the dough will give you some traction with the unfloured work surface. Another way is to roll each portion of dough firmly between the palms of both hands instead of on the work surface, flouring your hands if needed. Rolling this soft dough into nice round balls takes practice, but don't worry if your results are not perfect—your finished muffins will look a little more rustic but will taste just as delicious!

10. Place 6 English muffins on each prepared baking sheet, spacing them evenly. Cover the rolls of dough with clean kitchen towels and put them in a slightly warm *but not hot* place (see "How to Proof English Muffins," page 55) until they have doubled in size, which will take 1 hour to 1 hour and 45 minutes if the dough has not been refrigerated and will take about 2 to 2½ hours if the dough has been refrigerated.

11. When the English muffins have doubled in size, the dough will feel a little less sticky to the touch. Also, when you press gently on the dough, it will feel light and airy, not dense, and you may see some bubbles. Meanwhile, preheat the oven to 425°F.

12. Put the pans in the oven and bake the muffins for 8 minutes (see "How to Bake," page 16). Remove the pans from the oven and flip each muffin over to the other side. Use your hand to give each muffin a firm pat to flatten it slightly—but do it quickly and be careful of the hot steam! (You can protect your hand with a folded dish towel if you like.) Rotate the pans and return them to the oven, switching them between the racks. Bake the muffins until they are golden and baked through with a few browned patches, about 8 minutes more (about 16 minutes total baking time).

13. Remove the pan from the oven and cool on a wire rack for at least 30 minutes, then slice each English muffin crosswise in half and toast. For longer storage, place whole muffins in plastic freezer bags, then thaw before slicing and toasting.

After you have portioned the dough for English muffins and shaped them into round balls, the muffins must proof in a slightly warm spot until doubled in size. If there is a spot in your kitchen that is around 70°F, you can just leave the muffins there, covered with kitchen towels.

If your kitchen is cooler than this, you can turn your oven on to 200°F and put a couple of inverted baking sheets on top of the stove. Then put some folded towels on top of the inverted baking sheets. Finally, put the baking sheets with the shaped English muffins (which are covered with kitchen towels) on top of the folded kitchen towels. (This set-up protects the dough from getting too warm; you don't want the muffins to proof too quickly.) Leave the oven on for 30 to 45 minutes or so until the area has warmed up, then turn the oven off for the remaining proofing time. Allow the muffins to proof until doubled in size, about 1 hour to 2½ hours, depending on whether or not the dough was refrigerated before shaping.

When you are ready to preheat the oven to 425°F, be sure to remove the baking sheets with the balls of English muffin dough from the top of the stove first so that they don't get overly warm.

how to proof english muffins

the dahlia doughnut

DAHLIA DOUGHNUTS AND MONKEY BREAD

dahlia doughnuts with cinnamon sugar, mascarpone, and jam

MAKES ABOUT 30 DOUGHNUT HOLES; SERVES 6

These brioche doughnuts are a fun, decadent way to finish a meal or to start your day. When Giada de Laurentiis named them her favorite doughnut on Food Network, it was a struggle to keep up with how many we were selling. Everyone should have such problems!

After the doughnuts are fried and drained, we pop them into a small paper bag filled with a few tablespoons of cinnamon sugar, then fold over the top of the bag. The Dahlia server then runs the bag of warm doughnuts to the customer at the table, shakes the bag to coat the doughnuts with cinnamon sugar, and cuts off the top of the paper bag with scissors. Little pots of vanilla mascarpone and house-made jam seal the deal. Serve the doughnuts with any good-quality jam or try the jam and jelly recipes in this book.

Originally, at the bakery, we used round cutters to make doughnut holes, but the brioche scraps became overwhelming as the doughnuts grew in popularity. Now the bakers simply use knives and yardsticks to cut the sheet of brioche into neat little squares with no leftover scraps. At home, it's easy enough to use a round cutter, but if you prefer you can cut 1½-inch squares instead.

After you sugar the doughnuts, if you want to keep them warm for a short while before serving, put them on a rack set inside a baking sheet in a preheated 200°F oven. But the best way is to set out dishes of mascarpone and jam on the kitchen counter and eat the doughnuts right out of the fryer as soon as they've been cinnamon-sugared.

The brioche dough for the doughnuts must be made ahead and chilled for at least 6 hours or overnight, so plan accordingly.

NOTE: IT'S IMPORTANT TO KEEP THE OIL AS CLOSE AS POSSIBLE TO 350°F THE ENTIRE TIME THE DOUGHNUTS ARE BEING FRIED. THIS DOUGH IS VERY TEMPERATURE SENSITIVE, AND THE DOUGHNUTS MAY FORM LARGE BUBBLES INSIDE IF THE TEMPERATURE IS NOT EXACTLY RIGHT. ALTHOUGH WE USUALLY CONSIDER A PAN FITTED WITH A FRYING THERMOMETER AND FILLED WITH A FEW INCHES OF OIL A PERFECTLY GOOD METHOD FOR DEEP FRYING AT HOME, FOR THIS RECIPE, A TABLETOP DEEP FRYER WITH A CONTROLLED THERMOSTAT IS HIGHLY RECOMMENDED. YOU CAN PURCHASE A SMALL BUT PERFECTLY ADEQUATE DEEP FRYER FOR $50 TO $60 (SEE SOURCES).

NOTE: BE SURE TO CUT YOUR DOUGHNUTS INTO 1¼- TO 1½-INCH ROUNDS (OR, IF YOU PREFER, SQUARES). IF YOUR DOUGHNUTS ARE A DIFFERENT SIZE, THE FRYING TIME SPECIFIED IN THE RECIPE WILL NOT BE ACCURATE.

SPECIAL EQUIPMENT: AN ELECTRIC-THERMOSTAT-CONTROLLED DEEP FRYER WITH A FRYER BASKET (RECOMMENDED), 1¼- TO 1½-INCH ROUND CUTTER

Vegetable oil spray as needed

1 batch Basic Brioche Dough for Doughnuts (page 61), chilled for at least 6 hours or overnight

Canola or other neutral-flavored vegetable oil as needed for deep frying

for serving

1 cup (7 ounces/200 grams) sugar

2 tablespoons ground cinnamon

Vanilla Bean Mascarpone (page 63)

Good-quality jam (your favorite, or see pages 353 to 364)

1. Spray a parchment-lined baking sheet with vegetable oil spray and set aside.

2. Mix the sugar and cinnamon together and spread the mixture in a baking pan (such as 9 × 13) and set aside.

3. Remove the dough from the refrigerator and place it on a lightly floured work surface. Using a lightly floured rolling pin, roll the dough to a ¼-inch thickness. (Check the thickness with a ruler, because if your dough is more than ¼ inch thick, the doughnuts will not fry properly.) Use a 1¼-inch to 1½-inch round cutter to cut the doughnuts, cutting the rounds as close together as possible to get the best yield. (For the best-textured doughnuts, do not reroll the scraps.)

4. Place the doughnuts on the prepared baking sheet and cover loosely with a clean kitchen towel or a piece of plastic wrap sprayed with vegetable oil spray and placed greased side down over the doughnuts. Allow the doughnuts to rise at room temperature (or in a slightly warm place if your kitchen is cool) until they have increased their size by about 50 percent (the dough should increase by half again; you can use a ruler to check), about 1 hour. (Be careful not to let the dough overproof at this point. The dough should not double!) After the doughnuts have risen, place them in the refrigerator for at least 30 minutes or up to 3 hours before frying.

5. Fill a tabletop electric deep fryer with oil according to the manufacturer's instructions and preheat it to 350°F. When the frying oil is at the correct temperature, start out by frying only 1 or 2 doughnuts to get the knack.

6. Keep the rest of the doughnut holes in the refrigerator, right until they are ready to go into the oil. The dough must be kept cold until it is slipped into the oil; otherwise it may overproof and form bubbles. The oil must be kept at 350°F at all times, as this dough is very temperature sensitive.

7. After you drop a few doughnuts into the hot oil, use a slotted spoon to gently and steadily flip them back and forth until they begin to take on some color. The doughnuts will float and not sink. This step "sets" the doughnut and keeps it from forming a bubble on the side that is not immersed in the oil. When the doughnuts have taken on a little color, continue to cook them on both sides (flipping them less frequently now) until both sides are browned. When both sides are evenly golden brown (about 2 minutes *total* frying time), use the slotted spoon to remove the doughnuts from the oil and drain them on paper towels. To check that you have cooked the doughnuts long enough, use a knife to cut one of the doughnuts open. If it's not cooked through, adjust the timing to fry the rest of the doughnuts a little longer. After the fried doughnuts have drained briefly, transfer them to the baking pan with the cinnamon-sugar mixture and roll to coat them on all sides.

8. Continue to fry the doughnuts in small batches (no more than 4 at a time, because you have to pay attention to flipping them). If needed, keep the fried and sugared doughnuts warm for a brief time in a preheated 200°F oven. When all the doughnuts have been fried and coated with cinnamon sugar, transfer them to a platter and serve immediately, accompanied with ramekins of vanilla bean mascarpone and jam. To eat a doughnut, cut it open with a small knife and spoon in some of the jam and mascarpone.

Frying the doughnuts

Dropping the doughnuts into a paper bag

Pouring cinnamon sugar into the bag

Shaking the bag to coat the doughnuts with cinnamon sugar

basic brioche dough for doughnuts

MAKES ENOUGH DOUGH FOR ABOUT
30 DOUGHNUT HOLES OR 6 MONKEY BREADS

This dough was developed specifically for making Dahlia doughnuts, and is not as rich and buttery as a classic brioche, so don't use it for making a top-knotted *brioche à tête.*

Before starting this recipe, be sure your butter is softened and your eggs and milk are at room temperature. If you put the milk in a saucepan and warm it slightly to bring it to room temperature (see "How to Bring Ingredients to Room Temperature," page 000), use a digital or probe thermometer to be sure that it is not warmer than 80°F.

To find a warm place in your kitchen for the brioche dough to rise, see "How to Proof Brioche for Doughnuts and Monkey Bread," page 62.

SPECIAL EQUIPMENT: ELECTRIC MIXER

¼ cup plus 1 tablespoon (2½ ounces/70 grams) milk at room temperature (not more than 80°F)

1 teaspoon active dry yeast

1⅓ cups (7⅓ ounces/207 grams) bread flour

2 tablespoons sugar

¾ teaspoon kosher salt

2 large eggs at room temperature

5 tablespoons (2½ ounces/70 grams) unsalted butter, softened, plus more for buttering the bowl

1. Combine the milk and yeast in the bowl of an electric mixer, using the whisk attachment to combine. Set aside for about 10 minutes to allow the yeast to proof.

2. Add the flour, sugar, salt, and eggs to the bowl of the mixer and fit it with the dough hook. Mix on medium speed, stopping to scrape the bowl down a few times, and continue mixing until the dough wraps itself around the dough hook and pulls away from the sides of the mixing bowl, about 20 minutes. Stop the mixer, scrape the dough off the dough hook using a rubber spatula or a plastic dough scraper, and put the dough back into the bottom of the mixer bowl.

3. Turn the mixer (still fitted with the dough hook) back to medium speed and begin adding the butter a couple tablespoons at a time, allowing the butter to be fully incorporated after each

Brioche contains a large proportion of butter and must rise in a spot with a warm but not hot temperature. Professional bakeries have proof boxes for keeping the rising brioche dough at the ideal 90°F, but the home cook will have to find another way to create a warm environment. One way is to turn your oven to 200°F and place a folded towel on a baking sheet. Set the bowl of brioche dough, loosely covered with plastic wrap, or the pan of shaped but unbaked monkey breads on the towel, then set this on top of the range, which will have warmed up from the heat of the oven. (You can leave the monkey breads uncovered because they will rise over the top of the pan.) Allow the brioche dough or the pan of monkey breads to proof the amount of time directed in the recipes, but if at any point during the rising time the bottom of the bowl or the bottom of the pan begins to feel hot, turn the oven off.

If your oven and range top are separate, you will need to find another spot to proof. Pastry chef Garrett's trick is to turn on your clothes dryer for a while and set the dough, on its towel-lined baking pan, on top. If you want to use the inside of your oven as the warm spot, you must be careful that it is not too hot. Put an oven thermometer inside and turn it to 200°F, then turn the oven off. When the oven thermometer reads 90°F, place your bowl or pan inside.

Whether your dough is proofing on top of a low oven or inside an off oven, be sure to move the bowl or pan to another spot when you preheat your oven for baking.

addition, until all of the butter has been added. (If the butter sticks to the sides of the mixer bowl, use a rubber spatula to scrape it back into the dough and keep mixing. Eventually it will incorporate into the dough.) When all the butter has been incorporated, remove the dough from the mixing bowl and place it in a clean, lightly buttered bowl and cover loosely with plastic wrap. Place the dough in a warm place and allow to double in size, about 3 hours.

4. When the dough has doubled, remove it from the container and place it on a lightly floured work surface. The dough will be soft and sticky—a plastic pastry scraper is a useful tool for getting the dough out of the bowl. Flour your hands and punch or slap the dough to get rid of any air bubbles. Rebutter the bowl and put the dough back in it. Loosely cover the bowl with plastic wrap and refrigerate for 6 hours or overnight.

vanilla bean mascarpone

Are you a cream-filled doughnut person (like me) or a jelly-filled doughnut person (like my wife)? Now you can have both.

We serve Dahlia doughnuts with ramekins of house-made jam and vanilla bean mascarpone. Try a dollop of this rich Italian triple cream cheese, flecked with vanilla bean seeds and lightly sweetened, next to a wedge of fruit pie or a slice of plain cake, or just topping a bowl of fresh summer berries.

1 vanilla bean

1 cup (8 ounces/230 grams) mascarpone

¼ cup (2 ounces/55 grams) sugar

⅛ teaspoon kosher salt

½ cup (4 ounces/110 grams) heavy cream

1 teaspoon pure vanilla extract

Split the vanilla bean in half lengthwise and scrape out the seeds with the tip of a small knife. Put the vanilla bean scrapings in a bowl and reserve the pod for another use. (See "How to Make Vanilla Bean Sugar," page 64.) Add the mascarpone, sugar, and salt to the bowl and mix together using a rubber spatula. Gradually add most of the cream (hold back a few tablespoons), stirring with the rubber spatula until the mixture is smooth and there are no lumps of mascarpone. Add the remaining cream and the vanilla extract and, using a whisk, whisk until the mixture thickens and resembles a thicker, richer version of softly whipped cream. Cover the vanilla bean mascarpone and keep refrigerated until you are ready to use it (up to 5 days).

Vanilla beans, which are the seed pods of an orchid, are expensive, but their sweet fragrance and intensely pure vanilla flavor can't be beat. Vanilla beans are first fermented, then dried, so they last a long time. Store them in a covered container at cool room temperature.

You won't want to waste any part of your precious vanilla beans, so make vanilla bean sugar with the scraped-out pods. Put the pod in a large jar or other container that has an airtight lid, and cover it with sugar. You can keep adding pods to the container of sugar whenever you have them. If the pod has been steeped in liquid for a recipe, rinse and dry it before adding it to the sugar. Be sure to keep adding sugar as needed, to keep the pods buried. Store the vanilla sugar for at least 2 or 3 weeks before using.

You can use the vanilla sugar as is, but for the most bang for your buck, when pods are completely dry and a little crumbly, put everything in the food processor and process until the pods are ground up. Sift the sugar through a fine-mesh sieve to remove pieces of vanilla pod, then store the vanilla bean sugar in an airtight container. (This processed sugar is now actually superfine sugar, and it's fine as an equal substitution for granulated sugar.)

You can use vanilla sugar pretty much anywhere granulated sugar is called for in a recipe, whenever you want to add vanilla flavor. Vanilla bean sugar is especially nice in the fillings for fruit pastries and crisps. If you are using vanilla bean sugar in a recipe that calls for a vanilla bean, if you like, you can omit the vanilla bean. Or if the recipe calls for 2 vanilla beans, you can use only 1 vanilla bean and the vanilla sugar.

The exceptions are when sugar is going to be cooked to a high temperature (for candy making) or caramelized and you don't want any tiny bits in your sugar that may increase the danger of crystallization, or when superfine sugar is preferred and crystallization is an issue, as for jam and jelly making. In these cases, use regular granulated sugar or superfine sugar.

Vanilla beans are expensive and may cost $3 apiece or more in a supermarket. If you bake often, and are willing to buy 10 to 16 beans at a time (you can split them up with a friend), you can often find better deals online or at a large wholesale store such as Costco, sometimes at less than a dollar apiece. See Sources.

monkey bread

We developed this recipe to use up brioche scraps left over from prepping the Dahlia doughnuts. Now we make extra dough just to make this delicious cinnamon pull-apart.

Tulip papers are similar to paper muffin pan liners, but they are larger and rise higher over the wells of a muffin pan, and they look more dramatic and glamorous. It takes extra effort to purchase tulip papers, but we think it's worth it because the monkey breads won't rise as high in a standard muffin liner and the finished pastry won't look as attractive. Also, as the dough rises and expands in the oven, you need the extra room a tulip paper provides to get all that streusel on top.

To find a warm place in your kitchen for the monkey breads to rise see "How to Proof Brioche for Doughnut and Monkey Bread," page 62.

For a festive holiday brunch, you could double this recipe to make 12 monkey breads (don't forget to double the streusel recipe as well). Use 2 muffin pans and stagger 6 in each pan.

You can take the recipe to the point of putting the brioche squares in the freezer and leave them in the freezer overnight instead of for 30 minutes. Finish prepping your monkey breads the next morning (don't forget you'll need a 2½-hour rising time before baking), and they can be freshly baked in time for an afternoon brunch.

The brioche dough must be made ahead and chilled for at least 6 hours or overnight, and the monkey breads need to rise for about 2½ hours before baking, so plan accordingly.

SPECIAL EQUIPMENT: MUFFIN PAN AND TULIP PAPERS (SEE SOURCES)

1 batch Basic Brioche Dough for Doughnuts (page 61), chilled for at least 6 hours or overnight

½ cup (4¼ ounces/121 grams) sour cream

¼ cup (2 ounces/60 grams) sugar

2 teaspoons ground cinnamon

Cinnamon Vanilla Streusel (page 68)

Dreamy Caramel Sauce (page 69)

1. Remove the dough from the refrigerator and place it on a lightly floured work surface. Using a rolling pin, roll the dough to a ¼-inch thickness. Use a knife to cut the sheet of brioche into roughly ¾-inch squares. (You need pieces that are approximately ¾ inch in size. Don't worry about the pieces of brioche being completely uniform in size or shape.) Arrange the brioche pieces in a single layer on a parchment-lined baking sheet and place it in the freezer until the dough is completely frozen, about 40 minutes.

2. When you are ready to bake the monkey breads, line 6 wells of a 12-cup muffin pan with tulip liners. Place the liners in alternating cups so the monkey breads are spaced apart from each other. (The monkey breads will rise and overflow the cups a bit as they bake, and this way they won't flow into each other.)

3. In a large bowl, combine the sour cream, sugar, and cinnamon, whisking to combine. Add the frozen pieces of brioche and mix well until all the pieces are well coated.

4. Divide the brioche mixture evenly among the tulip liners. Place the muffin pan in a warm place until the breads double in size, about 2½ hours. When the monkey breads are doubled, they will rise to the tops of the muffin cups (not to the tops of the tulip liners, which extend well above the muffin pan), and they will be slightly domed. While the breads are rising, preheat the oven to 375°F.

5. Sprinkle the top of each monkey bread with streusel, dividing the streusel evenly among the cups. (This will seem like more streusel than you need, but use it all, because the tops of the monkey breads rise dramatically in the oven.)

6. Put the muffin pan in the oven and bake until the brioche is cooked and the monkey breads are deep golden brown on top, 24 to 26 minutes. Remove the pan from the oven and allow to cool on a wire rack for 5 to 10 minutes. Remove the monkey breads from the muffin cups and serve warm with ramekins of caramel sauce for dipping.

Making caramel is potentially dangerous, because hot sugar can give you a serious burn. Never touch hot sugar, and keep a bowl of ice water nearby in case you accidentally get some hot sugar on yourself.

You can caramelize dry sugar, or you can dissolve it first in a little water. Unless you're caramelizing only a small amount of sugar, it's a little easier to control the process if you dissolve the sugar first.

In a pan over low heat, stir the sugar and water until you have a clear solution, occasionally brushing down the sides of the pan with a clean pastry brush dipped in water. When the sugar has dissolved completely, turn the heat up to high to allow the sugar to caramelize. After the heat is turned up, don't disturb the sugar-water solution by stirring, or you may cause crystallization. It's important to prevent crystals from forming, because if they do, the mixture will seize up, forming a slushy clump, and you'll have to throw it away and start over.

If a dark brown color forms in one corner of the pan, carefully swirl the pan to distribute the color. When the syrup is uniformly golden brown, immediately remove the pan from the heat. Sugar burns quickly, and it will continue darkening even after removed from the heat.

how to caramelize sugar

cinnamon vanilla streusel

MAKES ENOUGH FOR 6 MONKEY BREADS OR
1 QUART STREUSEL ICE CREAM

Streusel, a crumbly mixture for topping cakes and pastries, means "sprinkled" or "strewn" in German. Here's a simple version with the homey flavors of brown sugar, butter, and sweet spices.

SPECIAL EQUIPMENT: FOOD PROCESSOR (OPTIONAL)

6 tablespoons (1¾ ounces/50 grams) all-purpose flour

2 tablespoons packed brown sugar

1½ teaspoons pure vanilla extract

½ teaspoon ground cinnamon

½ teaspoon ground ginger

½ teaspoon kosher salt

2 tablespoons (¼ stick) unsalted butter, softened

1. Put the flour, brown sugar, vanilla extract, spices, and salt in the bowl of a food processor. Add the butter, breaking it up into several small clumps and scattering it around. Pulse several times and keep pulsing until the mixture looks shaggy. When you turn off the machine, you should be able to squeeze some of the mixture together with your fingers to make clumps.

2. If you prefer to make this by hand, put the flour, brown sugar, vanilla extract, spices, and salt in a bowl and stir to combine. Add the softened butter in clumps, then use your fingers to work the butter into the dry ingredients until the mixture is shaggy.

3. If you are making monkey breads, transfer the streusel to a bowl, cover, and refrigerate until you are ready to top the cakes. If you are making streusel ice cream, follow the instructions in the recipe for baking and cooling the streusel.

dreamy caramel sauce

We love caramel sauce drizzled over Pear Tarts (page 222) or used as a dipping sauce for Monkey Bread (page 65), but it's also delicious ladled over a scoop or two of vanilla ice cream.

The burners on different types of ranges produce varying levels of heat. The amount of time it takes to caramelize sugar will vary depending on how hot your burner is when set to high heat. Pay attention to the color of the sugar more than to the amount of time.

When selecting a heavy-bottomed saucepan, choose one that is deep enough to hold the cream and allow it to sputter when it's added to the caramelized sugar. A 3- or 4-quart heavy saucepan is perfect (see "Pots and Pans," page 30).

You can make caramel sauce ahead and store it, covered, in the refrigerator for a few days. Warm it in a double boiler before serving.

1⅓ cups (9 ounces/250 grams) sugar

⅓ cup (2½ ounces/75 grams) water, plus more for brushing as needed

1 cup (8 ounces/235 grams) heavy cream

2 tablespoons (¼ stick) unsalted butter at room temperature

Read "How to Caramelize Sugar" (page 67) before beginning. Place the sugar and water in a heavy-bottomed saucepan over medium-low heat, whisking occasionally until the sugar is completely dissolved, 3 to 4 minutes, brushing down the sides of the pot with a clean pastry brush dipped in water as needed. After the sugar is dissolved, raise the heat to high and bring the mixture to a boil, undisturbed, until the syrup turns a deep amber, 6 to 12 minutes or more, depending on the heat of your burner. If you see the sugar caramelizing in only one corner, you can gently tilt or rotate the pan to distribute the color evenly, but do not whisk. When the syrup has colored nicely, remove the pan from the heat and immediately add the cream. Be careful and stand back, because the mixture will sputter. Do not stir until the mixture settles. Return the pan to low heat and stir with a wooden spoon until the strands of caramel melt. Remove from the heat and stir in the butter. Serve warm.

good morning!

MORNING PASTRIES

<<< *On the sheet pan from left to right: Carrot Muffins with Brown Butter and Currants; Cornbread Bacon Muffins; Blueberry Buttermilk Muffins; Best Bran Muffins*

cornbread bacon muffins

Every year for the last three years we've run an event called Baconopolis in our event space, the Palace Ballroom, and it sells out, to the steady drumbeat of the blogsters and the tweeters, to a 300-person capacity almost as soon as the post goes up on our website. At Baconopolis we taste and compare different bacons like Seattle's own Bavarian Meats, Nueske's from Wisconsin, and Black Pig bacon from Sonoma. Participants taste each bacon on its own and then graze through a multitude of bacon-packed treats. This moist cornbread muffin that packs a wallop of maple-glazed-bacon flavor is one of the recipes we developed for Baconopolis, and it soon became a Dahlia Bakery staple.

Use your favorite bacon. Cook the bacon first so it can cool while you measure out the rest of the ingredients. For cornmeal, we like Bob's Red Mill.

SPECIAL EQUIPMENT: MUFFIN PAN AND PAPER LINERS, 2½-OUNCE SCOOP (OPTIONAL)

5 strips (6 ounces/170 grams) thick-sliced bacon, cut into ⅛-inch-thick julienne

⅓ cup plus 2 tablespoons (5 ounces/ 142 grams) maple syrup

3 large eggs at room temperature (see "How to Bring Ingredients to Room Temperature," page 12)

⅓ cup (2¾ ounces/78 grams) canola or other neutral-tasting oil

⅓ cup (2¾ ounces/78 grams) sour cream at room temperature

⅓ cup (3 ounces/85 grams) milk at room temperature

1 cup plus 2 tablespoons (5¾ ounces/ 160 grams) all-purpose flour

¼ cup plus 2 tablespoons (2¼ ounces/ 63 grams) packed brown sugar

1 tablespoon baking powder

¾ cup (4¾ ounces/130 grams) cornmeal

⅔ cup (3 ounces/84 grams) chopped toasted pecans (see "How to Toast and Chop Nuts," page 13)

1½ teaspoons kosher salt

1. Preheat the oven to 375°F. Line a muffin pan with paper liners and set aside.

2. Put the bacon in a pan over low heat and cook until the bacon is golden brown and the fat has rendered out. Drain the bacon, reserving both the bacon and the bacon fat, separately.

3. Return the bacon to the pan over medium heat and add 2 tablespoons of the maple syrup. Cook, stirring occasionally, until the syrup is reduced and coats the bacon, about 5 minutes, adjusting the heat as necessary so the syrup doesn't burn. Set the glazed bacon aside to cool.

4. In a bowl, using a whisk, combine the eggs, oil, bacon fat, sour cream, milk, and reserved $1/3$ cup maple syrup. Set the wet ingredients aside.

5. In a large bowl, sift together the flour, brown sugar, and baking powder. Stir in the cornmeal, pecans, and salt. Make a well in the dry ingredients. Add the wet ingredients and the glazed bacon to the well and fold the batter together using the whisk (see "How to Fold with a Whisk," page 14) just until everything is combined.

6. Scoop the muffin batter into the paper-lined muffin pan, using about 2½ ounces (generous ¼ cup) per muffin and dividing the batter evenly (see "How to Scoop Muffins, Cookies, and Cupcakes," page 74).

7. Bake until the tops of the muffins are golden brown and the muffins are baked through, 22 to 24 minutes, rotating the pan halfway through the cooking time. A wooden skewer inserted into a muffin should come out with a few crumbs clinging but no batter.

8. Remove the muffin pan from the oven and cool on a wire rack for about 10 minutes before unmolding.

Professional bakers use ice cream scoops of various sizes to scoop muffins, cookies, and cupcakes. It's a good way to ensure uniform portion size, and it's quick and convenient. If you like to bake, it's not a bad idea to invest in a few scoops of various sizes.

If you don't have a scoop, the recipe generally gives you both an ounce size (weight) and a cup size (volume). For example, a recipe may say "scoop 2½-ounce or ¼-cup portions of cookie dough." If you have a digital kitchen scale, you can check 1 or 2 cookie or muffin portions on the scale to get an idea of how big a single portion should be.

Of course, if you are scooping muffins or cupcakes, you are dividing all the batter among the 12 wells of the muffin pan, and the scoop (or ounce or cup) size is just a convenience to help you divide the batter quickly and evenly.

If you are scooping cookies, the baking time will be accurate only if your scoop (or ounce or cup) portion of cookies is the same size specified in the recipe. If you portion your cookies to a different size, you will have to keep an eye on them and adjust the baking time accordingly. (By the way, any time we specify how many cookies you can place on a baking sheet, we assume you are using an 18- by 13-inch pan. If you are using a smaller pan, you may need to bake in more batches.)

If you do have a scoop, but it's not the exact size, you can overfill or underfill it. So, if, for example, we specify using a 2½-ounce scoop and you have only a 3-ounce scoop, you can underfill it. If you have a kitchen scale, check the first scooped portion to be sure you really are scooping 2½ ounces with your 3-ounce scoop.

For more information on scoops and scoop sizes, see page 29.

carrot muffins with brown butter and currants

The warm, nutty flavor of brown butter is a natural companion to the earthy sweetness of carrots. Add currants, orange, and spice to create a muffin layered with flavor.

First make the brown butter and plump the currants in simmering water so the butter and currants will have time to cool to room temperature while you measure out the rest of the ingredients.

SPECIAL EQUIPMENT: MUFFIN PAN, PAPER MUFFIN LINERS, ELECTRIC MIXER, 3-OUNCE ICE CREAM SCOOP (OPTIONAL)

1 cup (2 sticks/8 ounces/227 grams) unsalted butter

½ cup (2 ounces/60 grams) dried currants

½ cup (4 ounces/115 grams) water

1¾ cups (10 ounces/285 grams) all-purpose flour

2 teaspoons baking powder

¾ teaspoon ground cinnamon

¾ teaspoon ground ginger

4 large eggs at room temperature (see "How to Bring Ingredients to Room Temperature," page 12)

1 cup (7 ounces/200 grams) granulated sugar

1½ teaspoons grated orange zest

2 teaspoons pure vanilla extract

¾ teaspoon kosher salt

1 cup (5 ounces/142 grams/about 2 medium) peeled and grated carrot (use the largest holes of a box grater)

Raw (turbinado), granulated, or crystal sugar and kosher salt as needed for sprinkling

1. Preheat the oven to 375°F. Line the muffin pan with paper liners and set aside.

2. To make the brown butter, place the butter in a small saucepan over medium-high heat and cook until the butter solids are browned and smell toasty, stirring constantly, about 3 minutes or a little longer. Watch carefully so the butter does not burn. As the butter browns, the foam rises to the top and dark brown particles stick to the bottom of the pan. As soon as the butter is dark golden brown, pour it into a small bowl and set aside to cool to room temperature. (You can put the bowl in the refrigerator to cool more quickly, but do not let the butter solidify.)

3. Combine the currants with the water in a small saucepan and bring to a simmer over medium-high heat. Simmer until the currants are plump, about 10 minutes. Remove the currants from the heat, drain, and transfer to a small bowl to cool to room temperature.

4. Into a bowl, sift the flour, baking powder, cinnamon, and ginger together twice, then set the dry ingredients aside (see "How to Sift," page 13).

5. In the bowl of an electric mixer, combine the eggs, sugar, orange zest, vanilla, and salt. Using the whisk attachment, whip on medium-high speed until thick and pale, about 3 minutes. The egg mixture should begin to "ribbon" but not hold the ribbon. (In other words, when you lift the whisk, you will start to see a ribbon forming, but it will dissipate quickly.)

6. Remove the bowl from the mixer. Without stirring, place the carrots and currants on top of the egg mixture. Then pour the dry ingredients on top and, using a rubber spatula, gently fold everything together. Finally, fold in the browned butter, combining everything thoroughly but gently.

7. Scoop the muffins into the paper-lined muffin cups, dividing it evenly, using about 3 ounces, or about ⅓ cup, of batter per muffin (see "How to Scoop Muffins, Cookies, and Cupcakes," page 74).

8. Lightly sprinkle about ¼ teaspoon raw sugar and a pinch of kosher salt on top of each muffin. Bake until the muffins are cooked through and golden, about 18 minutes, rotating the pan once halfway through the baking time. A wooden skewer inserted into a muffin should come out with a few crumbs clinging but no batter.

9. Remove the pan from the oven and cool on a wire rack about 10 minutes before unmolding.

best bran muffins

These muffins have a hearty, satisfying flavor and the best texture you can get in a bran muffin, due to the soft, rehydrated currants, the mashed banana, and an overnight rest for the batter. The banana is there for moisture, not flavor—you will taste it only subtly.

The batter for these muffins must be made a day ahead, so plan accordingly.

SPECIAL EQUIPMENT: MUFFIN PAN, PAPER LINERS, POTATO MASHER (OPTIONAL), 4-OUNCE ICE CREAM SCOOP (OPTIONAL)

½ cup (2½ ounces/70 grams) dried currants

¾ cup (6 ounces/173 grams) water

1½ cups (7¼ ounces/206 grams) all-purpose flour

1 teaspoon baking powder

¾ teaspoon ground cinnamon

¼ teaspoon baking soda

3 cups (4 ounces/115 grams) bran, plus extra for sprinkling

½ teaspoon kosher salt

1 medium (5½ ounces/156 grams) ripe banana

2 large eggs

1 cup (7⅛ ounces/200 grams) canola or other neutral-tasting oil

⅔ cup (5 ounces/142 grams) packed brown sugar

¼ cup (2 ounces/63 grams) molasses

1½ cups (12 ounces/340 grams) buttermilk

1 teaspoon pure vanilla extract

Raw (turbinado), granulated, or crystal sugar as needed for sprinkling

1. Combine the currants with the water in a small saucepan and bring to a simmer over medium-high heat. Simmer until very soft, 10 to 15 minutes, reducing the heat as needed to keep the water at a simmer. Drain the currants, transfer them to a small bowl, and allow to cool to room temperature.

2. In a large bowl, sift together the flour, baking powder, cinnamon, and baking soda. Stir in the bran and the salt. Set aside.

3. Put the banana in a mixing bowl and mash it using a potato masher or a fork. (You should have about ⅓ cup/3½ ounces mashed banana.) Add the eggs, oil, brown sugar, and molasses. Whisk the mixture until the ingredients are emulsified, then mix in the buttermilk and vanilla.

4. Make a well in the center of the dry ingredients, pour in the banana-oil-buttermilk mixture, and add the currants. Use the whisk to fold everything together (see "How to Fold with a Whisk," page 14), mixing only until the ingredients are combined. Do not overmix.

5. Cover the bowl with plastic wrap and refrigerate overnight.

6. When you are ready to bake the muffins, preheat the oven to 375°F. Scoop the muffins into paper-lined muffin pans, using about 4 ounces (½ cup) batter per muffin (see "How to Scoop Muffins, Cookies, and Cupcakes," page 74).

7. Sprinkle the tops of the muffins with raw sugar and bran (about ¼ teaspoon each). Bake until the muffins are golden and baked through, 24 to 26 minutes, rotating the pan once halfway through the baking time. A wooden skewer inserted into a muffin should come out with a few crumbs clinging to it but no batter. Remove the muffin pan from the oven and cool on a wire rack about 10 minutes before unmolding.

blueberry buttermilk muffins

The marriage between the tartness of buttermilk and sour cream and the sweetness of perfect, in-season blueberries is hands-down the essence of this classic. When available, replace the blueberries with wild huckleberries. We forage for these annually from the Cascade and Olympic mountains while making sure to stay out of the local black bears' domain. It's a good way to get some exercise so you can slather on the butter.

When making the muffin batter, whip the butter and sugar until very light and carefully add the dry and wet ingredients until just mixed. The resulting muffins will have a delicate cake-like texture, punctuated with juicy purple berries.

SPECIAL EQUIPMENT: MUFFIN PAN, PAPER MUFFIN LINERS, ELECTRIC MIXER, 3-OUNCE ICE CREAM SCOOP (OPTIONAL)

1¾ cups (9 ounces/256 grams) all-purpose flour

½ teaspoon baking powder

½ teaspoon baking soda

½ cup (4½ ounces/127 grams) sour cream at room temperature (see "How to Bring Ingredients to Room Temperature," page 12)

¼ cup (2¼ ounces/64 grams) buttermilk at room temperature (see Note)

½ teaspoon pure vanilla extract

½ teaspoon kosher salt

½ cup (1 stick/4 ounces/114 grams) unsalted butter, softened

¾ cup (5⅝ ounces/159 grams) granulated sugar

2 large eggs at room temperature

1¼ cups (6 ounces/170 grams) blueberries

Raw (turbinado), granulated, or crystal sugar as needed for sprinkling

1. Preheat the oven to 375°F. In a bowl, sift together the flour, baking powder, and baking soda (see "How to Sift," page 13). Reserve ¼ cup of dry ingredients for coating the blueberries later. Set the dry ingredients aside.

2. In another bowl, mix together the sour cream, buttermilk, vanilla extract, and salt. Set the wet ingredients aside.

3. In the bowl of an electric mixer, combine the butter and sugar and mix on medium-high speed with the paddle attachment until pale and well whipped, about 3 minutes. About halfway through the whipping time, stop the machine and scrape down the sides of the bowl and the paddle.

4. Turn the mixer down to medium speed and add the eggs one at a time, allowing each egg to be completely incorporated before the next addition.

5. Add the dry ingredients and the wet ingredients to the batter in the bowl of the mixer in 3 additions, alternating wet and dry and ending with dry. Mix only until blended. Do not overmix.

6. Put the blueberries in a small bowl and toss them with the reserved ¼ cup dry ingredients to coat the berries. Remove the bowl from the mixer and gently fold in the berry-dry-ingredient mixture using a rubber spatula.

7. Scoop the muffin batter into paper-lined muffin pans, using about 3 ounces (generous ⅓ cup) of batter per muffin (see "How to Scoop Muffins, Cookies, and Cupcakes," page 74). Lightly sprinkle the top of each muffin with about ½ teaspoon raw sugar.

8. Bake until the muffins are golden, slightly domed, and baked through, 23 to 25 minutes, rotating the pan once halfway through baking. A wooden skewer inserted into a muffin should come out with a few crumbs clinging but no batter. Remove the muffin pan from the oven and cool on a wire rack for about 10 minutes before unmolding.

NOTE: BUTTERMILK HAS A LONG SHELF LIFE AND IS SOMETIMES SOLD IN SMALL (PINT) CONTAINERS. FOR LONGER STORAGE, YOU CAN FREEZE LEFTOVER BUTTERMILK IN SEVERAL SMALL PORTIONS. REMOVE THE QUANTITY YOU NEED FROM THE FREEZER AND THAW BEFORE USING FOR BAKING. THE BUTTERMILK WILL SEPARATE WHEN THAWED, BUT YOU CAN SMOOTH IT OUT IN THE BLENDER.

cherry almond scones

We developed this recipe a couple decades ago for Etta's brunch menu. It's still one of my favorite scones because, since you start them in a hot oven, they get well browned and the edges get a little crisp and caramelized.

Scones work best made one recipe batch at a time. If you need more, make more batches.

Brush the scones with cream, then sprinkle with plain old granulated sugar, not raw sugar, for a slightly shiny pale glaze. Serve the warm scones with softened butter and honey or jam if desired.

An inexpensive pastry blender, a tool consisting of several thick parallel wires attached on both ends to a wooden or metal handle, is a nice old-fashioned, low-tech device for cutting butter into flour by hand. A plastic dough scraper is a good tool for turning the dough out of the bowl, and a metal bench knife is helpful for cutting the dough into wedges.

SPECIAL EQUIPMENT: PASTRY BLENDER (OPTIONAL), SCRAPER (OPTIONAL), BENCH KNIFE (OPTIONAL)

2½ cups (13 ounces/370 grams) all-purpose flour

¼ cup (1¾ ounces/49 grams) sugar, plus more for sprinkling

1 teaspoon baking powder

1 teaspoon grated lemon zest

¾ teaspoon kosher salt

¼ teaspoon baking soda

10 tablespoons (1¼ sticks/5 ounces/142 grams) cold unsalted butter, cut into ½-inch dice

½ cup (2⅞ ounces/7 grams) dried tart cherries, coarsely chopped

½ cup (1⅞ ounces/54 grams) sliced blanched almonds, toasted and cooled (see "How to Toast and Chop Nuts," page 13)

1 cup (8¾ ounces/239 grams) buttermilk (see Note on page 80)

¼ teaspoon pure vanilla extract

¼ teaspoon pure almond extract

About ¼ cup (2 ounces/58 grams) heavy cream, for brushing

1. Preheat the oven to 425°F. In a large bowl, combine the flour, sugar, baking powder, lemon zest, salt, and baking soda. Cut the butter into the dry mixture, using a pastry blender or your fingertips, until the mixture looks like coarse cornmeal. Mix in the cherries and the almonds.

2. Gradually pour in the buttermilk and extracts and mix with a rubber spatula until the dough just comes together. (You can finish mixing the dough when you turn it out onto the work surface.) Turn out the dough onto a lightly floured work surface and knead lightly and quickly with your hands until the dough is smooth and the buttermilk is evenly incorporated into the dry ingredients, but do not overwork the dough. Pat the dough with your hands into a 9-inch round about 1 inch thick. Cut the dough into 8 wedges with a floured knife or metal bench knife.

3. Place the scones on a parchment-lined baking sheet. Brush them with the heavy cream and sprinkle them generously with the sugar. Bake for 10 minutes, rotate the baking pan, then reduce the oven temperature to 350°F and finish baking until golden brown and cooked through, about 15 minutes more. Remove from the oven and cool briefly on a wire rack. Serve the scones while they are still warm.

toasted hazelnut whole wheat scones with maple glaze

Fragrant with hazelnuts, light in texture but full of wholesome whole wheat flavor, and dripping with a creamy maple glaze, a batch of these scones will brighten any morning.

If you prefer not to make the maple glaze, brush the scones with heavy cream and sprinkle with sugar as for the Cherry Almond Scones (page 81).

Another idea, if you're not making the maple glaze, is to serve the scones warm from the oven (you don't need to cool them if you're not adding glaze), split them in half, and spread them with maple butter. To make maple butter, just blend 2 tablespoons maple syrup with ½ cup softened butter.

For the best fragrance and flavor, be sure to toast your hazelnuts long enough that they are toasted all the way through.

SPECIAL EQUIPMENT: PASTRY BLENDER (OPTIONAL), BENCH KNIFE (OPTIONAL)

scones

1¾ cups (8 ounces/227 grams) all-purpose flour

1 cup (5 ounces/140 grams) whole wheat flour

¼ cup (2 ounces/60 grams) packed brown sugar or ⅓ cup (2 ounces/60 grams) maple sugar

2 teaspoons baking powder

¾ teaspoon kosher salt

14 tablespoons (1¾ sticks/7 ounces/200 grams) cold unsalted butter, cut into ½-inch dice

1¼ cups (6¾ ounces/195 grams) hazelnuts, toasted (see "How to Toast and Chop Nuts," page 13), skinned (see "How to Skin Hazelnuts," page 84), and finely chopped

1 cup (8¾ ounces/239 grams) buttermilk, cold (see Note on page 80)

2 teaspoons pure vanilla extract

maple glaze

¾ cup (3¼ ounces/90 grams) powdered sugar

4 tablespoons (½ stick/2 ounces/57 grams) unsalted butter

¼ cup (2½ ounces/71 grams) pure maple syrup

½ teaspoon pure vanilla extract

¼ teaspoon kosher salt

2 tablespoons heavy cream

Hazelnuts have papery brown skins. After toasting hazelnuts, while they are still warm, remove as much of the skin as you easily can. Here are two methods:

- Put the toasted hazelnuts in a kitchen towel and rub them together using the towel.

- Put the warm hazelnuts in a plastic container with a lid (in batches so there is plenty of room) and shake vigorously, shaking off the skins.

In either case, you'll have to transfer the nuts from the towel or container, leaving the skins behind and discarding the skins. Don't worry about removing every last little bit of skin. Getting off whatever you can remove easily is fine. A few bits of remaining skin will add more color and flavor to your finished pastry.

1. Preheat the oven to 400°F.

2. Combine both flours, the brown sugar, baking powder, and salt in a large bowl. Using a pastry blender or your fingertips, cut the butter into the dry ingredients until the mixture resembles coarse breadcrumbs. Stir in the hazelnuts using a rubber spatula.

3. In a small bowl, combine the buttermilk and vanilla extract, then gradually stir in the buttermilk mixture until the dough just comes together into a soft, slightly moist dough. Turn the dough out onto a lightly floured work surface and gently knead it with your hands for a minute or two to help it cohere, but do not overmix.

4. Divide the dough into 2 equal pieces and pat each piece with your hands into a flat round about ½-inch thick. Cut each round into 6 wedges with a floured knife or metal bench knife.

5. Place the scones an inch apart on a parchment-lined baking sheet and bake until golden and cooked through, 20 to 25 minutes, rotating the pan halfway through the cooking time. Transfer the pan from the oven to a wire cooling rack and allow the scones to cool for 10 to 15 minutes, until they are only slightly warm but not hot.

6. While the scones are cooling, make the glaze. Sift the powdered sugar into a bowl. Put the butter in a small pan and melt over medium heat. As soon as the butter is melted and hot, pour it into the bowl with the powdered sugar and add the maple syrup, vanilla extract, and salt. Whisk until smooth, whisking in the cream last.

7. When the scones have cooled long enough so that they won't melt the glaze, spoon the glaze over the scones, letting it drip off the sides, then serve.

parsley chive scones

Most scones are sweet. Here's a savory scone flecked with green herbs, the perfect companion to a plate of scrambled eggs, a creamy seafood stew, or even pot roast. Try splitting these scones while they are still warm, smearing them with softened butter, and sprinkling the butter with big-flake sea salt.

You want the bottoms of these scones to turn a nice golden brown, but if they seem to be browning too fast, double-pan them by sliding another baking sheet underneath.

SPECIAL EQUIPMENT: PASTRY BLENDER (OPTIONAL), BENCH KNIFE (OPTIONAL)

2½ cups (13 ounces/370 grams) all-purpose flour

2 tablespoons sugar

1½ teaspoons kosher or sea salt

½ teaspoon freshly ground black pepper

2½ teaspoons baking powder

½ teaspoon baking soda

10 tablespoons (1¼ sticks/5 ounces/142 grams) cold unsalted butter, cut into ½-inch dice

1 teaspoon grated lemon zest

2 tablespoons thinly sliced fresh chives

⅓ cup (½ ounce/14 grams) finely chopped fresh flat-leaf parsley

1 cup (8¾ ounces/239 grams) buttermilk (see Note on page 80)

1. Preheat the oven to 400°F.

2. Combine the flour, sugar, salt, pepper, baking powder, and baking soda in a large bowl. Using a pastry blender or your fingertips, cut the butter into the dry ingredients until the mixture resembles coarse breadcrumbs. Stir in the lemon zest, chives, and parsley using a rubber spatula. Gradually add the buttermilk, stirring, until the dough just comes together into a soft, slightly moist dough.

3. Turn the dough out onto a lightly floured work surface and gently knead the dough with your hands for a minute or two to help it cohere, but do not overmix. Divide the dough into 2 equal pieces and pat each piece with your hands into a flat round about ½-inch thick. Cut each round into 6 wedges with a floured knife or metal bench knife.

4. Place the scones on a parchment-lined baking sheet and bake until golden and cooked through, 20 to 25 minutes. Transfer the pan from the oven to a wire cooling rack and allow to cool briefly. Serve warm.

serious biscuits

These are the same biscuits we make for the biscuit sandwiches served at Serious Biscuits, downstairs from our pizza joint, Serious Pie Westlake, but at Serious Biscuits we cut the dough into bigger squares, about 3½ inches, bake them, split them in half, and fill them with everything from fennel sausage with fried egg, melted fontina, and spicy-sweet pepper relish to crispy fried chicken with fried egg and savory black pepper gravy. If you want to make your own biscuit sandwiches, just cut the squares a little bigger than directed in this recipe, bake them, split them in half, and use the English Muffin breakfast sandwich recipes (pages 34 to 47) for ideas on how to fill them.

This smaller, 2½-inch biscuit is perfect for breakfast or brunch. If you've made any of the jams or jellies on pages 353 to 364, this is the time to bring them out along with plenty of softened unsalted butter.

When getting started on the recipe, dice the cold butter first and keep it chilled in the refrigerator while you assemble the rest of the ingredients. Also, be sure your buttermilk is very cold.

An inexpensive pastry blender, a tool consisting of several thick parallel wires attached on both ends to a wooden or metal handle, is a nice old-fashioned, low-tech device for cutting butter into flour by hand. A metal bench scraper or bench knife is useful for cutting the dough into squares (see page 28).

Rolling biscuit dough into a rectangle and cutting the biscuits into squares is more efficient than cutting out round biscuits, and there are no scraps to reroll, though if you prefer you could certainly cut these biscuits into 2½-inch rounds.

These southern-style biscuits have plenty of salt. Kosher salt is coarser than table salt. If you are substituting table salt, be sure to cut the quantity of salt at least in half.

SPECIAL EQUIPMENT: PASTRY BLENDER (OPTIONAL), METAL BENCH KNIFE (OPTIONAL)

5½ cups (1 pound 14 ounces/865 grams) all-purpose flour

2 tablespoons baking powder

2 teaspoons baking soda

2 tablespoons kosher salt (see headnote)

1½ cups (3 sticks/12 ounces/340 grams) cold unsalted butter, cut into ½-inch dice, plus a few tablespoons melted butter for brushing

3 cups (1 pound 9 ounces/708 grams) cold buttermilk (see Note on page 80)

Using her fingers to cut the butter into the dry ingredients

Adding the cold buttermilk

Starting to mix the dough with her hands

Finishing mixing the dough with her hands

Turning the dough out onto the work surface

Kneading the biscuit dough

Patting the biscuit dough into a rectangle

Using a rolling pin to roll the dough to a 3/4-inch thickness

Cutting the biscuit dough into squares

1. Preheat the oven to 475°F.

2. In a large bowl, using a whisk, combine the flour, baking powder, baking soda, and salt. Add the cold butter to the bowl and, using a pastry blender, 2 forks, or your fingertips, cut the butter into the dry ingredients until the butter is the size of peas. Add the cold buttermilk and use a rubber spatula or both hands to mix the dough until everything is just combined. Do not overmix.

3. Scrape the dough out onto a lightly floured work surface and knead 4 or 5 times, just until you have a smooth surface area on top. Use your hands to shape the dough into a rough rectangle, then use a rolling pin to roll out the dough to a rectangle ¾ inch thick. Use a knife or metal bench knife to cut the rectangle into 2½-inch squares. You should get about 20 biscuits.

4. Place the biscuits on parchment-lined baking sheets, spacing them about an inch apart. Brush the tops of the biscuits with melted butter.

5. Put the biscuits in the oven and bake until golden brown, about 14 minutes, rotating the pan halfway through the baking time. Remove the pan from the oven and cool on a wire rack for a few minutes. Serve the biscuits warm.

malted buttermilk biscuits

You'll find two biscuit recipes in this book. Quite frankly there's an argument between two headstrong pastry chefs. Garrett's Malted Buttermilk Biscuit has a crispier edge and a finer crumb, while Stacy's Serious Biscuit is a more southern-style softer and fluffier biscuit. Try 'em both and let me know your favorite at TomDouglas.com.

For sprinkling over the tops, we like the crunch of a sea salt such as fleur de sel. Serve the biscuits warm, with plenty of softened unsalted butter.

Barley malt (see page 19) has a malty flavor, and it's similar to but not as strong as molasses. You can substitute honey if you prefer.

Before you start the recipe, put the butter in the freezer for 15 minutes. Using a grater to grate the very cold butter right into the dry ingredients is a trick that allows you to cut the butter in quickly, without allowing it to warm up.

Because you want your biscuits to rise tall, be sure you don't roll the dough to less than 1 inch of thickness. It's all too easy to roll the dough too thin before you realize it, so use a ruler to check.

This recipe calls for 2 teaspoons of kosher salt for making the dough. Kosher salt is coarser than table salt, so an equal measurement of table salt will taste saltier. If you choose to substitute table salt, be sure to cut the amount of salt down, about in half (see "Salt," page 22).

SPECIAL EQUIPMENT: 2½-INCH ROUND COOKIE CUTTER

3¼ cups (1 pound/454 grams) all-purpose flour

2 tablespoons sugar

1 tablespoon plus 1 teaspoon baking powder

2 teaspoons kosher salt

1 cup (2 sticks/8 ounces/227 grams) unsalted butter, frozen for 15 minutes, plus a few tablespoons melted butter for brushing

1 cup (8⅝ ounces/243 grams) buttermilk, cold (see Note on page 80)

1 tablespoon barley malt or honey

Sea salt as needed for sprinkling

1. Preheat the oven to 400°F.

2. Put the flour, sugar, baking powder, and salt in a large bowl and use a whisk to combine the dry ingredients. Using a box grater, grate the very cold butter directly over the bowl. Use a rubber spatula to mix and distribute the butter evenly throughout the dry ingredients, then use your fingers to break up any large clumps of grated butter.

3. In a small bowl, combine the buttermilk and barley malt. Stir to blend thoroughly. Slowly pour the buttermilk mixture over the butter-flour mixture, stirring with the rubber spatula just until the dough comes together. Do not overmix. You can finish mixing when the dough is turned out onto the work surface.

4. Remove the dough from the bowl and place on a lightly floured work surface. Knead the dough lightly and quickly a few times to incorporate the buttermilk evenly into the dry ingredients, but do not overwork the dough. Then gently press the dough together into a flattened ball.

5. Using a rolling pin, roll the dough to a thickness of 1 inch. Cut out biscuits using a 2½-inch round cutter (you should get around 9 biscuits). Then, to reroll the scraps, push the scraps of dough together, and gently pat down with your hands to even out the surface, being sure to keep the dough at a thickness of 1 inch. Use the cutter to cut out more biscuits (you should get about 3 more), discarding any remaining scraps.

6. Place the biscuits on a parchment-lined baking sheet, spacing them about an inch apart. Brush the top of each biscuit with melted butter and sprinkle with sea salt.

7. Bake until golden and cooked through, about 20 minutes, rotating the pan halfway through the baking time. Remove the pan from the oven and cool on a wire rack for a few minutes. Serve warm.

banana chocolate chunk walnut loaf

This lightly sweetened, delicately textured banana bread, studded with crisp bits of toasted walnuts and rich chunks of dark chocolate, is delicious served slightly warm. After you remove the loaf from the oven, allow it to cool for about 45 minutes before slicing. The bread will have cooled enough for the texture to be set, but the chocolate chunks will still be soft and almost melted. Or you can cool the bread completely to room temperature before slicing, then warm the slices in the oven, wrapped in foil. For an indulgent treat, spread a slice of warm banana bread with sweet butter and sprinkle it with flaky sea salt.

Chocolate chunks are available at many supermarkets and online. Look for a top-quality brand such as Scharffen Berger.

If you save ripe bananas in the freezer, use them here. Just be sure to use 1 cup of banana puree. (If any liquid separated from your frozen and thawed banana puree, stir it in; don't discard it.)

Measure your loaf pan to be sure it is the same size specified in the recipe, or your baking time may differ.

SPECIAL EQUIPMENT: ELECTRIC MIXER, MEDIUM LOAF PAN (8½ × 4½ × 2½ INCHES)

Unsalted butter, softened, or vegetable oil spray as needed for the pan

½ cup (2¾ ounces/79 grams) bittersweet chocolate chunks (see "Our Favorite Chocolates," page 21)

⅓ cup (1¼ ounces/35 grams) walnuts, toasted (see "How to Toast and Chop Nuts," page 13), cooled, and roughly chopped

1¼ cups (6⅜ ounces/180 grams) all-purpose flour, plus more for the pan

1¼ teaspoons baking soda

¼ teaspoon kosher salt

About 1 pound (2 to 3, depending on size/454 grams) very ripe bananas

¼ cup (1⅝ ounces/47 grams) canola or other neutral-tasting oil

½ cup (3½ ounces/100 grams) sugar

1 large egg

¼ cup (2 ounces/58 grams) sour cream

1. Preheat the oven to 350°F. Either butter the loaf pan or spray it with vegetable oil spray, then flour the pan (see "How to Prepare a Cake or Loaf Pan," page 261). Chill the pan in the refrigerator to set the coating while you make the batter.

2. Put the chocolate chunks and walnuts in a small bowl. Add 2 tablespoons of the flour and toss to coat. Set aside.

3. Sift the remaining 1 cup plus 2 tablespoons of flour and the baking soda into a bowl. Stir in the salt. Set the dry ingredients aside.

4. Peel the bananas, cut them into chunks, and place them in the bowl of an electric mixer. On low speed, using the paddle, beat the bananas to a smooth puree until no large lumps remain. (At this point, measure the banana puree. You should have 1 cup. If you don't have 1 cup, adjust by adding more ripe banana or discarding some.) Still on low speed, add the oil, sugar, egg, and sour cream. Mix until everything is combined and the banana is well incorporated.

5. Add the dry ingredients and mix just until incorporated. Add the reserved chocolate-walnut mixture and combine briefly with the paddle just until evenly mixed into the batter.

6. Scrape the batter into the prepared pan.

7. Bake until the banana bread is cooked through and a skewer inserted into the loaf comes out with a few moist crumbs clinging but no batter, 65 to 70 minutes. For the best rise, do not open the oven door while the banana bread is baking. The loaf will be dark golden brown and there will probably be a crack running through the top. Remove the pan from the oven and cool on a wire rack for about 15 minutes. Unmold the banana bread, running a small knife around the sides to loosen if necessary (see "How to Unmold Cakes, Tarts, and Loaves," page 262), then cool on a wire rack to slightly warm (at least another 30 minutes) or room temperature before slicing and serving.

fresh corn cornbread with cornmeal crumble

This is not a typical cornbread, but rather a lightly sweetened quick bread, studded with fresh corn kernels and topped with an herb-scented streusel. Try a slice with breakfast or brunch or with an afternoon cup of coffee or tea.

To shave kernels from an ear of corn, use a sharp paring knife.

Measure your loaf pan to be sure it is the same size specified in the recipe or your baking time may differ.

SPECIAL EQUIPMENT: MEDIUM LOAF PAN, 8½ × 4½ × 2½ INCHES

½ cup (1 stick/4 ounces/113 grams) unsalted butter, plus more for the pan

1 cup (5¼ ounces/150 grams) all-purpose flour, plus more for the pan

¾ cup (4 ounces/114 grams/about 1 medium ear) corn kernels

¼ cup (1¼ ounces/35 grams) cake flour

¾ cup (5⅜ ounces/154 grams) sugar

1 teaspoon baking powder

½ cup (3 ounces/85 grams) cornmeal

½ teaspoon kosher salt

2 large eggs at room temperature

1 cup (7½ ounces/212 grams) buttermilk at room temperature (see Note on page 80)

1 teaspoon pure vanilla extract

Cornmeal Crumble with Lemon Thyme (quantity for 1 loaf quick bread, page 100)

1. Preheat the oven to 325°F. Butter and flour the loaf pan, then chill the pan in the refrigerator to set the coating while you make the batter (see "How to Prepare a Cake or Loaf Pan," page 261).

2. Bring a small saucepan of lightly salted water to a boil and set up a bowl of ice water. Add the corn to the pot and cook for 2 minutes. Drain the corn and immediately plunge it into the ice water. Drain the corn and set aside.

3. In a small pan, melt the butter. Set the melted butter aside to cool to room temperature, but do not allow it to solidify.

4. In a large bowl, sift together the flours, sugar, and baking powder (see "How to Sift," page 13). Stir in the cornmeal and salt. Set the dry ingredients aside.

5. Put the eggs, buttermilk, and vanilla into another bowl and whisk just enough to break up the eggs.

6. Pour the egg mixture into the bowl of dry ingredients and fold in using a whisk. Add the corn kernels and fold in. Add the cooled melted butter last, gently folding with the whisk (see "How to Fold with a Whisk," page 14).

7. Scrape the batter into the prepared loaf pan. Evenly distribute the crumble on top of the batter. Here and there, gently squeeze some of the crumble mixture in your hand to make larger clumps. Press down gently on the crumble topping to make sure it adheres to the batter during baking.

8. Bake until cooked through and the top is golden brown, about 1 hour and 8 or 10 minutes, rotating the pan halfway through the cooking time. To check for doneness, a wooden skewer inserted into the loaf should come out with a few moist crumbs clinging to it but no batter.

9. Remove the loaf pan from the oven and cool on a wire rack for about 15 minutes. Unmold the loaf, running a small knife around the sides to loosen it if necessary, and cool on the rack for at least another 30 minutes before slicing and serving (see "How to Unmold Cakes, Tarts, and Loaves," page 262).

cornmeal crumble with lemon thyme

A bit of chopped lemon thyme and grated lemon zest adds a pleasing herb-citrus zing to this streusel, which is equally delicious covering a bubbling fruit crisp (page 216) or topping a loaf of fresh corn cornbread (page 98).

If you can't find lemon thyme, just substitute regular fresh thyme leaves, but don't use dried thyme—it's too strong. If you prefer a cornmeal crumble without the touch of herbal flavor, just omit the thyme.

(If you don't have a food processor, you can combine the ingredients in a bowl using a pastry blender or your fingertips.)

SPECIAL EQUIPMENT: FOOD PROCESSOR OR PASTRY BLENDER (OPTIONAL)

for 1 quick bread loaf

⅓ cup (1⅞ ounces/54 grams) all-purpose flour

2 tablespoons plus 2 teaspoons (1 ounce/27 grams) cornmeal

3 tablespoons plus 1 teaspoon (1½ ounces/43 grams) sugar

1 teaspoon fresh lemon thyme or thyme leaves, roughly chopped (use fresh thyme only)

½ teaspoon grated lemon zest

½ teaspoon pure vanilla extract

¼ teaspoon kosher salt

2 tablespoons plus 2 teaspoons (1⅓ ounces/38 grams) unsalted butter, softened

for one 9-inch crisp

⅔ cup (3¾ ounces/108 grams) all-purpose flour

5 tablespoons plus 1 teaspoon (2 ounces/54 grams) cornmeal

⅓ cup (2⅔ ounces/76 grams) sugar

2 teaspoons fresh lemon thyme or thyme leaves, roughly chopped (use fresh thyme only)

1 teaspoon grated lemon zest

1 teaspoon pure vanilla extract

½ teaspoon kosher salt

5 tablespoons plus 1 teaspoon (2⅔ ounces/76 grams) unsalted butter, softened

Put the flour, cornmeal, sugar, thyme leaves, lemon zest, vanilla extract, and salt in the bowl of a food processor. Add the butter, breaking it up into several small clumps and scattering it around. Pulse about 5 times and scrape down. Repeat 1 or 2 more times. The mixture should not come together like a ball of dough but should look shaggy. You should be able to squeeze some of the mixture together with your fingers to make clumps. Transfer the crumble to a bowl, cover, and refrigerate until you are ready to use it.

grandma douglas's schnecken

My family has made these schnecken for most every holiday for as long as I can remember. Schnecken, which means "snails" in German, are basically pecan-cinnamon buns. Once the schnecken were turned out hot from the pan and the top of the buns covered with gooey pecan caramel, the real struggle began—fighting my seven siblings for first crack at our favorite piece. It might have been the first time I realized that my rotundness and arm length gave me a distinct advantage over my sisters as I groped for the warm center of this classic cinnamon pull-apart. After the center pieces were gone, I went for the ultra-caramelized golden brown corners.

It's convenient to prepare the schnecken to the point of forming the rolls and setting them into the prepared pan a day ahead. Cover the pan with plastic wrap and store them, unbaked, in the refrigerator overnight. When you are ready to bake the schnecken, remove the pan from the refrigerator and set it in a warm place for about an hour. Then bake as directed in the recipe.

Kosher salt is coarser than table salt. If you are substituting table salt, cut the quantity in half.

SPECIAL EQUIPMENT: 9 × 13-INCH BAKING PAN

dough

½ cup (1 stick/4 ounces/113 grams) unsalted butter, plus more for the bowl and pan

1 cup (8½ ounces/242 grams) milk

5 tablespoons (2¼ ounces/63 grams) granulated sugar

1 tablespoon active dry yeast

1½ teaspoons kosher salt

1 large egg plus 1 large egg yolk

3 to 3½ cups (13½ to 15½ ounces/383 to 439 grams) all-purpose flour as needed

sugar-pecan topping

¾ cup (1½ sticks/6 ounces/170 grams) unsalted butter

¾ cup (4½ ounces/128 grams) packed brown sugar

¼ cup (3 ounces/85 grams) light corn syrup

¾ cup (3 ounces/85 grams) chopped pecans

cinnamon-sugar filling

4 tablespoons (½ stick/2 ounces/ 57 grams) unsalted butter

1 cup (7 ounces/200 grams) granulated sugar

1 tablespoon ground cinnamon

Placing a baking sheet over the pan of schnecken

1. To make the dough, melt the ½ cup butter in a small saucepan over medium-low heat. Add the milk and sugar and heat just to lukewarm (about 110°F), stirring to dissolve the sugar. Pour the warm milk mixture into a bowl. Stir in the yeast. Allow the mixture to sit for 10 minutes, then stir in the salt.

2. Beat the whole egg and egg yolk together and add to the yeast mixture. Stir in the flour 1 cup at a time until you have a sticky dough. Scrape the dough out onto a floured work surface and knead for about 5 minutes, until you have a nice smooth dough. Butter a large bowl. Place the dough in the prepared bowl and cover with plastic

Inverting the pan of schnecken

Lifting off the baking pan. The schnecken are now unmolded.

wrap. Put the bowl in a warm place and allow the dough to rise for 2 hours, until tripled in volume.

3. Meanwhile, brush a 9 × 13-inch baking pan with some melted butter (or spray it with vegetable oil spray). To prepare the sugar-pecan topping, melt the butter with the brown sugar and corn syrup in a small saucepan over medium-low heat, stirring to combine. Remove from the heat and spread the mixture in the bottom of the pan. Sprinkle with the chopped pecans.

4. Punch down the dough and turn it out of the bowl onto a lightly floured work surface. Knead for a minute, then use a lightly floured rolling pin to roll the dough into a rectangle about 15 × 12 inches and ⅛ inch thick. To make the cinnamon-sugar filling, melt the butter in a small saucepan over medium-low heat and allow it to cool. Brush the butter thoroughly over the surface of the dough. In a bowl, mix together the sugar and cinnamon. Sprinkle the cinnamon sugar evenly over the melted butter. Roll the rectangle up, like a jelly roll, along one long edge.

5. Slice the log of rolled dough into 1-inch-thick slices and arrange the slices, cut sides up, in the prepared pan. Cover the pan with a piece of plastic wrap (you can spray the plastic wrap first with vegetable oil spray to be sure it doesn't stick to the dough) and allow it to rise in a warm place for about 40 minutes.

6. Preheat the oven to 350°F. Bake the schnecken until golden brown, 35 to 40 minutes, rotating the pan halfway through the baking time. Check them occasionally during the baking time, and if they seem to be browning too quickly, loosely cover them with a sheet of aluminum foil.

7. Remove the pan from the oven and cool on a wire rack for 5 to 10 minutes. Turn the schnecken out of the pan while still warm by inverting the pan over a large platter or baking sheet. Serve the schnecken warm.

sour cream coffee cake with cinnamon streusel

This is a homey, old-fashioned coffee cake originally from *Tom Douglas' Seattle Kitchen.* I love the counter-punch of the crunchy topping against the soft cake center. Make sure you get plenty of golden brown around the edges. Warm from the oven, a big square of this cake is perfect for its namesake—a hot cup of joe.

You can use blueberries, raspberries, or blackberries. If you're going to use frozen berries, choose individually quick frozen, the kind that are loose in the package, not frozen together in syrup. Pitted sweet cherries are another option. If you like, add a cup of chopped walnuts, pecans, or hazelnuts to the streusel mixture.

SPECIAL EQUIPMENT: 9 × 13-INCH BAKING PAN, PASTRY BLENDER (OPTIONAL), ELECTRIC MIXER

streusel

½ cup (2½ ounces/70 grams) all-purpose flour

½ cup (4 ounces/114 grams) packed brown sugar

1 teaspoon ground cinnamon

6 tablespoons (¾ stick/3 ounces/ 85 grams) cold unsalted butter, diced, plus more for the pan

cake

2½ cups (13 ounces/370 grams) all-purpose flour

2 teaspoons baking powder

1 teaspoon baking soda

1 cup (2 sticks/8 ounces/227 grams) unsalted butter, softened, plus more for the pan

1 cup (6⅝ ounces/188 grams) granulated sugar

3 large eggs

1 cup (7¾ ounces/220 grams) sour cream

1 tablespoon pure vanilla extract

1 teaspoon kosher salt

2 cups (about 8 ounces/227 grams for fresh berries and about 11 ounces/ 310 grams for frozen) blueberries, raspberries, or blackberries, picked over

1. Preheat the oven to 350°F. Butter a 9 x 13-inch baking pan and set aside.

2. To make the streusel, combine the flour, brown sugar, and cinnamon in a bowl. Add the diced butter and blend with a pastry blender or your fingers until crumbly. Set aside.

3. To make the cake, sift together the flour, baking powder, and baking soda into a bowl and set the dry ingredients aside (see "How to Sift," page 13). In an electric mixer with the paddle attachment, cream the butter and sugar together until light and fluffy. Scrape down the bowl. Add the eggs, one at a time, beating well after each addition and scraping the bowl down as needed. Mix in the sour cream, vanilla extract, and salt. Add the dry ingredients, a third at a time, mixing just until everything is blended together. Remove the bowl from the mixer and, using a rubber spatula, gently fold in the berries. The batter will be thick.

4. Scrape the batter into the prepared pan and spread it evenly with the spatula. Sprinkle the streusel evenly over the surface of the cake.

5. Bake until the top of the cake is golden brown and a wooden skewer inserted into the center of the cake comes out with a few crumbs clinging but no batter, 45 to 50 minutes, rotating the pan halfway through the baking time. Remove the pan from the oven and cool on a wire rack for 10 to 15 minutes. Cut the cake into 12 squares and serve warm.

jump-start your day

MORE BREAKFAST AND BRUNCH RECIPES

<<< *Bowl of yogurt; jar of Dahlia Bakery Granola; jar of
Braeburn Apple Compote with Golden Raisins*

dahlia bakery granola

Although this is a long list of ingredients, it's been streamlined from the original recipe, which, for example, contains five different types of seeds and nuts. After you try this recipe once, you can play around with your own favorite combinations of nuts and dried fruits.

If you don't want to buy two types of oats, just use 3½ cups rolled oats and omit the steel-cut oats.

Toast the hazelnuts long enough to get most of the skins off, but don't let them get too dark, because they will spend more time in the oven as the granola bakes.

As soon as the granola is completely cool, store it in an airtight container; otherwise it may absorb moisture and lose its crispness. You can store granola for a few weeks at room temperature or freeze it for a month. A large glass jar with a screwtop lid is ideal for room-temperature storage. If freezing granola, use resealable plastic freezer bags.

If your granola does get a little soggy, spread it on a baking sheet and bake in a preheated 200°F oven for 10 to 15 minutes. Remove the pan from the oven and allow it to cool to room temperature on a wire rack. It will crisp again after it cools.

Vegetable oil spray for greasing the baking sheets

3 cups (10½ ounces/300 grams) rolled oats, such as Quaker Old Fashioned

½ cup (3 ounces/90 grams) steel-cut oats

½ cup (1½ ounces/50 grams) shredded sweetened coconut, such as Baker's Angel Flake

½ cup (3 ounces/90 grams) hazelnuts, toasted (see "How to Toast and Chop Nuts," page 13) and skinned (see "How to Skin Hazelnuts," page 84)

¼ cup (1½ ounces/40 grams) sesame seeds

½ cup (6 ounces/170 grams) honey

¼ cup (2 ounces/60 grams) packed brown sugar

¼ cup (3 ounces/90 grams) maple syrup

¼ cup (2 ounces/60 grams) canola or other neutral-tasting oil

¼ cup (2 ounces/60 grams) freshly squeezed orange juice

¼ cup (2 ounces/60 grams) sugar

1 teaspoon ground cinnamon

1 teaspoon pure vanilla extract

1 cup (6½ ounces/185 grams) dried apricots, cut into ¼-inch dice

½ cup (3 ounces/90 grams) dried cherries

1. Preheat the oven to 300°F. Spray two 18 × 13-inch baking sheets with vegetable oil spray and set aside.

2. Combine the rolled and steel-cut oats, coconut, hazelnuts, and sesame seeds in a large bowl and set aside. In another bowl, combine the honey, brown sugar, maple syrup, oil, orange juice, sugar, cinnamon, and vanilla and whisk until well combined. Pour the honey-liquid mixture over the dry ingredients and toss with a rubber spatula to coat everything evenly.

3. Divide the granola between the prepared pans, spreading it evenly. Bake until deep golden brown, 50 to 60 minutes, stirring with a wooden spoon or heatproof silicone spatula every 15 to 20 minutes so the granola browns evenly. Remove the baking sheets from the oven and set them on wire racks to cool. (The granola will seem wet when you take it from the oven but will crisp up as it cools.)

4. When the granola is completely cool, transfer it from the baking sheets to a large clean bowl and stir in the dried apricots and cherries. Store the granola in airtight containers at room temperature or freeze.

granola yogurt parfait cups with braeburn apple compote with golden raisins

MAKES 4 PARFAITS

Layered in large plastic glasses, these pretty parfaits make a quick grab-and-go breakfast from the Dahlia Bakery's display case. We like to alternate two layers of each ingredient in the glass in this way—granola, yogurt, compote, granola, yogurt, compote—but you can layer the ingredients any way you find attractive.

Full-fat Greek yogurt is our favorite, but you can use 2% or nonfat. If your apple compote was made ahead and has been refrigerated, put it in a saucepan and warm it gently over low heat until it is room temperature or slightly warmer. (There is butter in the apple compote, and it congeals in the refrigerator, so don't serve the compote cold.)

Instead of the apple compote, you can layer yogurt and granola with any delicious jam. Try the blueberry (page 353) or peach-vanilla (page 354) jam.

SPECIAL EQUIPMENT: FOUR 12-OUNCE GLASSES

2 cups (10 ounces/285 grams) Dahlia Bakery Granola (page 110)

2 cups (1 pound/454 grams) yogurt, preferably Greek style

Braeburn Apple Compote with Golden Raisins (page 113) at room temperature or slightly warmer

Attractively layer the granola, yogurt, and apple compote, dividing everything evenly among the 4 glasses, and serve.

braeburn apple compote with golden raisins

Making a batch of homemade fruit compote, like this apple and golden raisin version, is an easy way to add something special to your breakfast bowl of oatmeal or yogurt. A big spoonful of apple compote will also jazz up a dish of rice pudding (page 312) or a scoop of maple ice cream (page 333).

Make this compote with any apple that's good for cooking. Some of our favorites are Braeburn, Pink Lady, Gravenstein, Cameo, and Honeycrisp.

You can make the compote ahead and store it in the refrigerator, but since the butter will congeal when chilled, put the compote in a saucepan and gently warm it to room temperature or warmer before serving.

½ cup (2½ ounces/75 grams) golden raisins

½ cup (4 ounces/115 grams) freshly squeezed orange juice

1 pound (2 large apples/450 grams) apples, such as Braeburn

⅓ cup (2½ ounces/75 grams) packed brown sugar

2 tablespoons honey

2 tablespoons (¼ stick) unsalted butter

¼ teaspoon ground cinnamon

1 teaspoon pure vanilla extract

1 teaspoon freshly squeezed lemon juice

⅛ teaspoon kosher salt

1. Put the raisins and orange juice in a small saucepan and bring to a simmer over medium-high heat. Simmer until the raisins are plump and there is only enough liquid left to coat the bottom of the pan. Remove the pan from the heat and set aside.

2. Peel and core the apples and cut them into ½-inch dice. Here's an easy way to make ½-inch chunks of apple: After you peel and core the apples, cut each apple into eighths, then stack 3 or 4 apple slices at a time and cut them into ½-inch pieces. You should have about 2 cups of diced apple. Set aside.

3. In a sauté pan or skillet, combine the brown sugar, honey, and butter with 2 or 3 tablespoons of water and bring to a simmer over medium-high heat, stirring with a heatproof spoon or spatula. Reduce the heat to medium and let bubble for 2 to 3 minutes. The sugar mixture will look very thick and glossy. Add the apples and cinnamon and return the mixture to a simmer.

Thirty or so years ago in Paris in the 7th arrondissement on the rue du Cherche-Midi in a bakery called Poilâne, I stumbled into a passion. I was welcomed in by sweet women dressed in white full-length aprons with matching caps and large serrated knives in their hands saying "Bonjour, monsieur." Speaking fast and completely in French, which Sister Mary Richards, my high school language teacher, would be annoyed to find out I didn't understand a word of, one of the women motioned me over to wood-shelved walls stocked full of 2-kilo sourdough loaves, all emblazoned with a large *P*. "Monsieur, monsieur, s'il vous plaît," and with a wave of her 12-inch Saber knife, I figured out that she was asking how much of this golden brown loaf with a grayish center and mahogany bottom I would like her to slice for me.

That was the first taste of bread that ever made a real difference in my life. Completely yeasty, firm interior structure, crust with the chew of beef jerky, and when toasted the perfect base for orange marmalade or smoked salmon or chèvre and arugula or just butter and sel gris. Wow, this was bread nirvana! From that moment I knew there was a bakery in my future and we were going to try and reach the bar that had been set by Lionel Poilâne and his father.

The Dahlia bread bakery does that today, led by head baker Gwen LeBlanc and her fabulous crew. They employ a variety of leavening methods to extend fermentation and develop unique flavors and textures. Many of the breads are a 3-day process from start to finish, and if I do say so myself, they're worth the wait. Pecan flaxseed with organic wheat, onion seed rye, kalamata olive ciabatta, and russet potato are just some of the daily offerings tempting our customers. Maybe we'll do a book on those someday?

(When you add the apples, they will thin out the sugar mixture; this is okay.)

4. Continue to cook the apples over medium-high heat, stirring frequently, until the syrup becomes thick and glossy again. The apples will be soft but not mushy. Remove the pan from the heat and add the reserved raisins (with any remaining liquid), then stir in the vanilla, lemon juice, and salt.

5. Serve warm or at room temperature.

seatown's "golden spurtle" steel-cut oatmeal

Bob's Red Mill is an Oregon-based company and one of our favorite sources for whole grains of every description. When oatmeal is on the breakfast menu at Seatown, my seafood and rotisserie joint located in the Pike Place Market, the cooks use Bob's Red Mill steel-cut oats, and they call the finished hot cereal by the same name Bob's Red Mill puts on its steel-cut oats label, Golden Spurtle. Bob's Red Mill people really know their oats, as proven in 2009 when they won the Golden Spurtle trophy at the Worldwide Porridge Making Championship in Scotland! Competing against chefs from the UK, as well as Sweden and Canada, they were the first and only American competitor. Quite an achievement for this hardworking Pacific Northwest company!

Serve each bowl of oatmeal with a dollop of apple compote (page 113) and a sprinkle of Roasted Maple Molasses Pecans (page 116). Or you can serve the oatmeal topped with a dollop of any of our jellies and jams (pages 353 to 364). If you're in a decadent mood, add a spoonful of Vanilla Bean Mascarpone (page 63).

1 cup steel-cut oats

1 tablespoon brown sugar

½ teaspoon kosher salt

3 cups water

1. Put the oats, brown sugar, and salt in a saucepan and add the water. Bring to a boil over medium-high heat, then reduce the heat to a slow simmer. Simmer until the oats are soft and cooked, stirring occasionally and adjusting the heat to keep it at a slow simmer, about 30 minutes. If the oatmeal is getting too thick toward the end of the cooking time, add a little more water.

2. Cover the pan, remove from the heat, and allow to sit for 5 minutes. Serve hot.

roasted maple molasses pecans

Easy to make, and with just the right amount of sweetness, these lightly candied nuts are delicious on a bowl of steaming oatmeal. We also like to scatter them on our Maple Banana Cream Pie (page 176), but they'd be just as good garnishing a pumpkin pie, a wintertime spinach salad, or a cheese tray.

You probably won't need all the candied pecans for any of these suggested uses unless you can't stop picking at them (that's what happens to me), but they keep well for 3 to 4 days in an airtight container.

Adding the butter to the pecans after they come out of the oven is a trick that keeps them from feeling sticky.

Vegetable oil spray for the baking sheet

2 tablespoons honey

2 tablespoons pure maple syrup

1 teaspoon molasses

1 teaspoon pure vanilla extract

Pinch of salt

8 ounces (225 grams) pecan halves

1 tablespoon unsalted butter, melted

1. Preheat the oven to 375°F and line a baking sheet with a piece of parchment sprayed with vegetable oil spray. Or you can line your baking sheet with a flexible nonstick silicone mat (see Equipment, page 25) and omit the vegetable oil spray.

2. Combine the honey, maple syrup, molasses, vanilla extract, and salt in a large bowl. Add the pecans and toss to combine well. Spread the pecans in a single layer on the prepared baking sheet. Bake for 15 minutes, stirring the nuts with a wooden spoon halfway through the cooking time. Remove the pecans from the oven and pour them into a bowl. Stir in the melted butter, then spread the pecans out on a clean baking sheet lined with parchment to cool.

jackie's favorite strata with wild mushrooms, sausage, and chard

MAKES 8 ENTRÉE SERVINGS OR 12 SIDE-DISH SERVINGS

Using European slow-rise techniques, the bread bakers at the Dahlia Workshop make rustic breads every day to serve in the restaurants and sell in the Dahlia Bakery. Although we didn't include these bread recipes (because they're time consuming and difficult to make at home), here's the strata based on a loaf of rustic bread that my wife, Jackie, makes every year for Christmas morning breakfast. When she brings this golden brown casserole filled with savory custard, fennel-scented Italian sausage, sautéed shiitakes and chanterelles, melted white cheddar, and leafy green chard to the table, our family knows it's really Christmas.

Jackie makes her strata with a crusty Dahlia House loaf, but you can use any European-style rustic bread. Jackie uses Beecher's Flagship cheddar, but you can use your favorite white or yellow cheddar.

After the chard is blanched, be sure you squeeze out all the liquid or your strata will be too wet.

Before baking, you must refrigerate the strata for at least a few hours to allow the bread cubes to absorb the custard, so plan accordingly. If you prep the strata to this point and chill it overnight, you can pop it into the oven the next day and serve it for breakfast, brunch, or lunch.

SPECIAL EQUIPMENT: 9 × 13-INCH BAKING PAN OR SHALLOW 3-QUART CASSEROLE

1 loaf of rustic bread, about 1½ pounds (680 grams), thick crusts removed with a serrated knife

1 pound bulk Italian sausage

2 tablespoons olive oil, plus 2 teaspoons if your sausage is lean

2 tablespoons unsalted butter, plus more for the pan

1 medium (10 ounces/283 grams) onion, chopped

12 ounces wild or domestic mushrooms such as shiitake, chanterelle, button, or oyster mushrooms, tough ends trimmed, cleaned, and sliced

1 pound chard, washed and stems removed

2 teaspoons thinly sliced fresh chives

2 teaspoons chopped fresh thyme leaves

12 ounces (about 3 cups) white or yellow cheddar cheese, grated

5 large eggs

2½ cups heavy cream

¾ teaspoon kosher salt

¼ teaspoon freshly ground black pepper

1. Butter a 9×13-inch baking pan. Using a serrated knife, cut the bread into ¾- to 1-inch cubes and set aside. You should have 6 loosely packed cups of bread cubes. (Note: it is important to have this amount of bread and not more. If you have too much bread, your strata will be too firm and not creamy inside.)

2. To cook the sausage, place a skillet over medium-high heat and add the sausage, breaking it up into clumps with a spatula. (If your sausage doesn't contain much fat, you may need to add 2 teaspoons of olive oil to the skillet.) Cook the sausage, turning the clumps over with a spatula as needed, until no pink remains, about 10 minutes. Remove the pan from the heat and transfer the sausage to a large sieve set over a bowl to drain off the fat. Discard the fat and set the cooked sausage aside.

3. Melt 1 tablespoon of the butter in another skillet over medium-high heat. Add the onion and cook, stirring as needed, until soft and starting to brown, about 5 minutes. Remove the onion from the skillet and place in a large bowl. Add the remaining 1 tablespoon butter and the 2 tablespoons olive oil to the skillet and return it to medium-high heat. When the butter is melted, add the mushrooms and cook, stirring as needed, until the mushrooms are tender and the juices have evaporated, 6 to 8 minutes. Transfer the mushrooms to the bowl with the onions.

4. To blanch the chard, bring a pot of salted water to a boil and have ready a large bowl of ice water. Add the chard and cook until tender, about 2 minutes. Drain the chard through a sieve, then immediately plunge the chard into the ice water. Drain again. Using your hands,

squeeze out as much excess water as possible from the chard. Roughly chop the chard and add it to the bowl with the mushrooms and onion. Add the cooked and drained sausage, bread cubes, chives, and thyme to the bowl. Reserve ¾ cup of the cheese, then add the remaining cheese to the bowl and stir to combine. Transfer the contents of the bowl to the baking pan and spread the mixture evenly in the pan.

5. To make the custard, in another bowl, whisk the eggs together lightly, then add the cream and whisk to combine. Add the salt and pepper and whisk to combine.

6. Pour the custard over the bread mixture in the baking dish. Use a spatula to press down on the bread and submerge everything in the custard as much as possible. Sprinkle the remaining ¾ cup cheese over the surface. Cover the baking dish with plastic wrap and refrigerate for a couple hours or overnight.

7. When you are ready to bake the strata, remove the plastic wrap and preheat the oven to 350°F. Bake the strata, uncovered, until it is golden and puffed and the custard is set (insert a small knife into the custard to check that it looks set and not liquidy), 55 to 60 minutes. Remove the pan from the oven and allow to cool on a wire rack for about 10 minutes, then cut into squares and serve warm.

a cookie in each hand

ABOUT COOKIES

Be careful not to overbake cookies. They are small and can overbake in just a few minutes.

When putting two baking sheets in the oven at the same time, be sure to rotate the pans and switch them between the racks. Depending on the heat circulation in your oven, the time it takes the cookies to bake when two pans are in the oven at the same time may be slightly different than the time given in the recipe, and one pan may take longer to bake than the other (see "How to Bake," page 16).

The chocolate chunk and oatmeal apricot cookies are big cookies. If you prefer to make smaller cookies, use 1½-ounce scoops rather than 2½-ounce scoops. Keep an eye on the cookies while they are baking as they will take a minute or two less time to bake.

Most cookies, after they are cooled, can be stored airtight at room temperature for a few days.

Generally cookie doughs freeze well. For example, you can wrap the sugar cookie dough tightly in plastic wrap and freeze, then thaw overnight in the refrigerator before you roll it out. But some doughs do not freeze well, such as the pine nut amaretti and the coconut macaroons, which are based on whipped egg whites. Also, the dough for the chocolate truffle cookies is best scooped and baked as soon as it is made rather than being stored in the refrigerator or freezer.

The chocolate chunk and the oatmeal apricot cookie doughs can be wrapped in plastic and frozen. Allow them to thaw in the refrigerator overnight before shaping and baking. Another way to freeze these cookies is to scoop the dough onto a parchment-lined baking sheet that is then placed in the freezer. When the scoops of dough are frozen solid, they can be removed from the baking sheet, placed in resealable plastic bags, and stored in the freezer until needed. When you are ready to bake them, pull the scoops from the freezer and place them on a baking sheet in the refrigerator overnight to thaw. Before baking the chilled scoops of either the chocolate chunk or oatmeal cookie dough, be sure to flatten each cookie to about ½-inch thickness.

all-american chocolate chunk cookies

This all-American cookie packed with chunks of top-quality chocolate never seems to go out of style. In our business we see food trends come and go; thank goodness the all-American chocolate chunk is here to stay.

I like eating this cookie about 20 minutes out of the oven, when it has set enough to be slightly chewy in the middle and crisp on the edges, but the chocolate chunks inside are still soft and almost melted.

Chocolate chunks are usually easy to find in supermarkets, or you can order them online. For the best-tasting cookies, look for a top-quality brand of chocolate chunks such as Scharffen Berger (see "Our Favorite Chocolates," page 21). Or, instead of buying chunks, you can carefully cut up bars of chocolate into ½-inch chunks using a sharp knife. We use a combination of milk chocolate and bittersweet chocolate chunks in our cookies, but if you prefer you can use just one or the other.

Moist brown sugar, the kind that comes in a resealable plastic bag rather than a box, is preferred for this recipe.

Kosher salt is coarser than table salt. If you substitute table salt, cut the quantity in half.

SPECIAL EQUIPMENT: ELECTRIC MIXER, 2½-OUNCE ICE CREAM SCOOP (OPTIONAL BUT RECOMMENDED)

3 large eggs at room temperature (see "How to Bring Ingredients to Room Temperature," page 12)

2 teaspoons pure vanilla extract

3½ cups (1 pound plus 1 ounce/ 482 grams) all-purpose flour

1 teaspoon baking soda

1 teaspoon baking powder

1½ teaspoons kosher salt

1 cup plus 5 tablespoons (10½ ounces/ 298 grams) unsalted butter, softened

1 cup plus 2 tablespoons (8¾ ounces/ 250 grams) packed moist brown sugar

1¼ cups (9 ounces/250 grams) granulated sugar

1½ cups (9 ounces/255 grams) milk chocolate chunks

1½ cups (9 ounces/255 grams) bittersweet chocolate chunks

1. Preheat the oven to 375°F.

2. Break the eggs into a small bowl, add the vanilla extract, and whisk by hand to combine. Set aside.

3. In a large bowl, combine the flour, baking soda, baking powder, and salt. Set the dry ingredients aside.

4. In the bowl of an electric mixer with the paddle attachment, combine the butter and both sugars. Cream on medium-high speed until very light and fluffy, 4 to 5 minutes. Stop the mixer and scrape down the bowl using a rubber spatula. Beating on medium speed, add about half of the egg-vanilla mixture and beat until fully incorporated. Scrape down the bowl and add the remaining egg-vanilla mixture, beating briefly to combine.

5. Add the dry ingredients to the electric mixer, beating on low speed until they look evenly distributed. Scrape down the bowl and mix for another 10 seconds or just until everything is combined. Do not overmix. Add the chocolate chunks and mix until just combined. Remove the paddle and scrape down the bowl using a rubber spatula, making sure all the dry ingredients down to the bottom of the bowl are incorporated.

6. Remove the bowl from the mixer and use an ice cream scoop to portion the cookies in 2½-ounce (about ¼-cup) portions, placing them evenly apart on parchment-lined baking sheets, 6 cookies per pan (see "How to Scoop Muffins, Cookies, and Cupcakes," page 74). (Note: there is no need to flatten the mounds of cookie dough before baking unless you have chilled the dough before scooping.)

7. Bake the cookies until mostly golden brown but slightly paler in the middle of the cookie (if you were to pick one up gently with a spatula, it would be browned on the bottom), 16 to 18 minutes, rotating the pan halfway through the baking time. If you have 2 pans of cookies in the oven at the same time, also switch them between the racks. For the best texture, do not overbake.

8. Remove the pan from the oven and cool on a wire rack for at least 10 minutes before using a metal spatula to remove the cookies from the baking sheet.

cranberry apricot oatmeal cookies

Here's another all-American "cookie jar" cookie. These oatmeal cookies are flavored with brown sugar and spices and packed with apricots, raisins, and cranberries. They're deliciously moist with just the right amount of chew.

As with most cookies, it's important not to overbake them. When the cookies are done, they'll be browned around the edges but still slightly pale in the middle. If you lift a cookie up gently with a spatula, it will be golden on the bottom. The cookies will continue to set up as they cool.

Moist brown sugar, the kind sold in a resealable plastic bag rather than a box, is preferred for this recipe.

SPECIAL EQUIPMENT: ELECTRIC MIXER, 2½-OUNCE ICE CREAM SCOOP (OPTIONAL BUT RECOMMENDED)

2 cups plus 2 tablespoons (10¼ ounces/290 grams) all-purpose flour

1 teaspoon baking soda

1 teaspoon ground cinnamon

1 teaspoon ground ginger

½ teaspoon ground cloves

2½ cups (9¼ ounces/260 grams) rolled oats, such as Quaker Old Fashioned

½ teaspoon kosher salt

1 cup (5¾ ounces/164 grams) diced dried apricots (⅛- to ¼-inch dice)

⅓ cup (2¼ ounces/64 grams) golden raisins

⅓ cup (2¼ ounces/64 grams) dried cranberries

1 cup plus 2 tablespoons (2 sticks plus 2 tablespoons/9 ounces/250 grams) unsalted butter, softened

1¼ cups (10⅝ ounces/300 grams) packed moist brown sugar

¾ cup plus 2 tablespoons (6⅛ ounces/173 grams) granulated sugar

1 teaspoon pure vanilla extract

2 large eggs at room temperature (see "How to Bring Ingredients to Room Temperature," page 12)

1. Preheat the oven to 375°F.

2. In a bowl, sift together the flour, baking soda, and spices. Stir in the oats and salt. Set the dry ingredients aside.

3. In another bowl, combine the apricots, raisins, and cranberries. Set the dried fruits aside.

4. In the bowl of an electric mixer on medium-high speed, using the paddle attachment, combine the butter, both sugars, and the vanilla extract, creaming on medium speed until very pale and fluffy, 4 to 5 minutes. Scrape down the bowl.

5. Add the eggs, one at a time, beating to incorporate each egg and scraping down the bowl as needed.

6. On low speed, add the dry ingredients in 3 additions and mix until just combined. Do not overmix. Add the dried fruits and mix until just combined. Remove the paddle, remove the bowl from the mixer, and scrape down the bowl with a rubber spatula, being sure to mix in any dry ingredients in the bottom of the bowl.

7. Use an ice cream scoop to portion the cookies in 2½-ounce (about ¼-cup) scoops, placing them evenly apart on parchment-lined baking sheets, 6 cookies per sheet (see "How to Scoop Muffins, Cookies, and Cupcakes," page 74). Use your hand to pat down each mound of dough to about ½-inch thickness.

8. Place the pan in the oven and bake the cookies until golden brown around the edges and still slightly pale in the middle, 14 to 18 minutes, rotating the pan halfway through the baking time. If you have 2 pans in the oven at the same time, also switch them between the racks.

9. Remove the baking sheet from the oven and allow to cool on a wire rack for at least 10 minutes before using a metal spatula to remove the cookies from the pan.

chocolate butter pecan sandwich cookies

These chocolate pecan cookies are one of the best-loved cookies in the bakery—chocolaty, buttery, melt-in-your-mouth wafers sandwiched around a mellow, creamy, brown butter pecan filling.

A sandwich cookie, by nature, will take more effort to make than a drop cookie, because you have to make double the quantity of cookies (each sandwich is composed of two), make the filling, let the cookies cool, then sandwich them together. Despite these extra steps, there's nothing particularly difficult about this recipe.

For the best flavor, use a top-quality cocoa such as Valrhona.

Because this cookie dough is soft and sticky, the dough must chill for at least 1 hour before you shape and bake the cookies, so plan accordingly.

The total amount of pecans in this recipe is 1¼ cups. You can toast, cool, and chop all of the nuts, then divide them as specified between the filling and the dough.

The recipe calls for kosher salt, but if you substitute table salt, cut the amount of salt in the filling in half.

SPECIAL EQUIPMENT: FOOD PROCESSOR, ELECTRIC MIXER, ⅓-OUNCE ICE CREAM SCOOP (OPTIONAL BUT RECOMMENDED FOR THE MOST UNIFORM COOKIE SANDWICHES)

brown butter pecan filling

6 tablespoons (¾ stick/3 ounces/ 85 grams) unsalted butter

1 cup (4½ ounces/128 grams) toasted, cooled, and chopped pecans (see "How to Toast and Chop Nuts," page 13)

¾ cup (3¾ ounces/105 grams) powdered sugar

1½ teaspoons pure vanilla extract

1 teaspoon kosher salt

chocolate pecan cookies

¾ cup plus 1 tablespoon (4½ ounces/ 126 grams) all-purpose flour

¼ cup plus 2 tablespoons (1½ ounces/ 43 grams) unsweetened cocoa powder

¼ teaspoon baking soda

½ cup plus 1 tablespoon (1 stick plus 1 tablespoon/4⅛ ounces/118 grams) unsalted butter, softened

¾ cup plus 2 tablespoons (6⅛ ounces/ 175 grams) granulated sugar

1 large egg at room temperature (see "How to Bring Ingredients to Room Temperature," page 12)

¼ cup (1⅛ ounces/30 grams) toasted, cooled, and finely chopped pecans

1 teaspoon pure vanilla extract

½ teaspoon kosher salt

1. To make the filling, first brown the butter. Put the butter in a small saucepan over medium to medium-high heat. Allow the butter to melt, then continue to cook, stirring constantly, until the butter solids are browned and smell toasty, about 3 minutes or more. Watch carefully so the butter does not burn. As the butter browns, the foam rises to the top and dark brown particles stick to the bottom of the pan. As soon as the butter is a dark golden brown, remove it from the heat and pour it into a small bowl.

2. In the bowl of a food processor, combine the brown butter, pecans, powdered sugar, vanilla extract, and salt and pulse until a thick paste forms, scraping down the bowl of the food processor a few times during the pulsing. Remove the filling from the food processor, cover, and chill while you are making the cookie dough.

3. To make the cookie dough, sift the flour, cocoa, and baking soda together into a bowl (see "How to Sift," page 13). Set the dry ingredients aside.

4. In the bowl of an electric mixer with the paddle attachment, combine the butter and sugar and cream together on medium-high speed until very pale and fluffy, about 3 minutes. Scrape down the bowl.

5. Add the egg on medium-low speed and beat to incorporate.

6. Scrape the bowl and the paddle and add the pecans, vanilla extract, and salt.

7. Add the dry ingredients on low speed in 3 or 4 additions and mix until just combined. Do not overmix. Remove the bowl from the mixer and scrape down all the way to the bottom of the bowl with a rubber spatula to be sure everything is well mixed.

8. Chill the cookie dough for 1 hour or longer before shaping.

9. When you are ready to shape and bake the cookies, preheat the oven to 375°F. Portion the dough using a ⅓-ounce (or #100) ice cream scoop (see "How to Scoop Muffins, Cookies, and Cupcakes," page 74). (If you don't have a scoop, use about 2 teaspoons of dough per cookie.) You should get 48 cookies. Place the cookies ¾ to 1 inch apart on parchment-lined baking sheets and use your fingers to press them flat, a little less than ¼ inch thick. (You should be able to get 16 cookies on each baking sheet and bake in 3 batches.) Bake the cookies, one sheet pan at a time, until the cookies are cooked through and feel set, about 7 minutes. Do not open the oven door

while they are baking. Remove the pan from the oven and allow to cool for at least 10 minutes before removing the cookies with a metal spatula. Cool the cookies completely before filling.

10. To make a cookie sandwich, turn one cookie flat side up and spread with about 2 teaspoons of filling (you can use the same small ice cream scoop that you used for the cookie dough to portion out the filling), then top with another cookie, flat side down, pressing gently. Repeat until all the cookies are sandwiched together.

peanut butter sandwich cookies, aka "the nora ephron"

MAKES ABOUT 24 SANDWICH COOKIES (3 INCHES IN DIAMETER)

This may be the most sought-after cookie recipe in the book, the cookie that makes it into *Seattle Metropolitan* magazine's Food Lover's Guide year after year. Once, when director, screenwriter (*When Harry Met Sally*), and novelist Nora Ephron was in town, she stopped by the Dahlia Bakery and bought a few of these cookies. Later she e-mailed me, saying this was her all-time favorite and asked for the recipe. Naturally, I sent it to Nora along with a big package of cookies. When I asked Nora if I could name the cookie after her in my cookbook, she said, "Are you kidding me? This may be the greatest cookie ever ever ever."

A sandwich cookie takes more effort than a drop cookie, because you have to make both cookies and filling. In addition, this recipe involves a chilling step and requires the cookies to be double-panned. But the results are worth it for the best-textured peanut butter cookie with the creamiest peanut filling.

After arranging the scoops of cookie batter on a baking sheet, slip another baking sheet underneath to double-pan so the cookies bake more slowly and evenly. Since you can bake only eight cookies per baking sheet, and the cookies must be double-panned, you'll have to bake them in batches. Be sure to let the baking sheets cool thoroughly before reusing them.

We use two different peanut butters in this recipe. Skippy creamy peanut butter makes the filling smooth and creamy. Adams crunchy peanut butter, which like other natural peanut butters must be well mixed before using to incorporate the oil, has just the right almost-runny consistency and crunchy bits of peanuts to give the cookies the perfect texture. To re-create our peanut butter sandwich cookies, we suggest you use the same or similar brands. We prefer moist brown sugar from a resealable plastic bag rather than from a box.

This recipe requires a 2-hour or longer chill of the shaped cookie dough, so plan accordingly.

The amount of salt in the filling is a perfect balance to the creamy peanut butter, but if you are substituting table salt for the kosher salt called for in the recipe, be sure to cut the amount in half.

This recipe was inspired by the Bouchon Bakery.

SPECIAL EQUIPMENT: ELECTRIC MIXER, 1-OUNCE ICE CREAM SCOOP (OPTIONAL BUT RECOMMENDED FOR THE MOST UNIFORM COOKIE SANDWICHES)

peanut butter filling

1½ cups (14 ounces/400 grams) creamy peanut butter, such as Skippy

6 tablespoons (¾ stick/3 ounces/168 grams) unsalted butter, softened

2 tablespoons powdered sugar

2 tablespoons honey

1 teaspoon kosher salt

peanut butter cookies

1½ cups (8 ounces/227 grams) all-purpose flour

1 teaspoon baking soda

½ teaspoon baking powder

1⅔ cups (5¼ ounces/99 grams) rolled oats, such as Quaker Old Fashioned

½ teaspoon kosher salt

1 cup plus 2 tablespoons (2 sticks plus 2 tablespoons/11¼ ounces/320 grams) unsalted butter, softened

⅓ cup (3½ ounces/125 grams) crunchy natural peanut butter, such as Adams, well mixed

¾ cup (5¼ ounces/150 grams) granulated sugar

⅔ cup (5¼ ounces/150 grams) packed brown sugar

2 large eggs at room temperature (see "How to Bring Ingredients to Room Temperature," page 12)

1 teaspoon pure vanilla extract

1. To make the peanut butter filling, combine all the filling ingredients in a bowl using a whisk. Cover and chill the mixture until you are ready to fill the cookies.

2. To make the peanut butter cookies, in a bowl, sift together the flour, baking soda, and baking powder (see "How to Sift," page 13). Stir in the oats and salt. Set the dry ingredients aside.

3. In the bowl of an electric mixer with the paddle attachment, combine the butter, chunky peanut butter, and sugars and cream on medium-high speed until very fluffy and pale, at least 3 minutes, scraping down the mixing bowl as needed.

4. Turn the mixer to medium-low and add the eggs, one at a time, beating to incorporate each egg and scraping down the bowl as needed. Beat in the vanilla extract. Add the dry ingredients on low speed in 3 to 4 additions and mix until just combined. Do not overmix. Remove the bowl from the mixer and scrape down the bowl with a rubber spatula, going all the way to the bottom of the bowl to mix in the dry ingredients well.

5. Use an ice cream scoop to portion all the cookies in 1-ounce scoops (or use about 1 heaping tablespoon per cookie), placing the scoops on a parchment-lined baking sheet (see "How to Scoop Muffins, Cookies, and Cupcakes," page 74). You should have about 48 cookies. (You can place all the cookies close together for the chilling step—you will space them for baking later.) Chill the scooped cookies for at least 2 hours or longer.

6. When you are ready to bake the cookies, preheat the oven to 375°F. Arrange 8 cookies, spaced evenly apart and staggered, on each parchment-lined baking sheet. (Note: Do *not* flatten the cookies; they will flatten as they bake.) Set the baking sheet inside another baking sheet to double pan and place it in the oven. Bake until evenly golden, about 12 minutes, rotating the pan halfway through the cooking time. If you have 2 double-panned pans in the oven at the same time, also switch them between the racks. Remove the pan from the oven and cool on a wire rack for about 10 minutes before removing the cookies with a metal spatula. Allow the cookies to cool completely before filling them.

7. To make a cookie sandwich, turn one cookie flat side up and spread with a little less than 2 teaspoons of filling. (If you have a 1-ounce scoop, you can slightly underfill it to portion the filling or underfill a tablespoon.) Top with another cookie, flat side down, pressing gently. Repeat until all the cookies are assembled into sandwiches.

top: Using a small scoop to put peanut butter filling on a peanut butter cookie placed flat side up
middle: Pressing another peanut butter cookie on top of the filling, flat side down
bottom: Gently pressing on the top cookie to push the filling to the edges

chocolate truffle cookies with crackly crust

MAKES ABOUT **30** COOKIES (3½ INCHES IN DIAMETER)

Packed with bittersweet chocolate, cocoa, and chocolate chips, super-chocolaty and soft with a crackled top, just one of these cookies will more than satisfy the cravings of any chocoholic. Whipping the batter well as you incorporate the eggs will give the cookies their characteristic crackly tops. But don't overwork the batter after you add the flour, or the cookies will be tough.

SPECIAL EQUIPMENT: ELECTRIC MIXER, 2-OUNCE ICE CREAM SCOOP (OPTIONAL BUT RECOMMENDED)

1¼ cups (7⅛ ounces/205 grams) all-purpose flour

3 tablespoons plus 1 teaspoon (¾ ounce/20 grams) unsweetened cocoa powder

½ teaspoon baking powder

½ teaspoon salt

1 pound plus 4 ounces (567 grams) bittersweet chocolate, chopped (see "Our Favorite Chocolates," page 21, and "How to Chop Chocolate," page 12)

½ cup plus 2 tablespoons (1¼ sticks/5 ounces/140 grams) unsalted butter, softened

2¼ cups (1 pound plus ¼ ounce/460 grams) sugar

6 large eggs at room temperature (see "How to Bring Ingredients to Room Temperature," page 12)

1 tablespoon pure vanilla extract

Generous 2 cups (12 ounces/340 grams) bittersweet chocolate chips

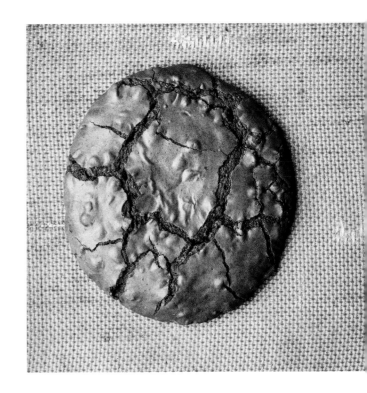

1. Preheat the oven to 350°F.

2. In a bowl, sift together the flour, cocoa, and baking powder (see "How to Sift," page 13). Stir in the salt and set aside. Place the chopped chocolate in a heatproof bowl over a saucepan of very hot but not boiling water (the bottom of the bowl should not touch the water), stirring occasionally until the chocolate is melted and smooth. Remove the bowl from the water and allow to cool for 5 to 10 minutes.

3. Combine the butter and sugar in the bowl of an electric mixer with the paddle attachment and cream on medium speed until well combined. Add the eggs, one at a time, mixing on medium speed until the eggs are incorporated.

4. Increase the speed to high and beat for a few minutes until the mixture is very light, creamy, and pale in color, scraping the bowl down as needed. Add the melted chocolate and the vanilla extract and mix just until combined. Remove the bowl from the mixer and fold in the dry ingredients using a rubber spatula. Fold in the chocolate chips.

5. Start scooping the cookies as soon as you finish making the batter. The batter is very soft at first, but it starts firming up quickly as it sits, which will make it more difficult to portion. The easiest way to portion the cookies is with a 2-ounce ice cream scoop. Pack the scoop only about three-quarters full. Or use a scant ¼ cup or 1½ ounces of cookie dough for each cookie.

6. Scoop the cookies onto parchment-lined baking sheets, placing them about 2 inches apart. Flatten each mound of dough slightly with your hand. (Tip: You can use a dampened hand, because the dough is sticky.)

7. Soon after the cookies are scooped, put them in the oven and bake them. If you are baking in batches, don't refrigerate the scooped dough, but leave them at room temperature. These cookies will not spread properly if the dough is chilled first.

8. Bake the cookies until they are evenly cracked all over the tops and softly set, 14 to 16 minutes, rotating the pan about halfway through the baking time. If you have 2 pans of cookies in the oven at the same time, also switch them between the racks.

9. Remove the pans from the oven and cool on a wire rack. Allow the cookies to cool completely before removing them from the baking sheets with a metal spatula. They stick to the paper a bit, but you can scrape them off with a sturdy metal spatula easily enough.

old-fashioned molasses cookies
with fresh ginger

MAKES 4 ½ DOZEN SMALL COOKIES

Grated fresh ginger gives these cookies their snappy flavor. They're at their delicious best when still very slightly warm from the oven.

The Dahlia Bakery offers a bigger version of this cookie so our customers can buy just one for their lunchtime treat, but this smaller size is perfect for serving with a bowl of ice cream or a cup of coffee or tea.

This recipe requires 1 hour or longer chilling time for the dough before shaping and baking, so plan accordingly.

SPECIAL EQUIPMENT: ELECTRIC MIXER

¾ cup (1½ sticks/6 ounces/170 grams) unsalted butter, softened

1 cup (7 ounces/200 grams) sugar, plus about ½ cup more for rolling

1 large egg

¼ cup (3½ ounces/99 grams) molasses

2 teaspoons peeled and grated fresh ginger

2 cups (9 ounces/255 grams) all-purpose flour

2 teaspoons baking soda

½ teaspoon kosher salt

½ teaspoon ground cinnamon

1. Preheat the oven to 350°F.

2. In the bowl of an electric mixer with the paddle attachment, cream the butter and sugar on medium speed until light and fluffy. Add the egg, molasses, and ginger and mix to combine. In a small bowl, combine the flour, baking soda, salt, and cinnamon. Add the dry ingredients to the wet ingredients and mix to combine. Refrigerate the dough for at least an hour before shaping the cookies.

3. Sprinkle about ½ cup sugar on a plate. Form ¾-inch balls of the dough and roll the balls in the sugar before placing them on parchment-lined baking sheets. Press the balls of dough flat with the palm of your hand. The cookies should be spaced 2 or 3 inches apart after they are flattened.

4. Bake until golden brown and set around the edges but still slightly soft in the center, 7 to 8 minutes, rotating the pan halfway through the baking time. If you have 2 pans of cookies in the oven at the same time, also switch them between the racks. Remove from the oven and allow the cookies to cool on the baking sheet before removing them with a metal spatula. The cookies will firm up as they cool.

tom's favorite coconut macaroons

This is not your Jewish deli macaroon. These are light, fluffy puffs of air that will make you smile.

I came up with this macaroon as a sweet end for the Chinese Feast menu in my *Big Dinners* cookbook, and the bakers have been making them (in a slightly larger size than this recipe) for the Dahlia Bakery ever since. Crisp on the outside with a nice chew inside, this is my kind of cookie.

The cookie batter must be chilled for at least 4 hours or overnight before the cookies are baked, so plan accordingly.

SPECIAL EQUIPMENT: ELECTRIC MIXER, FLEXIBLE NONSTICK BAKING MAT SUCH AS SILPAT (OPTIONAL), 1-OUNCE ICE CREAM SCOOP (OPTIONAL BUT RECOMMENDED)

2 large egg whites

Pinch of kosher salt

⅔ cup (4⅞ ounces/140 grams) sugar

2 tablespoons all-purpose flour

1 teaspoon pure vanilla extract

2¼ cups (6¾ ounces/191 grams) sweetened shredded coconut

Vegetable oil spray for the baking sheets (if not using a nonstick baking mat)

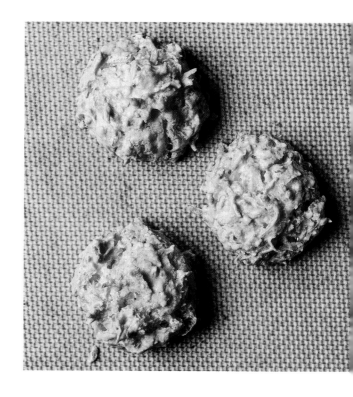

1. In the bowl of an electric mixer, using the whisk attachment, combine the egg whites and salt and whip to stiff peaks at high speed (see "How to Whip Egg Whites," page 14). Gradually add the sugar and continue to whisk for a few more minutes at high speed until the meringue is smooth and glossy and will form soft mounds. Add the flour and vanilla extract and whip briefly at medium speed until combined. Remove the bowl from the mixer and fold in the coconut with a rubber spatula. Cover the batter with plastic wrap and chill in the refrigerator for at least 4 hours or overnight.

2. When you are ready to bake the cookies, preheat the oven to 325°F. Line a baking sheet with parchment paper, then spray the paper with vegetable oil spray, because this batter is quite sticky. (Or you can use a flexible nonstick baking mat, such as a Silpat, and you won't need to spray it.) Using a 1-ounce scoop, place mounds of the batter, about 2 inches apart, on the prepared baking sheet. Or you can use a spoon to place mounds of batter, 1 tablespoon each, on the baking sheet. Keep the batter mounded up; don't flatten the cookies.

3. Bake until the cookies are evenly light golden brown, about 25 minutes, rotating the pan about halfway through the baking time. Remove from the oven and allow the cookies to cool on the baking sheet before removing them with a metal spatula.

toasted pine nut amaretti

This traditional Italian cookie is pure heaven when accompanied by a shot of espresso. These are not the world's most beautiful cookies, but they are among the most delicious if you like the flavors of almonds and pine nuts.

Amaretti are among the easiest cookies to make, but as for all pastries, the details are important.

Almond paste is usually sold in a can or as a plastic-wrapped tube. Unmold it from the can or unwrap it, then cut it into ½-inch cubes. Dicing the almond paste before putting it into the mixer is an important step for creating the proper texture of the cookie.

For the best-flavored cookies, give the pine nuts a long, slow toast at a low temperature, about 20 minutes at 300°F. Be sure the toasted pine nuts are completely cooled to room temperature before mixing them into the batter.

Because these cookies are a bit sticky, if you have a silicone mat such as a Silpat (see page 26), you can use it to line your baking sheet instead of parchment paper.

Kosher salt is coarser than table salt. If you are substituting table salt, cut the quantity in half.

SPECIAL EQUIPMENT: ELECTRIC MIXER, FLEXIBLE NONSTICK BAKING MAT SUCH AS SILPAT (OPTIONAL), 1-OUNCE ICE CREAM SCOOP (OPTIONAL BUT RECOMMENDED FOR THE NICEST SHAPE)

1 pound (about 1¾ cups/454 grams) almond paste

1½ cups (11 ounces/312 grams) sugar

1 cup (5 ounces/140 grams) toasted and cooled pine nuts (see headnote and "How to Toast and Chop Nuts," page 13)

1½ teaspoons kosher salt

3 large egg whites at room temperature (see "How to Bring Ingredients to Room Temperature," page 12)

1 teaspoon pure vanilla extract

1. Preheat the oven to 300°F.

2. Put the almond paste on a work surface and use a knife to cut it into ½-inch cubes. In the bowl of an electric mixer with the paddle attachment, combine the almond paste, sugar, pine nuts, and

salt and mix on medium-low speed until the pieces of almond paste are smaller than the size of peas and the mixture looks shaggy.

3. Add the egg whites and vanilla extract and mix until combined. Remove the bowl from the mixer and portion the cookie dough using a 1-ounce ice cream scoop (about 2 tablespoons per cookie). Place the cookies ½-inch apart on parchment-lined baking sheets. (Do not flatten the mounds.)

4. Bake the cookies until they are dark golden and cooked through, 45 to 50 minutes. Do not open the oven for the first 35 or 40 minutes of baking time, after which you can check the cookies occasionally until they are well browned and firm; rotate the pan if they are not browning evenly.

5. Remove the pan from the oven and cool on a wire rack for at least 10 minutes before removing the cookies from the pan with a metal spatula. (The cookies may stick, but you can scrape them off the paper easily enough with the metal spatula.) Allow the cookies to cool completely to room temperature before serving.

prizewinning pecan brownies

A few years ago, the bakery managers ran a contest open to all of our pastry bakers to see who could come up with a recipe for the best, most soul-satisfying brownies to produce for sale in the Dahlia Bakery, with a $250 spa gift certificate as the prize. After sampling bites of many delicious brownies in every style, from super-fudgy to delicately cakey, the panel of judges chose this recipe as the unanimous winner.

This is everything you want a brownie to be—from the crinkled crust on top to the soft but slightly chewy and intensely chocolaty interior balanced with just enough salt and studded generously with pecans.

Kosher salt is coarser than table salt. If you're substituting table salt, be sure to cut the quantity of salt in half.

SPECIAL EQUIPMENT: 9-INCH SQUARE BAKING PAN

¾ cup (1½ sticks/6 ounces/170 grams) unsalted butter, cut into chunks, plus more for the pan

4 ounces (113 grams) unsweetened chocolate, chopped (see "How to Chop Chocolate," page 12)

2 ounces (56 grams) bittersweet chocolate, chopped

1¼ cups (6 ounces/175 grams) all-purpose flour

½ teaspoon baking powder

1½ teaspoons kosher salt

2 cups (14 ounces/398 grams) sugar

2 large eggs

1 teaspoon pure vanilla extract

1½ cups (6 ounces/170 grams) roughly chopped toasted pecans (see "How to Toast and Chop Nuts," page 13)

1. Preheat the oven to 350°F. Butter the pan, then line the pan with a 9-inch-wide strip of parchment paper that fits the bottom of the pan and up 2 of the sides with a little overhang. Butter the paper.

2. Put both chocolates and the butter in a heatproof bowl that has been placed over a saucepan of gently simmering water over medium heat. (The bottom of the bowl should not touch the water.) Adjust the burner to keep the water barely at a simmer. Melt the chocolate and butter, stirring to combine using a rubber or silicone spatula, then remove the bowl from the heat and set aside.

3. Put the flour, baking powder, and salt in a bowl and use a whisk to combine. Set the dry ingredients aside.

4. In a large bowl, whisk the sugar, eggs, and vanilla extract together until smooth. Then add the chocolate-butter mixture and whisk again until smooth. Add the dry ingredients to the chocolate-egg mixture, folding with a rubber spatula until well combined. Fold in 1 cup of the pecans.

5. Scrape the batter into the prepared pan, smoothing the top with the rubber spatula. Sprinkle the remaining ½ cup of pecans evenly over the top.

6. Bake until the top looks dry and a skewer inserted into the brownies comes out mostly clean with a few crumbs clinging and maybe just a small streak of batter, 38 to 40 minutes, rotating the pan halfway through the baking time.

7. Remove the pan from the oven and cool on a wire rack for about an hour before unmolding. (The brownies will be soft when they are warm but will set up as they cool.)

8. To unmold the brownies, run a small knife along the 2 sides of the pan that are not lined with parchment paper, then invert onto a large cake cardboard or a parchment-lined baking sheet so the brownies slide out of the pan. Invert again onto a large cake cardboard or parchment-lined baking sheet so the brownies are right side up. Cut the brownies into 12 bars (4 cuts by 3 cuts) or 16 bars (4 cuts by 4 cuts) using a serrated knife.

MADE IN FRA

jackie's holiday fruitcake bars with dried cherries and brandy

Years ago, my wife, Jackie, found a recipe for fruitcake bars in an issue of *Martha Stewart Living*, tweaked it with her own combination of brandy-soaked fruits, toasted nuts, and sweet-smelling spices, and filled enough baking pans with batter to produce 100 cookie bars for our manager Christmas party. Everyone at the party went crazy for them. Whipping up a pan of these delicate, fruity, and nutty little bars is a breeze, so mark this page for your holiday baking list.

SPECIAL EQUIPMENT: 9 × 13-INCH BAKING PAN, ELECTRIC MIXER

1 cup (2 sticks/8 ounces/227 grams) unsalted butter, softened, plus more for the pan

2 cups (10¼ ounces/300 grams) all-purpose flour

¾ teaspoon ground allspice

¾ teaspoon ground cinnamon

¼ teaspoon ground cloves

¼ teaspoon freshly grated nutmeg

½ teaspoon kosher salt

1 cup (7 ounces/198 grams) brandy

1½ cups (8 ounces/227 grams) dried tart cherries

1½ cups (7 ounces/198 grams) prunes, medium-finely chopped

1 cup (4 ounces/140 grams) golden raisins

½ cup (2½ ounces/71 grams) dark raisins

½ cup (2½ ounces/71 grams) dried currants

2 cups (14 ounces/400 grams) packed brown sugar

3 large eggs

1 teaspoon pure vanilla extract

1 cup (4 ounces/118 grams) pecans, toasted, cooled, and medium-finely chopped (see "How to Toast and Chop Nuts," page 13)

Powdered sugar as needed for sprinkling

1. Preheat the oven to 350°F. Butter a 9 × 13-inch baking pan and line the bottom with a piece of parchment, leaving a few inches of parchment overhanging the 2 long sides of the pan, then butter the paper.

2. Whisk together the flour, spices, and salt in a bowl, then set the dry ingredients aside.

3. Put the brandy in a saucepan over medium-high heat and heat to a simmer. Remove the pan from the heat and stir in the fruit. Transfer the brandy-fruit mixture to a bowl and allow to cool to room temperature. Add 1 cup of the flour mixture to the fruit mixture and toss to combine. Set the fruit mixture and the remaining dry ingredients aside.

4. In an electric mixer with the paddle attachment, on medium speed, beat the butter and the brown sugar until light and fluffy. Add the eggs, one at a time, beating well to incorporate each egg before adding the next. Add the vanilla extract and mix. Turn the mixer to low speed and add the remaining dry ingredients. Mix until just combined. Remove the bowl from the mixer and, using a rubber spatula, fold in the reserved fruit mixture and the pecans. Scrape the batter into the prepared pan, using the rubber spatula to smooth the top.

5. Bake until cooked through and a skewer inserted into the fruitcake comes out with a few crumbs attached but no batter, 50 to 55 minutes, rotating the pan once halfway through the baking time.

6. Remove the pan from the oven and allow the cake to cool in the pan on a wire rack for 1 hour. Then use the overhanging parchment to lift the fruitcake (in one large piece) out of the pan. Transfer the fruitcake to the wire rack and allow to cool completely, still on the parchment paper, 45 to 60 minutes longer. Turn the cake over to peel off the parchment paper and turn it over again to put it right side up. (To transfer the fruitcake, use a couple large spatulas or slide the fruitcake onto a piece of cardboard to help move it around.)

7. Cut the fruitcake into 32 bars (8 cuts by 4 cuts), using a serrated knife. Use a small sieve to sprinkle the bars with powdered sugar before serving.

russian tea cakes

Our version of this ever-popular cookie, perfect for holiday baking, is rich with toasted pecans and butter. The recipe doubles easily, and, though most cookies can be stored airtight at room temperature for a day or two, Russian tea cakes store especially well, even for several days. Bake a big batch, roll the cookies in plenty of powdered sugar, and store them in cookie tins or in plastic containers with tight lids until you are ready to give them away.

The cookie dough may not seem sweet enough, but the powdered sugar coating will provide plenty of sweetness to the finished cookies. The cookies must be rolled in powdered sugar while they are still warm so the sugar sticks. You won't use up all the powdered sugar, but you need enough sugar in the pan to be able to roll the cookies and coat them well on all sides.

In the bakery we offer a larger version of this cookie, but small Russian Tea Cake "bites," like these, are sometimes sold stacked inside little boxes. A couple of small cookies go well with a cup of tea or coffee or a bowl of ice cream.

Since you'll be grinding the pecans in the food processor, it's fine to buy pecan pieces instead of halves.

SPECIAL EQUIPMENT: FOOD PROCESSOR, ELECTRIC MIXER

5 ounces (1¼ cups/143 grams) pecans, toasted and cooled (see "How to Toast and Chop Nuts," page 13)

¼ cup plus 1 tablespoon (2 ounces/ 56 grams) sugar

¾ cup (1½ sticks/6 ounces/170 grams) unsalted butter, softened

1 teaspoon pure vanilla extract

1½ cups (8 ounces/230 grams) all-purpose flour

¼ teaspoon kosher salt

About 4 cups (1 pound/454 grams) powdered sugar, for coating

1. Preheat the oven to 325°F.

2. Put the pecans and 1 tablespoon sugar in the bowl of a food processor and pulse until finely ground. Set the pecans aside.

3. In an electric mixer with the paddle attachment, beat the butter, the remaining ¼ cup of sugar, and the vanilla extract on medium speed until light and fluffy. Scrape down the bowl, then add the flour and salt. Mix with the paddle until combined. Add the pecans and mix again until combined. (The dough will seem dry at first, but it will come together.) Remove the bowl from the machine and use a rubber spatula to be sure all the dry ingredients are well mixed down to the bottom of the bowl.

4. Roll the dough into ¾-inch balls and place them about an inch apart on parchment-lined baking sheets. Bake the cookies for 22 to 26 minutes, until the bottoms are starting to turn golden, rotating the pan halfway through the baking time. If you have 2 pans in the oven at the same time, switch them between the racks. (You can gently lift a cookie up with an offset spatula to check that the bottom is starting to brown.) Remove the baking sheet from the oven and allow to cool on a wire rack for 3 to 4 minutes, long enough to set up, but don't allow them to cool completely or the sugar coating won't stick well.

5. Meanwhile, divide the powdered sugar between 2 shallow containers (such as 9 × 13-inch baking pans). While the cookies are still warm, use a metal spatula to transfer them from the baking sheets to the containers of powdered sugar, putting about 20 cookies in each container, and roll them in the powdered sugar to coat generously on all sides. Allow the cookies to cool completely to room temperature, then remove them from the powdered sugar and serve or store.

sparkling sugar cookies

MAKES 38 COOKIES (3 INCHES IN DIAMETER)

For the Dahlia Bakery, the bakers roll sugar cookie dough and cut out 4- to 5-inch cookies in myriad shapes, from Dungeness crabs to Valentine hearts to Thanksgiving turkeys, which are baked and then decorated with royal icing and sparkling colored sugars. If you would like to decorate the cookies, see the recipe for Royal Decorating Icing and "How to Decorate Sugar Cookies," which follow this recipe.

This cookie dough is tender enough that, after rolling and cutting, you can gently gather the scraps together and reroll them one time. Cut out more cookies, but don't reroll those scraps or the cookies will be tough. You can use any size and shape of cookie cutter that you like, but the yield will vary.

The dough must be chilled for at least 2 hours before being rolled, so plan accordingly.

SPECIAL EQUIPMENT: ELECTRIC MIXER, 3-INCH ROUND COOKIE CUTTER OR OTHER SHAPES

2 cups (4 sticks/1 pound/454 grams) unsalted butter, softened

2 cups (13½ ounces/383 grams) sugar

8 large egg yolks

3 tablespoons pure vanilla extract

½ teaspoon kosher salt

4½ cups (1 pound 7 ounces/650 grams) all-purpose flour

Royal Decorating Icing (page 151)

1. In an electric mixer, using the paddle attachment, cream the butter and sugar on medium speed until light and fluffy. Add the egg yolks, vanilla extract, and salt and beat until well combined. Gradually add the flour in 3 additions, mixing on low speed and scraping down the bowl with a rubber spatula to be sure all the dry ingredients are mixed in. Remove the dough from the mixer, shape into a flattened ball, and wrap in plastic wrap. Refrigerate the dough for 2 hours or longer.

2. When you are ready to bake the cookies, preheat the oven to 350°F.

3. On a lightly floured work surface, using a rolling pin, roll the dough out to a thickness of ¼ inch. (As you start to roll the dough, use a ruler to check, because for the best-textured cookies, you don't want to roll the dough too thin.) Use a 3-inch round cutter (or another shape) and cut as many cookies as you can from the sheet of rolled dough. Gently gather the scraps together and reroll the dough one time, cutting more cookies and discarding the scraps. Place the cookies about an inch apart on parchment-lined baking sheets.

Cookie cutters

4. Bake until very lightly browned around the edges, 15 to 18 minutes, rotating the baking sheet halfway through the baking time. If you have 2 pans in the oven at the same time, also switch them between the racks. Remove the baking sheet from the oven and cool on a wire rack for about 10 minutes before removing the cookies using an offset spatula. Allow the cookies to cool completely before decorating as desired.

Piping Royal Decorating Icing onto Sparkling Sugar Cookies using a parchment cone

Inverting a cookie into a pan of decorative sugar while the icing on the cookie is still wet

Adding another detail to a cookie

Be creative—this is the fun part!

royal decorating icing

Royal icing is a simple white icing made of powdered sugar and egg whites. The quantity here, intended for decorating cookies, makes a slightly thicker icing so it will hold its shape when piped onto sugar cookies from parchment cones or disposable plastic pastry bags.

The quantity for royal icing intended for dipping Éclairs (page 315) is a little thinner so that you can dip an éclair into it and then lift the éclair out and tilt it, allowing the excess glaze to run off the sides and coat the top of the éclair evenly.

In either case, if you want to adjust the thickness of the royal icing, add more powdered sugar to thicken or more egg white to thin, as needed.

If you prefer not to use raw egg whites for safety reasons, pint containers of pasteurized egg whites, both regular and organic, are available in the refrigerated section of supermarkets, usually right next to the fresh eggs. (Note: 1 large egg yields about 2 tablespoons of egg white.)

Use royal icing immediately after making it.

for decorating sugar cookies

3 cups (12 ounces/340 grams) powdered sugar, sifted

1 large egg white

1 tablespoon freshly squeezed lemon juice

1 teaspoon pure vanilla extract

Food coloring (optional)

Put the powdered sugar in a bowl and add the egg white, lemon juice, and vanilla extract. Combine with a whisk, whisking until smooth. If desired, add a few drops of food coloring and stir until the color is even.

for dipping éclairs

2 cups (8 ounces/227 grams) powdered sugar, sifted

1 large egg white

1 tablespoon plus 2 teaspoons freshly squeezed lemon juice

1 teaspoon pure vanilla extract

Put the powdered sugar in a bowl and add the egg white, lemon juice, and vanilla extract. Combine with a whisk until smooth. Transfer the icing to a small loaf pan or similar container and use for dipping éclairs.

To decorate the Sparkling Sugar Cookies (page 148), first make royal icing for decorating sugar cookies (page 151). If you like, you can color the icing with food coloring. You can use liquid food coloring, but we prefer gel or paste colors because they are more potent, and thus they require less coloring and won't affect the consistency of your icing. If using gel or paste food colors, you'll need to add only a tiny drop to your royal icing. If you want more than one color, divide the icing into small bowls and add the color of your choice to each bowl.

To decorate the cookies, you can make a paper cone, which is what our pastry bakers do, by cutting a triangle out of parchment paper and folding it to make a cone. If you don't know how to make a paper cone, it's easy to find instructions, often with video, online, or you can use a pastry bag with a small plain tip. Disposable pastry bags (see Sources) work well because you can cut off and save the tip and then throw the rest of the bag and any leftover icing away when you're done. You can even use a quart-size resealable plastic bag filled with icing and cut a bit off one corner to make an impromptu pastry bag.

Fill the paper cone or pastry bag with freshly made royal icing or fill a few cones or bags with different colors of icing (never fill a cone or pastry bag more than two-thirds full or it will be too difficult to handle) and pipe the icing onto the cookies as desired. Our pastry bakers often outline the silhouette of each cookie with a thin line of icing, or they may decorate the center of the cookie with overlapping lines of icing in different colors.

If you don't want to use a pastry bag, you can spread icing on the cookies using a small offset spatula or thin the royal icing as needed and use a pastry brush to brush it on the cookies.

If desired, sprinkle the cookies with decorative colored sugars while the icing is still wet. (Another way is to turn each cookie upside down and press it gently into a shallow dish of decorative sugar while the icing is still wet.) Allow the icing to set up at room temperature before serving the cookies.

how to decorate sugar cookies

ruby's bones

It's a rare dog who can resist the flavors of peanut butter and bacon, and Ruby, my wife, Jackie's, Brittany spaniel—not known for passing up a treat of any kind—was no exception. You'll find a glass jar of "bones" on the Dahlia Bakery counter every day.

Instead of using a bone-shaped cookie cutter, you can just cut the rolled out dough into small rectangles using a chef's knife. The treats won't look as cute, but I doubt anyone's pooch will mind.

SPECIAL EQUIPMENT: A BONE-SHAPED COOKIE CUTTER (OPTIONAL) (YOU CAN USE ANY SIZE CUTTER, BUT THE YIELD WILL VARY)

4 strips (3½ ounces/100 grams) thick-sliced bacon

½ cup (4 ounces/115 grams) water, plus a few tablespoons for cooking the bacon

¼ cup (2 ounces/ 60 grams) peanut butter

1 large egg

3 tablespoons (2 ounces/57 grams) honey

¾ teaspoon kosher salt

1 cup (5½ ounces/160 grams) all-purpose flour

1 cup (3 ounces/90 grams) wheat germ

½ cup (2½ ounces/70 grams) whole wheat flour

1. Preheat the oven to 350°F.

2. Cut the bacon into fine julienne, about ⅛ inch thick, and place in a skillet over medium-high heat. Add a few tablespoons of water and cook, rendering out the fat, until the bacon is light golden brown and starting to get crispy. Remove the pan from the heat and transfer the bacon, with all the fat, to a bowl and allow to cool for 5 to 10 minutes. Stir in the water, peanut butter, egg, honey, and salt. Set the wet ingredients aside.

3. In another bowl, combine the flour, wheat germ, and whole wheat flour. Add the wet ingredients and use a rubber spatula to combine everything into a soft dough.

4. Place the dough on a lightly floured work surface and use a rolling pin to roll it out to a thickness of about ¼ inch. Cut out dog bone shapes with a cookie cutter and place them at least

½ inch apart on a parchment-lined baking sheet. Gather the scraps together and reroll, cutting out more dog bones and placing them on the baking sheet.

5. Use a fork to prick each dog bone in 2 or 3 places. Place the baking sheet inside a second baking sheet to double-pan, then place in the oven and bake until the dog bones are golden brown, 35 to 40 minutes, rotating once halfway through the baking time. Turn the oven off and let the bones dry out in the oven until the oven returns to room temperature. Remove the bones from the oven and allow to cool on a wire rack, then store in an airtight container.

6. If you, or your dog, prefer a dog bone that is a little softer and chewier, skip the step of allowing the bones to cool in the oven and instead transfer them to a wire rack as soon as they are baked and allow them to cool to room temperature.

<<< Derby, eating "Ruby's Bones"

heavenly pies

PIES, RUSTIC PIES, CRISPS

ABOUT PASTRY DOUGHS

Making and baking pies and pastries takes time. Before pastry dough is made, butter and shortening must be chilled in the refrigerator or freezer. Then the dough must be chilled before being rolled. A single-crust pie shell must be blind-baked and cooled before being filled.

Often our pies and pastries are baked at lower temperatures and for longer times than you may see in other cookbooks. We think this slower baking cooks the dough all the way through and improves the texture of your finished pastry.

So, when making pastry, give yourself enough time and do some advance planning.

CHILLING AND FREEZING PASTRY DOUGH

You can make pastry dough ahead, wrap it in plastic, and refrigerate it for a day or two before using. For longer storage, at least a few weeks, you can freeze the dough, but allow it to rest and chill in the refrigerator for an hour or two first. Just remember to thaw the dough overnight in the refrigerator when you are ready to use it.

If you are making a single-crust pie shell, you can roll your dough and form your pastry shell, then wrap it in plastic wrap and either refrigerate or freeze it for the same amount of time. Frozen pastry shells can be baked directly out of the freezer, without being thawed.

Keep in mind that, for all pastry dough, freezing is not resting. If the recipe directs you to allow the pastry dough to rest in the refrigerator for a certain amount of time, be sure to refrigerate it before you freeze it; otherwise it may be tough.

BLIND-BAKING PASTRY SHELLS

Blind-baking a pastry shell means baking the shell before filling it. The pastry shell is lined with parchment paper and filled with weights—we use dried beans—before being baked. This prevents the sides of the pastry from sliding down and the bottom of the shell from puffing up while baking. After the pastry is cooked enough to be set, the parchment and beans are removed and the pastry shell is returned to the oven to brown the bottom of the shell.

For lining the pastry shell, use a square of parchment paper large enough to grab the corners of the paper later and pull the paper out of the shell. Then pour in enough dried beans to come up the sides. Push lightly on the beans so they are spread all the way to the edges.

After the pastry shell has been baked long enough to set the pastry, remove the pan from the oven and remove the parchment and beans, then return your pastry shell to the oven to finish browning. Save the beans; allow them to cool, then store them in a jar or other container. The dried beans can be used many times as pie weights (but will no longer be good for eating).

After blind-baking a single-crust pastry shell, you can allow it to sit at room temperature for several hours before filling it.

PIE PANS

We baked all our pies in glass (Pyrex) pie pans except our double-crust apple pie, which we bake in a metal pie pan (because we like the extra heat from a metal pan for a double-crust pie). Metal conducts heat faster than glass, so if you do the reverse, your baking times may vary slightly from ours.

MY TRIPLE COCONUT CREAM ADVENTURE AND OTHER PIE STORIES

Can a single pie really save a restaurant?

In November 1989, three months into what seemed like our own personal reality show—the opening of the 140-seat Dahlia Lounge restaurant in center city Seattle—reality actually hit. Jackie was eight months pregnant with our now-twenty-two-year-old daughter, Loretta. I was spending every available minute questioning each decision we made leading up to opening day. What was the magic menu mix that was going to draw more people through our front doors? Because we sure weren't cooking enough meals for us to survive. Some of the staff members were beginning to quit because they weren't making enough tips, while

how to measure ice cold water for pastry

Fill a container with ice and water. When you are ready to measure the ice-cold water for the pastry recipe, use a small strainer to strain the amount of ice water needed for the recipe. Measure out the amount with a measuring spoon or measuring cup, then transfer the strained ice-cold water to a small bowl or container. If the recipe calls for vinegar, you can measure the vinegar into the cold water at this point.

how to make starch water

Put 1 tablespoon of flour or cornstarch in a small bowl with ½ cup cold water and mix to combine. Use a pastry brush to brush this mixture on uncooked pastry, using as much as needed to seal. (You don't need to use it all up.)

Instead of making starch water, if you have saved an egg white in the refrigerator, you can beat it until frothy with a fork or a small whisk and use the beaten white to seal pastry.

others were going through the mutually tough process of getting laid off. Our crew of forty-two was steadily being whittled down until there were only twenty of us left, and we still had to hold our paychecks till "after the weekend." Money was painfully tight at home, and all the while the world seemed to be closing out our dream.

One of the few bright spots in those opening months was a wacky, homey dessert that made everyone smile. When things are tough, it helps to focus on even the smallest successes. From the day we opened, the Triple Coconut Cream Pie was a hit. People of every age would just plain flip out when they saw the fluffy triangular mound covered in white chocolate and toasted coconut arrive at their table. Eyes as big as saucers would glance back up at the waiter after the first bite, suggesting this was no grandma's coco pie. Every time I saw a mention of us in the newspaper, was asked to do a spot on TV or radio, or was asked for an auction donation, the "unbelievable coconut cream pie" was mentioned, with people implying that if you hadn't tried it you were an idiot.

The pie "connection" with our customers was indisputable. Many folks called to check that it was on the menu before they would make a reservation.

Slowly, we worked our way up from one pie a day in 1989 to the more than a hundred now served every day in our restaurants and out of our bakery. It seems that everywhere I go around town, someone has a story to share about his or her experience with our custardy wonder. We now have fifteen businesses, at thirteen of which on any given day you can order a lusty wedge of Triple Coconut Cream Pie. It does go without saying that the "Coco Pie" holds a special place in our hearts, and I hope the "little pie that could" brings family and friendship closer in yours!

And now for a few pie facts! Since we opened in 1989 . . .

- We've sold 345,290 Coco Pies.
- We've used 500,000 pounds of coconut, 690,580 large eggs, and 54,000 gallons of heavy cream to make the Coco Pie.
- We've served the Coco Pie four times to President Barack Obama.
- I've eaten 1,196 slices of Coco Pie (one a week for 23 years). Yum!
- Local charities have raised $1,000,000-plus by selling donated Coco Pies for big bucks at their auctions!

dahlia triple coconut cream pie

MAKES ONE 9-INCH PIE; SERVES 6 TO 8

This coconut cream pie has made many lists as one of the best pies in America. We've been serving it for twenty-three years, and, hyperbole aside, this is a damn good pie. The effort you put into making this pie will be rewarded when you taste its silky, coconuty filling topped with clouds of vanilla whipped cream and showered with crunchy toasted coconut.

I've always called this our triple coconut cream pie because there's coconut in the pastry cream, coconut in the crust, and more coconut sprinkled on top. Several years ago, the bakers had the idea to make the coconut pastry cream with half milk and half coconut milk, instead of using all milk. Now that there are two kinds of coconut in the pastry cream, it would be fair to call this a quadruple coconut cream pie, but "triple coconut cream" rolls off the tongue more easily. The funny thing is how many people have told me they love this pie even though they don't like coconut!

A good-quality heavy-bottomed saucepan (see "Pots and Pans," page 30) works best for making pastry cream.

You can make the pastry cream up to a day ahead and keep it covered and refrigerated, but fill and top the pie only when you are ready to serve it.

Large-chip unsweetened coconut, for the topping, is available in the bulk section of some supermarkets or natural food stores, or you can buy it online (see Sources). Or you can just substitute shredded sweetened coconut.

SPECIAL EQUIPMENT: 9-INCH PIE PAN, ELECTRIC MIXER, PASTRY BAG FITTED WITH A LARGE STAR TIP

coconut pastry cream

1 cup (8 ounces/230 grams) milk

1 cup (8 ounces/230 grams) canned unsweetened coconut milk, stirred

2 cups (6 ounces/170 grams) shredded sweetened coconut

1 vanilla bean, split in half lengthwise

2 large eggs

½ cup plus 2 tablespoons (4¼ ounces/125 grams) sugar

3 tablespoons (⅞ ounce/26 grams) all-purpose flour

4 tablespoons (½ stick/2 ounces/ 57 grams) unsalted butter, room temperature

One 9-inch blind-baked and cooled coconut pastry shell (page 164)

whipped cream topping

2½ cups (20 ounces/600 grams) heavy cream, chilled

⅓ cup (2¼ ounces/63 grams) sugar

1 teaspoon pure vanilla extract

garnish

2 ounces (57 grams) unsweetened chip or large-shred coconut (about 1½ cups), or sweetened shredded coconut (about ⅔ cup)

Chunk of white chocolate (4 to 6 ounces, to make 2 ounces of curls)

Filling the coconut pastry shells with coconut pastry cream

Piping the whipped cream topping on top of the coconut cream pies

Garnishing coconut cream pies with toasted coconut

1. To make the coconut pastry cream, combine the milk, coconut milk, and shredded coconut in a heavy-bottomed medium saucepan. Use a paring knife to scrape the seeds from the vanilla bean and add both the scrapings and the pod to the milk mixture. Place the saucepan over medium-high heat and stir occasionally until the mixture almost comes to a boil.

2. In a bowl, whisk together the eggs, sugar, and flour until well combined. Temper the eggs by pouring a small amount (about ⅓ cup) of the scalded milk into the egg mixture while whisking. Then add the warmed egg mixture to the saucepan of milk and coconut. Whisk over medium-high heat until the pastry cream thickens and begins to bubble. Keep whisking until the mixture is very thick, 4 to 5 minutes more. Remove the saucepan from the heat. Add the butter and whisk until it melts. Remove and discard the vanilla pod (or rinse it and save it for Vanilla Bean Sugar, page 64). Transfer the pastry cream to a bowl and place it over another bowl of ice water. Stir occasionally until it is cool. Place a piece of plastic wrap directly on the surface of the pastry cream to prevent a skin from forming and refrigerate until completely cold. The pastry cream will thicken as it cools.

3. When the pastry cream is cold, fill the pastry shell, smoothing the surface with a rubber spatula.

4. In an electric mixer with the whisk attachment, whip the heavy cream with the sugar and vanilla extract to peaks that are firm enough to hold their shape. Fill a pastry bag fitted with a star tip with the whipped cream and pipe it all over the surface of the pie.

5. For the garnish, preheat the oven to 350°F. Spread the coconut chips on a baking sheet. Toast in the oven for 7 to 8 minutes, watching carefully and stirring once or twice until lightly browned, since coconut burns easily. Remove the coconut from the oven and allow to cool, then sprinkle it over the top of the pie. Use a vegetable peeler to scrape about 2 ounces of the white chocolate into curls on top of the pie. If you prefer, you can cut the pie into wedges and put the wedges on plates, then garnish each wedge individually with coconut and white chocolate curls.

coconut pastry dough

This is the dough we use for the Dahlia Triple Coconut Cream Pie (page 161). When you blind-bake the pastry shell, be sure you bake it thoroughly, as directed in the instructions, or the crust may be tough.

Very cold butter makes a flakier crust. If your butter is not very cold, set the diced butter in the freezer for 10 to 15 minutes before making your dough.

Like most pastry doughs, this one must be chilled for at least 30 minutes before being rolled, and the shaped pastry shell must be chilled for at least an hour before being blind-baked, so plan accordingly.

SPECIAL EQUIPMENT: FOOD PROCESSOR, BENCH KNIFE OR SCRAPER, 9-INCH PIE PAN, DRIED BEANS FOR PIE WEIGHTS

1 cup plus 2 tablespoons (5¾ ounces/165 grams) all-purpose flour

½ cup (1¾ ounces/50 grams) shredded sweetened coconut

½ cup (1 stick/4 ounces/113 grams) cold unsalted butter,
    cut into ½-inch dice

2 teaspoons sugar

¼ teaspoon kosher salt

⅓ cup (2⅝ ounces/75 grams) ice-cold water, or more as needed
    (see "How to Measure Ice-Cold Water for Pastry," page 159)

1. In the bowl of a food processor, combine the flour, coconut, diced butter, sugar, and salt. Pulse to form coarse crumbs. Gradually add the water, a tablespoon at a time, pulsing each time. Use only as much water as needed for the dough to hold together when pressed gently between your fingers; don't work the dough with your hands—just test to see if it is holding. (The dough will not form a ball or even clump together in the processor—it will still be quite loose.)

2. Place a large sheet of plastic wrap on the counter and dump the coconut dough onto it. Pull the plastic wrap around the dough, forcing it into a rough flattened round with the pressure of the plastic wrap. Chill for 30 to 60 minutes before rolling.

3. To roll the dough, unwrap the round of coconut dough and put it on a lightly floured board. Flour the rolling pin and your hands. Roll the dough out into a circle about ⅛ inch thick. Occasionally lift the dough with a bench knife or scraper to check that it is not sticking and add more flour if it seems like it's about to stick. Trim to a 12- to 13-inch round.

4. Transfer the rolled dough to a 9-inch pie pan. Ease the dough loosely and gently into the pan. You don't want to stretch the dough at this point because it will shrink when it is baked. Trim any excess dough to a 1- to 1½-inch overhang. Turn the dough under along the rim of the pie pan and use your fingers and thumb to flute the edge. Chill the unbaked pie shell for at least an hour before baking. (This step prevents the dough from shrinking in the oven.)

5. When you are ready to bake the piecrust, preheat the oven to 400°F. Place a piece of parchment in the pie shell, with sides overhanging the pan, and fill with dried beans. (This step prevents the bottom of the shell from puffing up during baking.) Bake the piecrust for 20 to 25 minutes, or until the pastry rim is golden. Remove the pie pan from the oven. Remove the paper and beans and return the piecrust to the oven. Bake for another 10 to 12 minutes or until the bottom of the crust has golden brown patches. Remove from the oven and allow the pie shell to cool completely.

Our top-selling triple coconut cream pie is sold in three sizes at the Dahlia Bakery: the 9-inch full-size pie, which serves 6 to 8 people; a "baby" pie, which serves 2 to 4; and mini coco pie bites—the perfect little bite to pop right into your mouth! The pie bites sell like crazy and are especially popular as tray-passed desserts or for dessert buffets for weddings and other events. If you would like to make your own, here is the method for making 40 mini coco pie bites.

SPECIAL EQUIPMENT: 2¾- OR 3-INCH ROUND COOKIE CUTTER, 40 TARTLET PANS (80 FOR EASIEST BAKING), 2 INCHES IN DIAMETER

2 batches Coconut Pastry Dough

½ batch Coconut Pastry Cream

1 batch Whipped Cream Topping

1 batch Garnish

1. Roll out the coconut pastry dough and cut out 40 rounds using a 2¾-inch round cutter.

2. Press the rounds into 40 tartlet pans. The best way to bake the tartlets is to press another (empty) tartlet pan of the same size on top of the pastry-lined tartlets, then turn both tartlet pans upside down and set them on parchment-lined baking sheets. When the baking sheet is full of tartlet pans, set another baking sheet on top to weigh the tartlet pans down and keep the dough from shrinking while it is baked. If you don't have 80 tartlet pans, you will have to line each of the 40 pastry-lined tartlets with a small piece of parchment, fill them with dried beans, and bake them right side up.

3. Bake the tartlet shells in a preheated 350°F oven for about 24 minutes, until evenly golden brown. Remove from the oven and allow to cool. (Remove the paper and beans, if using.) Unmold the pastry shells from the tartlet pans.

4. Fill each pastry shell with a little less than a tablespoon of pastry cream. Whip the heavy cream with sugar and vanilla, toast the coconut, and shave the white chocolate curls as directed for the garnish in the coconut cream pie recipe. Top each mini pie bite with whipped cream, a little toasted coconut, and a white chocolate curl. Serve immediately.

silk chocolate cream pie with pecan crust

Lush, dark, and silky smooth, this pie is like the best chocolate pudding you ever tasted enclosed in a really crisp pecan pastry shell and topped with a cloud of whipped cream. Try making this, instead of a cake, to celebrate a special "decade" birthday.

Though the pie filling contains both milk and bittersweet chocolates (more milk than bittersweet in fact), you wouldn't guess it from the richly dark chocolate flavor. The milk chocolate is there for balance and sweetness. For the best flavor, it's essential to use high-quality brands for both types of chocolate and the cocoa (see "Our Favorite Chocolates," page 21).

A good-quality heavy-bottomed saucepan is highly recommended for making the chocolate filling (see "Pots and Pans," page 30).

The chocolate filling must chill for at least 2 hours before the pie is served, so plan accordingly.

SPECIAL EQUIPMENT: FOOD PROCESSOR, ELECTRIC MIXER, 9-INCH PIE PAN

chocolate filling

¾ cup (5 ounces/140 grams) chopped milk chocolate (see "How to Chop Chocolate," page 12)

½ cup plus 1 tablespoon (3 ounces/ 85 grams) chopped bittersweet chocolate

¼ cup (3 ounces/85 grams) light corn syrup

2 teaspoons pure vanilla extract

½ teaspoon kosher salt

5 large egg yolks

¼ cup plus 1 tablespoon (2¼ ounces/ 65 grams) packed brown sugar

¾ cup (6¼ ounces/175 grams) milk

¾ cup (6¼ ounces/175 grams) heavy cream

3 tablespoons (⅞ ounce/24 grams) unsweetened cocoa powder

One 9-inch blind-baked and cooled pecan pastry shell (page 170)

topping

1½ cups (12½ ounces/355 grams) heavy cream, chilled

2 tablespoons plus 1 teaspoon packed brown sugar

1 teaspoon pure vanilla extract

¼ cup chocolate shavings or ½ cup curls (1 ounce/30 grams) (see "How to Shave Chocolate," page 12, and "How to Make Chocolate Curls," page 13)

1. To make the chocolate filling, place both chocolates, the corn syrup, vanilla extract, and salt in the bowl of a food processor. Place a fine-mesh strainer over the food processor bowl. (You will use this setup after you cook the cream-yolk mixture in the next few steps.)

2. In another bowl, combine the egg yolks and brown sugar, whisking until slightly pale. Set aside.

3. In a heavy-bottomed saucepan over medium-high heat, combine the milk, cream, and cocoa powder and bring to a boil, stirring frequently with a whisk. To temper the yolks, add a third of the hot cream mixture to the yolk-sugar mixture and whisk briefly. Then add the yolk-sugar mixture to the saucepan, reduce the heat to medium, and stir vigorously with a heatproof rubber spatula, making sure to keep scraping all over the bottom and sides of the pot so the mixture doesn't stick. Then switch the rubber spatula to a whisk and continue to cook the mixture, stirring constantly with the whisk, until it thickens enough to coat the back of a spoon, about 4 minutes.

Pouring the chocolate filling from the bowl of the food processor into the pecan pastry crust

4. As soon as the hot cream-yolk mixture has thickened, pour it through the fine-mesh sieve set over the chocolate in the food processor, forcing all of the mixture through using a rubber spatula. Remove the strainer, put the lid on the processor, and run it for about 1 minute. Scrape the mixture down with a rubber spatula and run again until smooth, about 1 minute more.

5. Transfer the chocolate filling to the pastry shell, smoothing the top with a rubber spatula. Refrigerate the pie for at least 2 hours, or until set. (If you touch the top of the filling, you won't have chocolate on your finger if the filling is set.)

6. When the filling is set, make the topping. Combine the cream, brown sugar, and vanilla extract in the bowl of an electric mixer using the whisk and whisk until stiff peaks form. Top the pie with the whipped cream, using a rubber spatula to cover the whole surface of the pie evenly. Use an offset spatula to make decorative swirls in the cream. Sprinkle the chocolate shavings or curls decoratively over the cream, slice the pie, and serve.

A properly blind-baked pecan pastry shell is golden brown with a few dark patches.

pecan pastry dough

MAKES 1 SINGLE 9-INCH PIECRUST

I love the earthy flavor of pecans in this piecrust. The extra oil from the nuts helps it get nice and crisp, and the crispness, along with an extra hit of salt, makes this crust a good contrast with any sweet cream pie.

The salt is more than you usually see in a pastry dough, but it plays well against the flavor of the nuts. Kosher salt is coarser than table salt, so if you are substituting table salt, cut the quantity of salt in half.

Before you begin the recipe, dice the butter, cover it with plastic wrap, and place it in the freezer for 30 minutes.

The dough must be refrigerated for at least 2 hours before being rolled, and the pastry-lined pie pan needs to be chilled at least 30 minutes before baking, so plan accordingly.

Often pastry shells are blind-baked at a higher temperature than the 350°F specified here, so this pastry takes a long time to bake, over an hour. The reward for slow, patient, thorough baking is a really crisp pastry.

SPECIAL EQUIPMENT: FOOD PROCESSOR, 9-INCH PIE PAN, DRIED BEANS FOR PIE WEIGHTS

½ cup (2⅛ ounces/60 grams) pecans, halves or pieces

1⅓ cups (7 ounces/200 grams) all-purpose flour, plus more for rolling out the dough

1 tablespoon plus 2 teaspoons packed brown sugar

1½ teaspoons kosher salt

½ cup plus 2 tablespoons (5 ounces/ 150 grams) unsalted butter, cut into ½-inch dice, very cold (see headnote)

3 to 4 tablespoons (1⅜ to 2 ounces/39 to 58 grams) ice-cold water as needed (see "How to Measure Ice-Cold Water for Pastry," page 159)

1 teaspoon distilled white vinegar

1. Put the pecans in the bowl of a food processor and pulse until finely ground. Scrape down the sides and bottom of the food processor bowl to make sure none of the nuts are stuck to the bowl. Add the flour, brown sugar, and salt and pulse 2 to 3 times to mix the dry ingredients with the nuts. Add the butter and pulse 10 times or a few more until the pieces of butter are slightly smaller than peas.

2. Combine 3 tablespoons of ice-cold water with the vinegar in a small measuring cup, then gradually pour the water-vinegar mixture through the feed tube and pulse 3 or 4 more times, or until the mixture looks shaggy. Remove the lid and squeeze some of the dough, which should come together as a clump. If the mixture seems too dry, add the remaining tablespoon of cold water and pulse a few more times.

3. Remove the dough from the food processor and dump it onto a work surface. Use your hands to gather the dough into a flattened disk. Wrap the dough in plastic wrap and refrigerate for at least 2 hours before rolling.

Making a "thumb and index finger" fluted edge on a pecan pastry pie shell

4. Unwrap the chilled dough and place it on a lightly floured work surface. Using a rolling pin, roll the dough into a circle approximately 12 inches in diameter. Transfer the dough to a 9-inch pie pan. An easy way to transfer the dough is to fold the dough in half or quarters. Pick up the folded dough and place it in the pan, then unfold gently, easing it (and not stretching it) into the pan. Use your fingers to press the dough lightly against the sides of the pan all the way around so the dough won't slide down.

5. Trim the excess dough to a ¾- to 1-inch overhang. Fold the overhang up and over (toward the inside of the pan) and use your hands to press gently on the dough all around the circumference to form a neat pastry rim ¼ to ½ inch thick. Then use the narrowest side of the handle of a small tool such as a paring knife or a small offset spatula to press down on this pastry rim against the pan at 1-inch intervals to crimp and seal. Another way to finish the edge of the pecan dough is with a classic "thumb and index finger" fluted edge. Chill the shell for 15 to 30 minutes before blind baking.

6. Preheat the oven to 350°F. Line the pastry shell with a piece of parchment (make sure it is large enough that you will be able to grab the ends of the paper and pull it out later) and fill with dried beans. Bake until the bottom of the dough is baked through but not yet browned. (Note: The rim will be browned and the sides will be starting to brown, but the bottom will not have browned yet), 55 to 60 minutes. Remove the pan from the oven and remove the paper and the dried beans. Return the pie pan to the oven and bake until the bottom of the crust is lightly golden brown, about 15 minutes more. Remove from the oven and allow to cool completely on a wire rack before filling the pastry shell.

banana cream pie with chocolate and pecans

Who doesn't love banana cream pie? We upped the ante for this version with a layer of rich chocolate ganache, crunchy pecans, ripe banana slices, and creamy smooth vanilla pastry cream, all piled into a crisp pecan pastry shell. That makes this a project with several steps, but it's well worth the effort when you really want to show the love.

The vanilla pastry cream must be made and chilled 3 to 4 hours before the pie is assembled. For the nicest slices, chill the assembled pie a few hours before slicing.

SPECIAL EQUIPMENT: ELECTRIC MIXER, 9-INCH PIE PAN

Chocolate Ganache (page 175), slightly cooled but still liquid

One 9-inch blind-baked and cooled pecan pastry shell (page 170)

½ cup (2 ounces/60 grams) toasted and cooled chopped pecans (see "How to Toast and Chop Nuts," page 13)

3 medium (15 ounces/430 grams) bananas, ripe but firm

Vanilla Bean Pastry Cream (quantity for Banana Cream Pie, page 320), chilled for at least 3 to 4 hours

1 cup (8 ounces/230 grams) heavy cream, chilled

2 tablespoons sugar

½ teaspoon pure vanilla extract

⅛ teaspoon kosher salt

¼ to ½ cup dark chocolate curls or shavings (see "How to Shave Chocolate," page 12, and "How to Make Chocolate Curls," page 13)

1. Make the chocolate ganache and allow it to cool slightly, but pour it into the bottom of the baked pastry shell while it is still liquid. Place the pie pan in the refrigerator and chill for about 20 minutes, until the ganache is set up. (If you press on it gently, you won't have chocolate on your finger.)

2. Remove the ganache-filled pie shell from the refrigerator and sprinkle half the pecans evenly over the surface of the ganache. Slice the bananas ¼ inch thick and place half the banana slices evenly, overlapping, on top of the pecans.

3. Scrape the pastry cream into the pie shell, smoothing out the top with a rubber spatula. Top with the remaining banana slices in a single layer or overlapping.

4. In the bowl of an electric mixer with the whisk, combine the cream with the sugar, vanilla extract, and salt and whip to stiff peaks.

5. Top the pie with the whipped cream, using an offset spatula to smooth the cream all over the surface and to create some swirls.

6. Garnish the top of the pie with the chocolate shavings and the remaining pecans. Cover the pie loosely with a sheet of plastic wrap and chill for 2 to 3 hours before slicing.

chocolate ganache

Ganache is made by pouring hot cream over chopped chocolate. This mixture is whisked until smooth and can be used for a variety of purposes from sauce to glaze to truffle base. Ganache will taste exactly as delicious as the brand of chocolate you use, so use a good one. We prefer a dark chocolate that's 70% cacao (see "Our Favorite Chocolates," page 21).

Be sure your butter is at room temperature and soft—you should be able to squish the butter with your finger.

½ cup (2⅝ ounces/75 grams) finely chopped bittersweet chocolate (see "How to Chop Chocolate," page 12)

2 teaspoons honey

½ cup (4⅜ ounces/125 grams) heavy cream

1¾ tablespoons (⅞ ounce/25 grams) unsalted butter, softened

½ teaspoon pure vanilla extract

¼ teaspoon kosher salt

1. Put the chocolate and honey in a heatproof bowl and set aside. Put the cream in a saucepan over medium-high heat and bring it just to a boil. Remove the pan from the heat and immediately pour the cream over the chocolate. Allow the hot cream and chocolate mixture to sit for 1 minute, then stir with a whisk until smooth. As soon as the ganache is smooth, add the butter and stir with the whisk until the butter is incorporated. Add the vanilla extract and salt and stir to combine.

2. Place a sheet of plastic wrap directly over the surface of the ganache and set aside to cool slightly, but do not allow it to cool long enough to set. When you put the ganache in your pastry shell, it should be slightly cooled but still liquid enough to pour.

maple banana cream pie with
maple molasses pecans

If you love the warm, mellow flavor of maple, here's the pie for you. Try this at Thanksgiving instead of pumpkin pie.

If you're not in the mood for bananas, you can omit them and just make a maple cream pie.

After you make the pastry cream, chill it for at least 3 hours before you assemble the pie. For the nicest slices, chill the pie for another couple hours after it is assembled.

You can make pastry cream up to a day ahead and keep it refrigerated. Make the pie shell and blind-bake it up to several hours ahead. Make the maple molasses pecans up to 4 days ahead and store them airtight at room temperature. It won't take long to finish assembling the rest of the pie from this point.

SPECIAL EQUIPMENT: ELECTRIC MIXER, 9-INCH PIE PAN

3 medium (15 ounces/430 grams) bananas, ripe but firm

One 9-inch blind-baked and cooled pecan pastry shell (page 170)

Maple Pastry Cream (page 178), chilled for at least 3 hours

1 cup (8 ounces/230 grams) heavy cream, chilled

2 tablespoons sugar or maple sugar

½ teaspoon pure vanilla extract

⅛ teaspoon kosher salt

About 1 cup Roasted Maple Molasses Pecans (page 116)

1. Slice the bananas ¼ inch thick and place half the banana slices in one layer, or overlapping, over the bottom of the pastry shell. Scrape the maple pastry cream into the pastry shell on top of the bananas and smooth the surface using a rubber spatula. Top the pastry cream with the remaining banana slices in a single layer or overlapping.

2. Put the heavy cream, sugar, vanilla extract, and salt in the bowl of an electric mixer with the whisk attachment and whip to stiff peaks.

3. Top the pie with the whipped cream using an offset spatula to smooth the cream all over the surface and create some swirls.

4. Cover the pie loosely with a piece of plastic wrap and chill for 2 to 3 hours. Before serving, garnish the top of the pie with the maple molasses pecans, then slice and serve. If you prefer, you can slice and plate the pie, then garnish each wedge with some of the pecans.

maple pastry cream

Finding maple sugar takes a bit of extra effort, but this luscious pastry cream with a pure maple flavor and deep-ivory hue is well worth it. You can find maple sugar in well-stocked supermarkets or order it online (see Sources).

A good-quality heavy-bottomed saucepan works best for making pastry cream (see "Pots and Pans," page 30). After you add the egg yolks, be sure to cook the pastry cream until it is quite thick, like a thick pudding. For an ultra-lush pastry cream, we finish with softened butter. Adding butter using a food processor, instead of whisking it in by hand, makes a pastry cream that's silky and shiny. Be sure your butter is soft and at room temperature so it will incorporate quickly into the pastry cream.

Pastry cream must be chilled thoroughly before being used, at least 3 or 4 hours. You can make it a day ahead and chill it overnight.

SPECIAL EQUIPMENT: FOOD PROCESSOR, INSTANT-READ OR DIGITAL PROBE THERMOMETER (OPTIONAL)

¼ cup (1½ ounces/40 grams) maple sugar

¼ cup (1 ounce/30 grams) cornstarch

6 large egg yolks

1 cup (8 ounces/230 grams) whole milk

½ cup (4 ounces/115 grams) heavy cream

½ cup (5 ounces/140 grams) pure maple syrup

½ cup (1 stick/4 ounces/115 grams) unsalted butter, cut into 4 chunks, softened

1 teaspoon pure vanilla extract

½ teaspoon kosher salt

1. Put the maple sugar and cornstarch in a bowl and use a whisk to combine. Add the egg yolks and whisk vigorously until well combined and the color of the yolks pales slightly.

2. Meanwhile, combine the milk, cream, and maple syrup in a saucepan over medium-high heat and scald (just below the boiling point until it begins to steam and little bubbles appear around the edges). Remove the saucepan from the heat and temper the yolks by adding a few ladles of the hot milk-cream mixture to the sugar-yolk mixture, whisking to combine. Then scrape all the

sugar-yolk mixture from the bowl into the saucepan and place the pan back on the stove over medium-high heat. Return the mixture to a boil, whisking constantly. (If, at any time, you think the pan is getting too hot and the pastry cream is in danger of scorching, lower the heat as needed or just move the pan on and off the heat, whisking steadily all the time. (If you are using an electric coil burner, please see "How to Adjust for the Heat on an Electric Coil Burner," page 16.)

3. When the mixture comes to a boil, allow it to boil for about a minute while whisking constantly and vigorously. The pastry cream should be very thick, like a thick pudding. (If the pastry cream is not thick, continue to cook and whisk.) When the pastry cream is thick, remove the saucepan from the heat and transfer the pastry cream to a clean bowl.

4. Stir the pastry cream with a rubber spatula for a few minutes to cool it down to between 140° and 150°F on an instant-read thermometer. (The pastry cream will no longer be scalding hot—you will be able to keep a finger in it—but it must still be warm enough to incorporate the butter, which is added in the next step.)

5. Transfer the pastry cream to the bowl of a food processor. Add the butter and pulse several times until all the butter is incorporated and the pastry cream is smooth. Then add the vanilla extract and the salt and pulse to combine.

6. Transfer the pastry cream to a clean bowl and place it over a bowl of ice water. Stir occasionally until the pastry cream has cooled, then place a piece of plastic wrap directly over the surface (to prevent a skin from forming). Allow the pastry cream to chill completely before using it, 3 to 4 hours.

The top pie is Old-Fashioned Pumpkin Pie and the bottom pie is Sugar Pumpkin Crème Pie.

old-fashioned pumpkin pie

You'll notice there are two pumpkin pies in this book (the other is on page 194). This one is simpler and more classic—custardy and smelling of sweet spices. We love them both.

The last thing we want to do is make your holiday baking more difficult, but the joy of slicing and seeding your own pumpkin, roasting it, and creating a homemade pumpkin filling instead of opening a can cannot be overstated. To make things easier, you can roast the pumpkin the day before, puree it in a blender or food processor, and store it covered and refrigerated.

Sugar Pie is a variety of pumpkin with a good, sweet flavor and smooth, dense texture. Talk to the farmer at the farmers' market or the produce manager in the supermarket, and you will find other varieties of pie pumpkins (bred for eating, not jack-o'-lanterns) that can be used in this recipe, such as Baby Pam Sugar Pie, Small Sugar, or New England Pie pumpkin.

A 2¼-pound Sugar Pie (or similar variety) pumpkin, once cut, cleaned, roasted, and skinned, will yield about 1¾ cups pumpkin puree, the amount needed for this recipe. Or you can use half of a 4½-pound Sugar Pie pumpkin. Don't use larger pumpkins or varieties not meant for pie making, because they may be fibrous and watery. Or you can use a combination of Sugar Pie pumpkin and butternut squash in this pie. Just be sure you get about 1¾ cups puree.

If you prefer, you can substitute 1¾ cups pumpkin puree (about a 15-ounce can) for the roasted pureed pumpkin.

Serve with lightly sweetened whipped cream (page 193) or the Vanilla Bean or Buttermilk Ice Cream (page 326 or 330). Serve the pie at room temperature.

Note that you need a slightly larger pie pan (9½ inches) for this pie than for most of the pies in the book.

SPECIAL EQUIPMENT: BLENDER OR FOOD PROCESSOR

roasted pumpkin puree

1 Sugar Pie pumpkin, 2¼ pounds (about 1 kilogram)

2 tablespoons canola or other neutral-tasting oil

⅔ cup (3⅝ ounces/104 grams) packed brown sugar

⅓ cup (2⅜ ounces/69 grams) granulated sugar

1 tablespoon all-purpose flour

¾ teaspoon ground cinnamon

¼ teaspoon ground ginger

¼ teaspoon ground cloves

¼ teaspoon ground allspice

½ teaspoon kosher salt

1 cup (8⅜ ounces/237 grams) heavy cream

⅓ cup (2⅞ ounces/79 grams) whole milk

3 large eggs, lightly beaten

2 teaspoons pure vanilla extract

pastry shell and garnishes

One 9½-inch blind-baked and cooled flaky but tender pastry shell (page 183) (see How to Blind-Bake a Pastry Shell for the Old-Fashioned Pumpkin and Kentucky Bourbon Pecan Pies, page 190)

Powdered Sugared Pastry Leaves (optional; page 192)

Sugared Cranberries (optional; page 191)

1. To roast the pumpkin, preheat the oven to 400°F. Use a large heavy knife to quarter the pumpkin, then scrape out and discard all the fibers and seeds. Cut the pumpkin quarters in half crosswise to yield 8 pieces of pumpkin. Put the pumpkin pieces in a baking dish and toss with the oil. Arrange the pumpkin pieces rind side down, cover the pan with foil, and use the tip of a paring knife to cut a few small steam vents in the foil. Put the pan in the oven and roast until the pumpkin feels quite tender when poked with the tip of a paring knife, about 1 hour. Remove the foil and continue to roast until the pumpkin is very soft, 20 to 25 minutes more. Remove the pan from the oven. As soon as the pumpkin is cool enough to handle, use a paring knife to peel off and discard the skins. Put the pumpkin flesh in a blender or food processor and puree until smooth. You should have about 1¾ cups (14 ounces/400 grams) pumpkin puree. Set the pumpkin puree aside and leave the oven at 400°F.

2. In a large bowl, whisk the pumpkin puree, the sugars, the flour, spices, and salt together. Add the cream, milk, eggs, and vanilla extract and whisk again until everything is well combined and smooth. Pour the mixture into the pie shell and place it in the oven. Bake at 400°F for 15 minutes, then turn the oven down to 350°F and bake until the custard is set, 55 to 60 minutes more. When the pie is done, the center of the pie will *not* look soft and jiggly when you gently shake the pan. (You can insert the tip of a small knife into the custard to see if the filling is set, not liquid, but if you do so, the pie custard will crack as it cools.) Remove the pie from the oven and allow it to cool on a wire rack for at least 2 hours before slicing and serving. If you like, decorate the pie with Powdered Sugar Pastry Leaves and Sugared Cranberries.

flaky but tender pastry dough

This pastry dough calls for pastry flour, a special flour that you may not already have in your pantry, but the results are well worth acquiring it for a crust that's both flaky and tender. We prefer unbleached pastry flour, such as King Arthur. If you prefer, you can substitute cake flour for the pastry flour. (For more information, see "About Flour," page 22.)

The pastry or cake flour keeps the pastry dough tender, and the vinegar strengthens the gluten and adds elasticity. This pastry dough has more salt than most. Kosher salt is coarser than table salt. If you are using table salt instead, cut the amount of salt in half.

For the flakiest pastry, be sure your fats (butter and vegetable shortening) are very cold. Before you start your dough, dice the butter and portion the shortening into a few clumps and place the fats on a plate, then cover with plastic wrap. If you are using the electric mixer method, place the fats in the freezer for 2 hours. If you are using the food processor method, freeze the fats for only 30 minutes (a shorter time because the metal blade has to be able to cut through the butter).

A plastic dough scraper and metal bench knife are useful tools for making pastry dough. (For information on those tools as well as on pie pans and tart pans, see page 28.)

You can save the dough scraps for making decorations (see "How to Make Pastry Leaves and Decorations," page 192).

SPECIAL EQUIPMENT: ELECTRIC MIXER OR FOOD PROCESSOR

for a 9- or 9½-inch single-crust pie or a 10-inch tart shell

1⅓ cups (6⅛ ounces/175 grams) pastry or cake flour

⅓ cup (1¾ ounces/50 grams) all-purpose flour

1 tablespoon sugar

1½ teaspoons kosher salt

½ cup (1 stick/4 ounces/113 grams) unsalted butter, freezer-cold (see headnote), cut into ½-inch dice

2 tablespoons vegetable shortening (we use "trans-fat-free" shortening), freezer-cold (see headnote)

¼ cup (2 ounces/57 grams) ice-cold water, or more as needed (see "How to Measure Ice-Cold Water for Pastry," page 159)

1 teaspoon distilled white vinegar

for a 9-inch double-crust pie or 8 individual rustic pies

2⅔ cups (12¼ ounces/350 grams) pastry flour

⅔ cup (3½ ounces/100 grams) all-purpose flour

2 tablespoons sugar

1 tablespoon kosher salt

1 cup (2 sticks/8 ounces/226 grams) unsalted butter, freezer-cold (see headnote), cut into ½-inch dice

¼ cup (2 ounces/60 grams) vegetable shortening, freezer-cold (see headnote)

½ cup (4 ounces/114 grams) ice-cold water (see headnote), or more as needed

2 teaspoons distilled white vinegar

To Make the Flaky but Tender Pastry Dough in the Electric Mixer

1. In the bowl of an electric mixer with the paddle, combine the flours, sugar, and salt. Add the cold butter and shortening, mixing on low speed until the mixture looks shaggy and the pieces of butter are slightly smaller than peas. Stop the mixer and check the size of the butter, sifting through the mixture with your hands. If you find a few bigger chunks, quickly smear them between your fingers.

2. Put the ice-cold water and vinegar into a measuring cup or small container and stir to combine.

3. Add the water-vinegar mixture to the flour-fat mixture in the electric mixer on low speed and mix briefly with a few rotations of the paddle, but do not let the dough come together.

4. Turn off the mixer and scrape around the sides and the bottom of the mixer bowl to make sure there are no pockets of dry ingredients, rotating the paddle a few more times if needed, then squeeze a small amount of dough in your hand. The dough should come together as a clump. If the dough seems too dry, add a little more water a few teaspoons at a time and rotate the paddle a few more times.

5. Remove the dough from the mixer and shape, wrap, and chill as directed.

1. Put the flours, sugar, and salt in the bowl of a food processor and pulse a few times to combine. Add the cold butter and shortening to the dry ingredients. Use your hands to break up the shortening into several small clumps and get them coated with flour.

2. Pulse 9 to 12 times. Turn off the machine and take the lid off. The butter should be in pieces a little smaller than the size of a pea. If needed, put the lid back on and pulse a couple more times.

3. Put the ice-cold water and vinegar into a measuring cup or small container and stir to combine.

4. Gradually pour the water-vinegar mixture through the feed tube while pulsing 10 to 12 times. Take the lid off. Use your fingers to see if you can clump the mixture together to form a dough. (The dough should not come together to form a ball while you are pulsing it in the food processor, but it should form a clump pressed between your fingers.) Use a rubber spatula to scrape around the sides of the food processor bowl and the bottom of the bowl to see if there are any dry pockets of flour. If the dough seems too dry, you can add more water a few teaspoons at a time and pulse a few more times.

5. Remove the dough from the food processor and shape, wrap, and chill as directed.

HOW TO SHAPE, WRAP, AND CHILL FLAKY BUT TENDER PASTRY DOUGH FOR PIES, TARTS, AND RUSTIC PIES

Whether using the electric mixer or food processor method, dump the dough, which will still be crumbly and loose, onto a work surface. Use your hands to work the dough into a cohesive ball, then flatten the ball into a disk. (Note: Because this dough contains pastry or cake flour, which is a soft flour, and because it contains a little vegetable shortening, you can work it with your hands a few times, forming it into a ball and making it cohesive, without having to worry as much about toughening the dough, so feel free to work the dough enough to make it cohesive.) To shape the dough for chilling:

For a single-crust pie shell or tart pan, shape the single-crust quantity of dough into a flattened disk and wrap in plastic wrap.

For a double-crust pie, cut the double-crust quantity of dough in half and shape into 2 flattened disks, then wrap each in plastic wrap.

For hand pies or crostatas, use the double-crust quantity and shape the dough into a flattened rough rectangle, approximately 4×6 inches, then wrap in plastic wrap.

In all cases, after shaping and wrapping the dough, refrigerate it for at least 2 hours or overnight before rolling. (For longer storage, pastry dough also freezes well, but allow it to rest in the refrigerator for 1 or 2 hours before freezing.)

HOW TO ROLL, SHAPE, AND BLIND-BAKE FLAKY BUT TENDER PASTRY DOUGH

Because it contains a large proportion of pastry or cake flour, the Flaky but Tender Pastry Dough is softer and has less structure than other pastry doughs. Therefore, the rim of a pie shell made with this dough should be shaped (rolled and pressed) as directed here. A classic "thumb and index finger" fluted edge is not recommended for this dough because a tall pastry rim may collapse as the pie is being baked.

Also, we blind-bake our crusts at a lower temperature and for a longer time than you usually see in a pastry recipe, because we like the way the crust gets thoroughly cooked all the way through.

To shape a flaky but tender pie shell, use your hands to press gently on the dough all around the circumference . . .

to form a neat pastry rim.

To crimp the edge, use the narrowest side of the handle of a small tool to press down on the pastry rim at about 1-inch intervals.

HOW TO ROLL, SHAPE, AND CRIMP A SINGLE-CRUST PIE SHELL

SPECIAL EQUIPMENT: 9- OR 9½-INCH PIE PAN, DRIED BEANS FOR PIE WEIGHTS

Make the dough quantity for a 9-inch single-crust pie and chill as directed. When you are ready to roll the dough, unwrap the dough and place it on a lightly floured surface. Using a rolling pin, roll the dough out to a round about 12 inches in diameter and about ⅛ inch thick.

Transfer the dough to a 9-inch pie pan. An easy way to transfer the dough is to fold the dough in half or into quarters. Pick up the folded dough and place it in the pan, then unfold gently, easing (not stretching) it into the pan. Use your fingers to press the dough lightly against the sides of the pan all the way around so the dough won't slide down. Trim the excess dough to a ¾- to 1-inch overhang. Fold the overhang up and over (toward the inside of the pan) and use your hands to press gently on the dough all around the circumference to form a neat pastry rim ¼ to ½ inch thick. (The pastry rim should be flush with the edge of the pie pan and not overhanging it.) Then use the narrowest side of the handle of a small tool such as a small offset spatula or a small paring knife to press down on this pastry rim against the rim of the pan at about 1-inch intervals to crimp and seal.

(Also see "How to Make a Checkerboard Edge on a Pie Shell or a Hand Pie," page 189.)

Chill the pastry-lined pie pan for 15 to 30 minutes before blind baking.

HOW TO BLIND-BAKE A SINGLE-CRUST PIE SHELL

Preheat the oven to 350°F. Line the pastry-lined pie shell with a square of parchment (make sure it is large enough for you to grab the corners of the paper and pull it out later) and fill it with dried beans. Bake until the bottom of the dough is baked through but not browned, 55 to 60 minutes. When you lift a corner of the paper and beans to look at the dough on the bottom of the pan, the dough should be evenly whitish and matte. But don't lift the paper too soon or you may tear the dough.

When the dough on the bottom of the pan is set and cooked, remove the pie pan from the oven and remove the parchment and beans. Return the pie pan to the oven and bake until the pastry shell is evenly golden brown, about 15 minutes more. Remove from the oven and place the pan on a wire rack to cool completely before filling the pastry shell.

HOW TO ROLL, SHAPE, AND BLIND-BAKE A 10-INCH TART SHELL

SPECIAL EQUIPMENT: 10-INCH REMOVABLE-BOTTOM TART PAN, PASTRY SCRAPER, DRIED BEANS FOR PIE WEIGHTS

Unwrap the round of dough and place it on a lightly floured work surface. Using a rolling pin, roll the dough out to a round about ⅛ inch thick and 12 or 13 inches in diameter. Use flour as needed to roll the dough, lifting the dough occasionally using a pastry scraper as you work to check that the dough is not sticking to the work surface.

Transfer the dough to the tart pan. It's easiest to transfer the dough by folding it in half or into quarters. Pick up the folded dough and place it in the pan, then unfold gently. Ease the dough gently into the pan (don't stretch the dough or it will shrink when baked), gently pressing the sides in and down so they are flush against the sides of the pan. Trim the overhanging dough to ¼ to ½ inch. Use your thumb to press the dough against the metal rim and cut off the excess dough. Then, use a thumb and index finger (thumb against pastry inside the pan and index finger along the outside of the pan, rotating the pan as you go) to press gently all around the sides and to press the pastry into the grooves and make sure it is nice and straight and comes up to the top of the pan. Chill the pastry-lined tart shell for 15 to 30 minutes before baking.

Preheat the oven to 350°F. Line the tart shell with a square of parchment paper (make sure it is large enough for you to grab the corners of the paper and pull it out later), then fill it with dried beans. Put the tart shell in the oven and bake for 50 minutes. After 50 minutes, remove the tart pan from the oven and lift up a corner of the paper to look at the dough on the bottom of the pan, which should look evenly whitish and matte. (Do not check too soon, because if you lift the paper before the bottom is mostly cooked, you may tear the dough.) If the dough on the bottom of the pan does not looked cooked enough, return the pan to the oven and continue to bake for 5 more minutes.

When the dough on the bottom of the tart is cooked, remove the pan from the oven and lift out the paper and beans. Return the tart pan to the oven and bake until the tart is lightly golden brown, about 10 to 15 minutes more. Remove the pan from the oven and allow to cool completely at room temperature before filling the tart shell.

HOW TO ROLL AND SHAPE A DOUBLE-CRUST PIE

SPECIAL EQUIPMENT: 9-INCH PIE PAN

Unwrap the 2 disks of dough. Using a rolling pin and flour as needed, roll one piece into an 11- to 12-inch round about ⅛ inch thick and transfer it to the pie pan. It's easiest to transfer the dough by folding it in half or into quarters. Pick up the folded dough and place it in the pan, then unfold gently. Ease the dough gently into the pan so you don't stretch the dough. Trim the excess dough to a ¾-inch overhang.

Roll the other piece ⅛ inch thick to an 11-inch circle and trim to a 9-inch circle. (If you like, you can save the scraps for making pastry decorations; see page 192). Keep both the pastry-lined pie pan and the pastry circle for the top of the pie chilled in the refrigerator while you are prepping the filling ingredients. (If you have a large round cake cardboard—see page 26—you can use it to transfer a pastry circle back and forth, or use a parchment-lined baking sheet. You can also fold the pastry circle in half to transfer it.)

When you are ready to fill the pie, remove the pastry-lined pie plate from the refrigerator and add your filling.

Brush starch water (see "How to Make Starch Water," page 159) on the overhang of the bottom crust. Remove the pastry circle from the refrigerator and transfer it to the top of the pie. Pull the overhang of the bottom crust up and over the top crust and press to seal. You can press with your fingers, or crimp with a fork, or crimp by pressing with the narrowest edge of the handle of a small tool such as a paring knife or small offset spatula. (It's best not to make a fluted rim with Flaky but Tender pastry. Also note that rolling the bottom crust up over the top crust in this way helps keep any filling from leaking out between the crust and the pie plate during baking.)

Cut slits for steam vents using the tip of a paring knife. Add cut-out decorations to the top crust of the pie (see page 192) if desired. Brush the top of the pie with cream, sprinkle with sugar, and bake as directed in the recipe.

FOR CROSTATAS OR HAND PIES

Follow the rolling and baking instructions in the recipe.

HOW TO MAKE A CHECKERBOARD EDGE ON A PIE SHELL OR A HAND PIE

Another decorative edge that works well with Flaky but Tender Pastry Dough is the checkerboard edge. For a pie shell, after you have formed the pastry rim, use a paring knife to cut notches 1 inch apart, going all the way around the

To form a checkerboard edge on a pie shell, one tab of dough is folded inward, the other remains outward, the next is folded inward, and so on.

circumference of the pan, so that you have an even number of notches. Fold every other "tab" of dough inward toward the center of the pan—in other words, one tab of dough is folded inward, the next remains outward on the rim, the next is folded inward, and so on.

The edge of a hand pie can be sealed in a similar way if you want to do something fancier than just crimping the edge with a fork. Use a paring knife to cut notches 1 inch apart, then fold every other tab of dough inward toward the body of the hand pie.

HOW TO BLIND-BAKE A PASTRY SHELL FOR THE OLD-FASHIONED PUMPKIN AND KENTUCKY BOURBON PECAN PIES

To ensure a crisp, thoroughly baked crust, we generally blind-bake a single-crust pastry shell even when the pie shell will be baked again after the filling is added. If the filled pie will be baked in a low oven, as with the Sugar Pumpkin Crème Pie, there is no worry of overbaking the blind-baked shell. But since the Old-Fashioned Pumpkin Pie and the Kentucky Bourbon Pecan Pie will be baked, after they are filled, at higher temperatures, we blind-bake them for about 15 to 20 minutes less time than the master recipe directs for blind-baking single pie shells. This way the rim of the pie will not come out too dark after the additional baking of the filled pie.

For either of these pies, make the Flaky but Tender Pastry Dough quantity for a 9½-inch pie pan and line the pie pan with the rolled-out dough and chill as instructed in the recipe.

To blind-bake the crust for either of these two pies, preheat the oven to 350°F. Use vegetable spray to spray the piece of parchment paper that you are going to use to hold your pie weights (such as dried beans) and place it sprayed side down in the pastry shell. (This is done because you may be lifting out the paper and beans before the pastry is completely cooked through and you don't want to tear the pastry.) Fill the parchment-lined shell with dried beans and bake the shell for 50 minutes. Remove the pie pan from the oven and remove the paper and beans. Return the pie pan to the oven and bake 5 minutes more. Then remove the pie pan from the oven and allow to cool to room temperature on a wire rack. (The pastry shell will be slightly underbaked at this point but will finish baking after you add the filling and return it to the oven.)

sugared cranberries

These sparkly red berries add a festive touch to a pumpkin pie, and they're tasty too.

The simple syrup used to steep the berries can be saved in the refrigerator for about a week for sweetening drinks.

You can prepare the cranberries a day ahead and leave them uncovered, at room temperature, in the pan of sugar.

1 cup (8 ounces/230 grams) water

2 cups (13⅛ ounces/372 grams) sugar

2 cups (7¼ ounces/205 grams) cranberries

1. Combine the water and 1 cup of the sugar in a saucepan and bring to a boil over high heat, stirring to dissolve the sugar.

2. When the syrup is at a rolling boil, add the cranberries. Immediately remove from the heat and cover the pan. Allow the cranberries to steep for 15 minutes, then strain the cranberries from the syrup. Discard the syrup or save it for another use.

3. Spread the cranberries in a single layer on a wire mesh rack, discarding any that may have burst, and allow to dry for 30 to 60 minutes.

4. Pour the remaining 1 cup sugar into a shallow pan. Add the cranberries and stir them around to coat with the sugar, separating any clumps with your fingers.

HOW TO MAKE PASTRY LEAVES AND DECORATIONS

When making a single- or double-crust pie, after rolling and shaping your pie shell (and top crust pastry circle if using), you can use the scraps to make decorations for your finished pie. For a single-crust pie, pastry decorations are baked ahead and used to garnish the top of the filled pie. For a double-crust pie, raw pastry decorations are affixed to the top crust, and they bake as the pie is baking.

HOW TO MAKE PASTRY DECORATIONS FOR "HOT BUTTERED RUM" APPLE PIE

Cut out pastry decorations, such as leaf shapes, from the pastry scraps as detailed above. Use starch water (see page 159) to attach the unbaked decorations to the unbaked top crust of the pie. Brush the whole pie, including the decorations, with cream, sprinkle with sugar, and bake according to the recipe.

HOW TO MAKE POWDERED SUGARED PASTRY LEAVES FOR SUGAR PUMPKIN CRÈME PIE, OLD-FASHIONED PUMPKIN PIE, OR KENTUCKY BOURBON PECAN PIE

Collect the scraps from trimming your piecrust and roll them out to an ⅛-inch thickness. Use a paring knife or small cookie cutters to cut shapes as desired. (Leaf shapes are always nice on a pie.) Place the scraps on a parchment-lined baking sheet and bake in a preheated 350°F oven until lightly golden and cooked through, 12 to 15 minutes. Remove the pan from the oven and allow the cutouts to cool. Before placing them on top of a finished pie, dust the cutouts with powdered sugar.

sweetened whipped cream

It's easiest to whip cream if everything is very cold, including your bowl and whisk. If you like, you can adjust the amount of sugar to your taste.

SPECIAL EQUIPMENT: ELECTRIC MIXER (OPTIONAL)

1½ cups (12 ounces/340 grams) heavy cream

3 tablespoons (1¼ ounces/37 grams) sugar

1½ teaspoons pure vanilla extract

Place the cream, sugar, and vanilla extract in the bowl of an electric mixer and whip with the whisk until soft peaks are formed, or whip by hand with a whisk. Serve immediately.

sugar pumpkin crème pie

Blending crème anglaise (classic French custard sauce) with roasted pumpkin results in a pumpkin pie with a creamy but light and delicate filling. It takes a bit more time and effort than our recipe for Old-Fashioned Pumpkin Pie (page 181), but it's an interesting twist that gives the pie a lighter pumpkin flavor and texture.

A 2¼-pound Sugar Pie pumpkin, after being cut, cleaned, roasted, and skinned, will yield about 1¾ cups pumpkin puree, the amount needed for this recipe. Or you can use half of a 4½-pound Sugar Pie pumpkin. (Other varieties that you can use are noted on page 181. Don't use larger pumpkins or they may be fibrous and watery, and don't use other varieties of pumpkin, which are not meant for pie making.) Or you can use a combination of Sugar Pie pumpkin and butternut squash in this pie. Just be sure you get about 1¾ cups puree.

The most time-consuming part of this recipe is roasting the pumpkin. You can roast the pumpkin the day before, puree it in a blender or food processor, and store it covered in the refrigerator.

Serve each slice of pie with a spoonful of unsweetened crème fraîche or Sweetened Whipped Cream (page 193) or, even better, a scoop of tangy Buttermilk Ice Cream (page 330). Serve the pie at room temperature; don't chill it.

It's best to use a good-quality heavy-bottomed pan for crème anglaise (see "Pots and Pans," page 30). When you are ready to make the crème anglaise, put a fine-mesh sieve over a bowl and set it near the stove so you can strain the custard as soon as it is cooked. Place the pureed roasted pumpkin in the blender container and have it sitting nearby.

SPECIAL EQUIPMENT: BLENDER, FOOD PROCESSOR

roasted pumpkin

1 Sugar Pie pumpkin, 2¼ pounds (about 1 kilogram)

2 tablespoons canola or other neutral-tasting oil

1 teaspoon kosher salt

crushed gingersnaps and pastry shell

3 ounces (85 grams) store-bought gingersnaps, such as 365 brand (about 13 gingersnaps, depending on the size of the cookies)

2 tablespoons (¼ stick/1 ounce) unsalted butter, melted

One 9-inch blind-baked and cooled Flaky but Tender Pastry Shell (page 183)

pumpkin-crème anglaise filling

¾ cup (6 ounces/165 grams) whole milk

½ cup (4 ounces/115 grams) heavy cream

1 vanilla bean, split in half lengthwise

3 large egg yolks

1 teaspoon ground ginger

¾ teaspoon ground cinnamon

¼ teaspoon freshly graded nutmeg

⅛ teaspoon ground cloves

½ teaspoon kosher salt

1 cup (4¾ ounces/134 grams) packed brown sugar

3 large eggs

1 tablespoon pure vanilla extract

garnishes

Powdered sugared pastry leaves (optional; see page 192)

Sugared Cranberries (optional; page 191)

1. To roast the pumpkin, preheat the oven to 400°F. Use a large heavy knife to quarter the pumpkin, then scrape out and discard all the fibers and seeds. Cut the pumpkin quarters in half crosswise to yield 8 pieces of pumpkin. Put the pumpkin pieces in a baking dish and toss with the oil and salt. Arrange the pieces rind sides down, cover the pan with foil, and use the tip of a paring knife to cut a few small steam vents in the foil. Put the pan in the oven and roast until the pumpkin feels quite tender when poked with the tip of a paring knife, about an hour. Remove the foil and continue to roast until the pumpkin is very soft, 20 to 25 minutes more.

2. Remove the pan from the oven. As soon as the pumpkin is cool enough to handle, use a paring knife to peel off and discard the skins. Put the pumpkin flesh in the container of a blender and puree until smooth. You should have about 1¾ cups (14 ounces/400 grams) pumpkin puree. Set the pumpkin puree aside in the blender container.

3. Reduce the oven temperature to 300°F.

4. To make the crushed gingersnaps, put the cookies in a food processor and pulse to make fine crumbs. (You should have about ¾ cup crumbs.) Transfer the crumbs to a bowl and pour the melted butter over them. Mix together well with a fork or your fingers. Press the crumb mixture evenly over the bottom surface of the baked pie shell. (You can use the bottom of a heavy glass or a glass measuring cup to help you press the crumbs evenly.) Set the prepared pie shell aside.

5. Combine the milk and cream in a heavy saucepan. Scrape the seeds from the vanilla bean, place the scrapings in a bowl, add the yolks, spices, salt, and ½ cup of the brown sugar, and set the bowl aside. Put the scraped-out vanilla pod in the saucepan. Place the pan over medium heat and scald (just below the boiling point until it begins to steam and little bubbles appear around the edges). Remove the pan from the heat, cover, and allow to steep for 5 to 10 minutes.

6. Whisk the yolk-sugar mixture vigorously until well combined and lighter in color. Remove the lid from the saucepan and remove the vanilla pod. (You can discard the pod or save it for vanilla bean sugar, page 64.) Return the saucepan to medium heat and bring the milk mixture back to a scald. Add a ladle of the scalded milk mixture to the yolk mixture and whisk briefly, to temper the yolks and keep them from scrambling, then add the warmed yolk mixture to the saucepan and cook over medium heat, stirring constantly, until the mixture is thick enough to coat the back of a spoon, 2 to 3 minutes. Immediately pour the crème anglaise through a fine-mesh sieve into a clean bowl. (If necessary, use a rubber spatula or a whisk to force the crème anglaise through the sieve.)

7. Pour the crème anglaise into the blender container (which has the pumpkin puree in it). Add the remaining ½ cup brown sugar, the eggs, and the vanilla extract. Blend on high speed for 1 full minute. Turn off the blender and use a rubber spatula to scrape down the sides of the container, going all the way to the bottom of the container with your spatula to make sure everything is well mixed. Blend again for a few seconds if necessary.

8. Leave the pumpkin custard in the blender container and allow the mixture to rest and any bubbles to rise to the top, about 15 minutes. Use a small ladle to skim off and discard as many of the bubbles as you easily can. (You will lose a little of the custard mixture, which is okay. The point of this step is to keep the top of your pie as smooth and bubble-free as possible, but don't worry about getting every single small bubble.)

9. Pour the pumpkin filling into the pastry shell, transfer it to the oven, and bake until the custard is set, about 1 hour. When the pie is done, the custard should jiggle just slightly in the center when you shake the pan gently. (Don't bake this pie so long that the filling does not move at all.)

10. Remove the pie from the oven and allow to cool on a wire rack for at least 2 hours before slicing and serving.

11. If you like, decorate the top of the pie with powdered sugar pastry leaves and sugared cranberries.

kentucky bourbon pecan pie

Our Kentucky-born-and-raised pastry chef, Stacy Fortner, makes the best-ever pecan pie. Naturally she adds a good slug of her favorite Kentucky bourbon, Knob Creek. If you put the pecans into the shell first, they will rise to the top after you add the filling. The larger than usual amount of eggs gives this pecan pie an almost custardy texture.

Toast the pecans until they are lightly browned and fragrant, but don't let them get too dark as they will darken a little more as the pie bakes.

Serve the pie at room temperature with Sweetened Whipped Cream (page 193) or Vanilla Bean or Buttermilk Ice Cream (page 326 or 330).

Note that this recipe calls for a slightly larger pie pan than most of the pies in the book.

SPECIAL EQUIPMENT: 9½-INCH PIE PAN

1¾ cups (7 ounces/198 grams) pecan halves, toasted and cooled (see "How to Toast and Chop Nuts," page 13)

One 9½-inch blind-baked and cooled single-crust Flaky but Tender Pastry Shell (page 183)

4 large eggs

5 tablespoons (2½ ounces/71 grams) unsalted butter, melted and slightly cooled

⅔ cup (4⅞ ounces/140 grams) packed brown sugar

1 cup (12½ ounces/350 grams) light corn syrup

1 tablespoon plus 1 teaspoon molasses

2 tablespoons Kentucky bourbon, preferably Knob Creek

½ teaspoon kosher salt

1. Preheat the oven to 350°F.

2. Put the pecans in the prepared pie shell, taking a moment to turn them right side up, and set aside.

3. Put the eggs in a bowl and whisk lightly to break them up. Add the melted butter, brown sugar, corn syrup, molasses, bourbon, and salt, whisking until smooth. Pour the filling into the pastry shell. The pecans will emerge beautifully while the pie is baking.

4. Bake until the pie is cooked through and set, 50 to 55 minutes. To check that the pie is cooked enough, poke the tip of a small knife into the filling, which should look set up and not liquid. Remove the pie from the oven and allow to cool on a rack for about 1 hour before slicing and serving.

"hot buttered rum" apple pie

This pie is a project, but it's a very special pie. It might even be the best apple pie; wait—no—it *is* the best apple pie we've ever tasted!

Washington is apple country, with more than 175,000 acres of apple orchards located in the foothills of the Cascade Mountains in the eastern part of the state. Use a sweet-tart, firm apple for this pie, such as Gravenstein, Braeburn, Cameo, Granny Smith, or Pink Lady.

Start out by sautéing sliced apples in caramelized sugar. When you cut a slice of the finished pie, you'll find the apples are soft in texture but still hold their shape; the pie juices are deliciously flavored with rum, butter, vanilla, and spice; and everything is encased in a pastry that is both flaky and tender.

A bit of pectin sets the apple pie juices perfectly, but if you don't have pectin you can add a little more cornstarch instead.

After sautéing the apples, allow time for the apples to cool before filling and baking the pie. This is a good time to roll out your dough.

After assembling the pie, it takes about 2 hours to bake, which is a long time, but the slow baking ensures a deliciously crumbly, flaky crust.

Serve the pie with Vanilla Bean (page 326), Maple (page 333), or Streusel (page 327) Ice Cream.

SPECIAL EQUIPMENT: 9-INCH PIE PAN

6 to 8 apples, such as Gravenstein (about 3¾ pounds/1.7 kilograms)

⅓ cup (2½ ounces/70 grams) granulated sugar

¼ cup (1⅜ ounces/40 grams) packed brown sugar

¼ cup (2 ounces/58 grams) dark rum

4 tablespoons (½ stick/2 ounces/60 grams) cold unsalted butter, cut into ¼-inch dice

1 tablespoon plus 1 teaspoon cornstarch

2 teaspoons pure vanilla extract

1 teaspoon dry pectin or an extra ½ teaspoon cornstarch

½ teaspoon ground cinnamon

¼ teaspoon freshly grated nutmeg

¼ teaspoon kosher salt

Flaky but Tender Pastry Dough for a double-crust 9-inch pie (page 183), rolled out with the unbaked bottom crust fitted into a 9-inch pie pan with ¾-inch overhang and the top crust rolled into a 9-inch circle, both kept chilled

to finish the pie for baking

Starch water (see page 159)

Pastry decorations (optional; see page 192)

2 tablespoons heavy cream

2 tablespoons granulated sugar

1. Peel and core the apples and slice them ¼ to ½ inch thick. You should have about 8 cups of apple slices.

2. Place 2 large (at least 10-inch) sauté pans over medium-high heat and divide the ⅓ cup granulated sugar evenly between them. Cook the sugar, without stirring, until it melts and then caramelizes and turns amber in color, tilting the pans a little to swirl and distribute the color, adjusting the heat as needed. (As soon as the sugar melts, it will quickly start caramelizing, so be ready to add the apples as soon as the color of the sugar turns amber.)

3. Add the apples, dividing them between the 2 pans, and sauté until they are about half-cooked and the juices that are released boil away and reduce until no liquid remains, 8 to 10 minutes. Toss and stir the apples regularly while they are cooking so they cook evenly on both sides. When the apples are done, they should have some give but should not fall apart when you press one between your fingers.

4. Transfer the apples to a bowl and allow them to cool completely to room temperature.

5. Meanwhile, preheat the oven to 350°F.

6. When the apples are cooled, add the brown sugar, rum, butter, cornstarch, vanilla extract, pectin (if using), spices, and salt and toss to combine.

7. Put the apple filling in the pastry-lined pie plate. Place the pastry circle on top, roll the overhang up and over, and seal with starch water. Press or crimp the edge, then use a paring knife to cut a few vents in the top (see page 189). If using pastry decorations, attach them to the top crust of the pie with starch water. Brush the pie (and the decorations, if using) with the heavy cream and sprinkle with the 2 tablespoons sugar.

8. Put the pie on a baking sheet to catch any drips, place in the oven, and bake for 30 minutes. Tent the pie with foil and continue to bake for 1 hour. Remove the foil and bake for 30 minutes or until the pie is evenly golden brown. (The total baking time is 2 hours.) Remove the pie from the oven and allow to cool for at least 1 hour on a wire rack before slicing. The pie will still be warm, or you can cool it to room temperature, then slice and serve.

blackberry lemon thyme crostatas

You know summer is really here when the farmers' markets are bursting with ripe, juicy berries—red and yellow raspberries, small fragile strawberries, lush purple-juiced blackberries—and the bakers rush to put them on the bakery and restaurant menus at the peak of their short, intense season. Crostatas, or rustic pies, are an excellent way to use peak-of-summer berries or other fruit.

These small free-form crostatas make a lot of sense in the home kitchen. You can serve each of your guests an individual pie without having to buy tartlet pans or other special equipment. When you bring out these golden flaky-crusted little pies, bursting with purple fruit and topped with a scoop of ice cream (try the Buttermilk, page 330), a chorus of oohs and aahs will ring out around the table.

Crostatas are best served warm. You can bake them several hours ahead of serving and reheat in a preheated 375°F oven for 8 to 10 minutes.

We like the herbal note of thyme with the blackberries, especially the citrusy fragrance of lemon thyme if you can find it at a farmers' market or if you grow it in your garden, but you can omit the thyme if you prefer.

If you have made vanilla bean sugar (page 64), you can use it here in place of the regular sugar and omit the vanilla bean.

See "How to Shape Crostatas and Hand Pies," page 205.

SPECIAL EQUIPMENT: METAL BENCH KNIFE (OPTIONAL)

Flaky but Tender Pastry Dough (quantity for 8 rustic pies, page 183), formed into a flattened rough rectangle, about 4 x 6 inches, and chilled for at least 2 hours

¾ cup (5¼ ounces/150 grams) sugar

3 tablespoons cornstarch

1 tablespoon plus 1 teaspoon all-purpose flour

2 teaspoons chopped fresh lemon thyme or regular thyme leaves

½ teaspoon grated lemon zest

1 vanilla bean

1½ pounds (about 2 pints/680 grams) blackberries

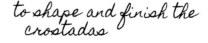
to shape and finish the crostadas

½ cup starch water (see page 159)

3 tablespoons (1½ ounces/43 grams) heavy cream

3 tablespoons (1½ ounces 43 grams) sugar

Mounding the blackberry filling in the center of a pastry round

Starting to fold the dough into pleats around the filling

Finishing the pleats on a crostata

1. Preheat the oven to 375°F.

2. Using a metal bench knife or a chef's knife, divide the dough into 8 equal pieces (cut it in half the long way and into quarters the short way) and shape each piece into a flattened disk. Using a rolling pin on a lightly floured surface, roll each disk into a 6½-inch round about ⅛ inch thick. Place the pastry rounds on parchment-lined baking sheets (4 rounds to a pan), cover loosely with plastic wrap, and refrigerate while you assemble the filling.

3. To make the filling, combine the sugar, cornstarch, flour, thyme, and zest in a small bowl. Slice open the vanilla bean pod lengthwise and, using a paring knife, scrape the vanilla seeds into the bowl. (Save the vanilla pod for another use, such as vanilla bean sugar; see page 64.) Stir the sugar mixture until well combined. Put the blackberries in a large bowl, add the sugar-cornstarch mixture, and toss to combine.

4. Remove 1 baking sheet with 4 pastry rounds from the refrigerator. (Leave the other 4 rounds in the refrigerator to stay chilled until you need them.) To shape a crostata, place about one-eighth of the berry mixture (about a generous ½ cup) in the center of a pastry round, leaving a 1-inch border of pastry all the way around. (If some of the sugar and cornstarch mixture or a slurry of berry juices plus sugar-starch has settled to the bottom of the bowl, be sure to divide this evenly among the mounds of berries.)

5. Using a pastry brush, brush the pastry border with starch water. Fold the pastry border up and

over the berries (the mound of berries will be only partially covered with dough), crimping the dough up with your fingers and allowing the dough to fold into pleats around the filling. When you have finished pleating, use your hands to press down gently but firmly on the folds of the crostata to seal it well so that it doesn't unfold and open while baking.

6. Repeat filling and shaping the remaining crostatas. When you are done, brush the pleated pastry rims of all the crostatas with some of the cream and sprinkle with the sugar. (If the pastry seems warm, chill the crostatas for 20 to 30 minutes before baking.)

7. Bake the crostatas until the pastry is evenly golden brown, 50 to 55 minutes, rotating the pans once halfway through the baking time and switching them between the racks. Remove the pans from the oven and cool on wire racks.

8. Serve the crostatas while still warm from the oven or allow them to cool to room temperature and reheat them when you are ready to serve.

Our crostatas are individual free-form pies, with a pleated rim and an open center, and our individual hand pies are folded over and sealed like turnovers.

For both crostatas and hand pies, keep your pastry rounds cold in the refrigerator for as long as possible until you are ready to shape and bake them. If you are making crostatas and you allow your dough to warm up before or while being shaped, the crostatas will be more likely to unfold in the oven instead of keeping their shape. If it takes you a while to shape all the crostatas, and the pastry has warmed up, refrigerate the shaped crostatas for 20 to 30 minutes before baking them.

Also when shaping the crostatas, brush them generously with the starch water and press down firmly on the pleated folds of dough to seal them well so that they don't unfold in the oven.

For the bing cherry hand pies, because of the liquid in the cooked filling, it is best to chill them for 30 minutes after they are shaped and before they are baked.

You will need 2 baking sheets so you can place 4 crostatas or 4 hand pies on each pan, for a total of 8 rustic pies. The roasted carrot, leek, and goat cheese hand pie recipe (page 212) yields 6 pies, so you can bake 3 pies on each of 2 baking sheets for a total of 6 pies. (We're assuming the use of a baking sheet that is 18 x 13 inches. If your baking sheets are smaller, you may need more of them or may need to bake in batches.)

crimson rhubarb crostatas

Slender stalks of rhubarb in the market are one of the first signs of spring. Washington farmers have been growing rhubarb since the late 1800s, and the town of Sumner, Washington, considers itself the nation's rhubarb pie capital.

Serve these hand-formed pies warm, topped with a dollop of Sweetened Whipped Cream (page 193) or crème fraîche or, even better, with scoops of Vanilla Bean (page 326) or Buttermilk (page 330) Ice Cream.

You can bake the crostatas several hours ahead of serving and reheat them in a preheated 375°F oven for 8 to 10 minutes.

See "How to Shape Crostatas and Hand Pies," page 205.

SPECIAL EQUIPMENT: METAL BENCH KNIFE (OPTIONAL)

Flaky but Tender Pastry Dough (quantity for 8 rustic pies, page 183), formed into a flattened rough rectangle, approximately 4 x 6 inches, and chilled for at least 2 hours

¾ cup (5½ ounces/156 grams) sugar, plus about 3 tablespoons (1½ ounces/ 43 grams) for sprinkling

2 tablespoons plus 1½ teaspoons cornstarch

1½ pounds (680 grams) rhubarb, tough ends trimmed

Starch water (see page 159)

About 3 tablespoons (1½ ounces/ 43 grams) heavy cream, for brushing

1. Preheat the oven to 375°F.

2. Unwrap the rectangle of dough and divide it into 8 equal pieces using a chef's knife or a bench knife. (Cut it in half the long way, then cut it into quarters the short way.) Pat each portion of dough into a flattened disk; then, using a rolling pin on a lightly floured surface, roll each disk into a 6½-inch round about ⅛ inch thick. Place the pastry rounds on parchment-lined baking sheets (4 rounds to a pan), cover loosely with plastic wrap, and refrigerate while you make the filling.

3. To make the filling, combine the ¾ cup sugar with the cornstarch in a small bowl and set aside. Cut the rhubarb stalks into ¼- to ½-inch dice, then place the rhubarb in a large bowl. Add the sugar-cornstarch mixture and toss to combine with the rhubarb.

4. Remove 1 baking sheet with 4 pastry rounds from the refrigerator. (Leave the other 4 rounds in the refrigerator until you need them.) To shape a crostata, place about one-eighth of the rhubarb mixture (about a generous ½ cup) in the center of the pastry round, leaving a 1-inch border of pastry all the way around. (If some of the sugar-cornstarch mixture is in the bottom of the bowl, be sure to divide it evenly among the mounds of rhubarb.)

5. Using a pastry brush, brush the pastry border with some of the starch water. Fold the pastry border up and over the rhubarb (the rhubarb will be only partially covered with dough), crimping the dough up with your fingers and allowing the dough to fold into pleats around the filling. When you have finished pleating, use your hands to press down gently but firmly on the folds of the crostata to seal it well so it doesn't open while baking.

6. Repeat filling and shaping the remaining crostatas. When you are done, brush the pleated pastry rim of all the crostatas with some of the cream and sprinkle with sugar. (If you think your pastry has warmed while you were working, chill the crostatas for about 20 to 30 minutes before baking.)

7. Bake the crostatas until the pastry is evenly golden brown, 50 to 55 minutes, rotating the pans once halfway through the baking time, and, if you have 2 pans in the oven at the same time, also switching them between the racks. Remove the pans from the oven and cool on wire racks.

8. Serve the crostatas while still warm from the oven or allow them to cool to room temperature and reheat.

bing cherry hand pies with pinot noir and vanilla

Cherries and Pinot Noir are natural companions. Open a good Oregon Pinot Noir from the Willamette Valley—Erath is one of my favorites—and drink the rest of the bottle with dinner.

This filling is a little more complex than in our other rustic pies, but the harmonious notes of cherry, caramelized sugar, red wine, vanilla, and star anise make for a sensational little pie well worth the extra trouble.

Serve these hand pies warm with a scoop of Vanilla Bean Ice Cream (page 326) or a spoonful of Sweetened Whipped Cream (page 193) or crème fraîche.

It's important to make sure you use only a couple tablespoons of cherry–Pinot Noir liquid, because a little hand pie can't hold as much juice as a regular pie. Be sure to cool the cherry filling to room temperature before forming the pies.

You can bake the hand pies several hours ahead and reheat them before serving in a preheated 375°F oven for 8 to 10 minutes.

A cherry pitter is a handy little tool, worth the small investment.

See "How to Shape Crostatas and Hand Pies," page 205.

SPECIAL EQUIPMENT: METAL BENCH KNIFE (OPTIONAL), CHERRY PITTER (OPTIONAL BUT RECOMMENDED)

Flaky but Tender Pastry Dough (quantity for 8 rustic pies, page 183), shaped into a flattened rough rectangle, approximately 4 x 6 inches, and chilled for at least 2 hours

1 vanilla bean

⅓ cup (2¾ ounces/75 grams) sugar

½ cup (4 ounces/110 grams) Pinot Noir or other dry red wine

1½ pounds (680 grams) Bing or other sweet cherries, stemmed, pitted, and halved (you should have about 4 cups pitted and halved cherries)

½ teaspoon ground star anise (see "How to Grind Spices," page 43)

½ cup (2¾ ounces/75 grams) tart dried cherries

2 teaspoons cornstarch

2 teaspoons pure vanilla extract

to finish the hand pies

Starch water (see page 159)

About 3 tablespoons (1½ ounces/ 43 grams) heavy cream

About 3 tablespoons (1½ ounces/ 43 grams) sugar

1. Unwrap the rectangle of dough and divide it into 8 equal pieces using a chef's knife or a metal bench knife. (Cut it in half the long way and in quarters the short way.) Pat each portion of dough into a flattened disk; then, using a rolling pin on a lightly floured surface, roll each one into a circle about 6 inches in diameter and ⅛ inch thick. Place the pastry circles on parchment-lined baking sheets (4 rounds to a pan) and set them aside in the refrigerator while you make the filling.

2. Split the vanilla bean lengthwise and scrape out the seeds with a paring knife. Reserve both the scraped-out seeds and the pod.

3. Put the sugar in a sauté pan or a wide, shallow, heavy-bottomed saucepan over medium-high heat and cook until you see the sugar starting to turn amber in color, 3 to 4 minutes. (Do not let the sugar get too dark.) Tilt the pan or stir quickly with a metal spoon to disperse the color evenly throughout the sugar. Remove the pan from the heat and, taking care to stand back as the mixture may sputter, immediately add ¼ cup of the wine. Return to the heat and cook just until the sugar dissolves. (The sugar will harden up when you add the wine, then it will dissolve.) Add the cherries and cook over medium to medium-high heat until they are soft but not falling apart and their juices have been released, 8 to 10 minutes. While the cherries are cooking, scrape the bottom of the pan with a metal spoon occasionally to dislodge and melt any candylike strands of sugar. Remove the pan from the heat.

4. Using a slotted spoon, remove the cherries and transfer them to a bowl, leaving the cooking liquid in the pan. If you have scooped more than a small amount of liquid out with the cherries, strain it back into the pan. Set the bowl of cooked cherries aside. To the cooking liquid in the pan, add the vanilla bean scrapings and the pod, the star anise, the remaining ¼ cup of wine, and the dried cherries. Return the pan to medium heat and cook until the dried cherries have plumped slightly and only about 2 tablespoons of liquid, reduced to a syrup, remains in the pan, 8 to 10 minutes. (To check that you have the right amount of liquid, pour the dried cherries and their liquid through a strainer into a bowl and measure the amount of liquid. If you have much more than 2 tablespoons of liquid, return the liquid to the pan and reduce it until you have only about 2 tablespoons.)

5. Remove the pan from the heat and transfer the dried cherries and their 2 tablespoons of syrup to the bowl with the reserved cooked Bing cherries. Add the cornstarch and vanilla extract and stir to combine. Place the bowl in the refrigerator and allow to cool. When the cherry mixture is cold, remove and discard the vanilla pod (or rinse, dry, and save for vanilla bean sugar, page 64). Now you are ready to fill and shape the hand pies.

6. Remove 1 baking sheet with 4 pastry rounds from the refrigerator. (Leave the other 4 rounds in the refrigerator to stay chilled until you need them.) Set one of the pastry rounds on a work surface. Brush some starch water around the border. Place about one-eighth of the cherry filling (about a scant ⅓ cup) off-center on the circle of dough (so that you can fold the top part of dough over, like a turnover). Fold the top part of the dough over the filling so the edges are flush, then seal the edges, crimping with the tines of a fork. If needed, even the edges by trimming with a paring knife. Repeat until all 8 pastry circles are filled and sealed.

7. Divide the hand pies between 2 parchment-lined baking sheets (4 pies to a pan). Brush the top of each pie with cream and sprinkle with sugar. Using the tip of a sharp knife, cut a few slits for steam in the top of each pie. Put the sheet pans back in the refrigerator for about 30 minutes before baking. While the pastries are chilling, preheat the oven to 375°F.

8. Bake the pies until evenly golden brown and bubbling through the vents, about 50 to 55 minutes, rotating the pans about halfway through the baking time and switching the pans between the oven racks. Remove the pans from the oven and cool on wire racks for at least 5 or 10 minutes before removing the hand pies using a metal spatula. (If the pies leaked cherry juice and are stuck to the paper, you can scrape them off using the metal spatula.)

9. Serve the pies while still warm or cool to room temperature and reheat before serving.

roasted carrot, leek, and goat cheese hand pies

These savory hand pies full of sweet roasted carrots, nuggets of soft, mellow chèvre, and bits of salty, pungent olives encased in a tender whole wheat crust make a hearty lunch or casual supper. Serve the pies with bowls of Tom's Tasty Tomato Soup (page 342).

Leeks can be gritty and dirty between the layers, so be sure to wash them well in a few changes of water.

Kosher salt is coarser than table salt, so if you are substituting table salt, cut the quantity in half.

You can make the filling a day ahead, cover, and refrigerate it overnight. You can make the dough a day ahead and chill it overnight. You can bake the hand pies a few hours ahead, leave them at room temperature, then reheat them before serving in a preheated 375°F oven for about 10 minutes.

SPECIAL EQUIPMENT: FOOD PROCESSOR

1 medium-large (about 14 ounces) leek, white and light green parts only, root end trimmed

2 teaspoons unsalted butter

¼ cup plus 2 teaspoons olive oil

½ cup water

2½ pounds carrots, peeled and cut into ¼- to ½-inch dice

1 tablespoon kosher salt

½ teaspoon freshly ground black pepper

1 tablespoon chopped fresh thyme leaves

2 teaspoons finely chopped garlic

½ cup (about 18) pitted kalamata olives, roughly chopped

4½ ounces (about ½ cup) soft fresh goat cheese (chèvre), divided into 6 equal ¾-ounce portions

Whole Wheat Pastry Dough (page 215), shaped into a flattened 5 x 6-inch rectangle and chilled for at least 1 hour

egg wash

1 large egg yolk

1 tablespoon cold water

Roasted carrots on the baking sheet

1. To make the carrot-leek filling, preheat the oven to 425°F.

2. Slice the leek in half lengthwise and wash it well. Thinly slice the leek crosswise, then finely chop it.

3. Heat the butter and 2 teaspoons of the olive oil in a sauté pan over medium-high heat. Add the chopped leek and sauté until limp, stirring as needed, about 3 minutes. Add the water to the pan, reduce the heat to low, cover, and cook until the leeks are soft, 10 to 15 minutes, stirring occasionally. Remove the pan from the heat and set aside, uncovered.

4. To roast the carrots, put them in a bowl, add the remaining ¼ cup of oil and the salt and pepper, and mix together. Spread the carrots on a baking sheet and place them in the oven. Roast until the carrots are soft, about 30 minutes, stirring occasionally. Remove the pan from the oven and sprinkle the carrots with the thyme and garlic. Return the pan to the oven and roast for about 10 more minutes, stirring once or twice, until the garlic and herbs are fragrant. Remove the carrots from the oven.

5. Put about half of the roasted carrots (about 1¾ cups) in the bowl of a food processor and puree until smooth. Transfer the carrot puree to a bowl and add the remaining carrots, leeks, and olives, mixing everything together with a rubber spatula. Taste for seasoning and add more salt and pepper if desired. Set the filling aside.

6. To form the hand pies, unwrap the rectangle of dough and place it on a lightly floured work surface. Use a chef's knife or a metal bench knife to divide the dough into 6 equal pieces. (Cut the dough in half lengthwise and into thirds crosswise.) Use a rolling pin to roll out 1 portion of dough into an 8½ x 6-inch rectangle, dusting the rolling pin and work surface with flour as needed. Set the rectangle aside and repeat with the remaining portions of dough. Place the rectangles of dough on parchment-lined baking sheets loosely covered with plastic wrap and refrigerate until you are ready to shape the hand pies.

7. Preheat the oven to 375°F. To shape a hand pie, put a rectangle of dough on the work surface with the short edge of the dough facing you. To make the egg wash, beat the egg yolk with the tablespoon of water. Use a pastry brush to brush a 1-inch border of egg wash all the way around the rectangle.

8. Place about ½ cup of the carrot-leek filling on the rectangle of dough, off-center, placing it closer to one of the shorter edges of the dough, but not covering the egg washed border. Slightly flatten the filling and break 1 portion of cheese into a few clumps, pressing the cheese lightly into the filling.

9. Then bring up the other short edge of the dough and fold it over the filling, covering the filling completely. Use a fork to crimp the edges of the dough and seal them well. (If needed, you can trim the edges with a knife.) Repeat until all the hand pies are formed and place them on

2 parchment-lined baking sheets, 3 pies to each baking sheet. Brush the tops of the pies with egg wash, then use a small sharp knife to cut a few slits in each one for steam vents.

10. Bake the hand pies until they are golden brown and the filling is hot, 30 to 35 minutes, rotating the pans and switching them between the racks halfway through the baking time.

11. Remove the pans from the oven and allow to cool on wire racks for a few minutes. Serve the hand pies warm.

whole wheat pastry dough

MAKES ENOUGH DOUGH FOR **6** ROASTED CARROT, LEEK, AND GOAT CHEESE HAND PIES

This sour-cream-enriched pastry dough, with the hearty flavor of whole wheat, is tender, not at all stodgy or heavy, and it goes together easily in the food processor.

For this dough, as for many other pastry doughs, a good rule of thumb is, if in doubt as to whether the dough is too dry, it's better to go ahead and add the extra tablespoon or more of water.

Before you begin the recipe, dice the butter, cover it with plastic wrap, and freeze it for 30 minutes.

The dough must chill in the refrigerator for at least 1 hour or more before being rolled, so plan accordingly.

SPECIAL EQUIPMENT: FOOD PROCESSOR

1½ cups (6¾ ounces/190 grams) all-purpose flour

1½ cups (7 ounces/200 grams) whole wheat flour

1 tablespoon sugar

1 teaspoon kosher salt

½ cup (1 stick/4 ounces/113 grams) unsalted butter, freezer-cold (see headnote), cut into ½-inch dice

¼ cup (2¼ ounces/60 grams) sour cream

¾ cup plus 1 to 2 tablespoons ice-cold water, as needed (See "How to Measure Ice-Cold Water for Pastry," page 159)

1. Put the flours, sugar, and salt in the bowl of a food processor and pulse to combine. Add the butter and pulse several times, until the butter is in crumbs slightly smaller than pea size. (Remove the lid of the processor and check to see if the butter is crumbled evenly. If you find a few larger chunks of butter, you can quickly smear them between your fingers.)

2. Add the sour cream and pulse a few times, then add ¾ cup of ice-cold water and pulse a few times. Remove the lid from the processor and see if you can form a clump by pressing some dough with your fingers. (Note that the dough will not form a ball in the processor, but you should be able to clump the dough together with your fingers.) If the dough seems too dry, add more cold water, a tablespoon at a time, pulsing a few times to incorporate the water.

3. Take the lid off the processor, dump the dough out onto a work surface, and gather it together with your hands into a flattened rectangle, roughly 5 × 6 inches. Wrap the dough in plastic and chill for at least 1 hour before using.

peak-of-the-season crisp with brown sugar oats

MAKES ONE 9-INCH PIE PAN; SERVES 5 OR 6

At my house, this is the most frequently used recipe out of my first book, *Tom Douglas' Seattle Kitchen*. The recipe calls for berries, but I've used it as a guideline for my own variations—plum and gooseberry, peach and blueberry, nectarine and black pepper, apple-cranberry-pear-date, apple and huckleberry, and so on. The only way you can go wrong is to use less than terrific fruit. I really do suggest staying in the season instead of buying fruit from halfway around the world.

When we serve crisps in the restaurants, we set them up to bake in individual ramekins, but a 9-inch pie pan is the simplest way to bake a crisp at home.

You can use any combination of berries in this recipe. If you like, you can add 1/3 cup chopped toasted nuts (pecans, hazelnuts, walnuts) to the crisp topping.

Serve the crisp while still warm in wide shallow soup bowls topped with big scoops of Vanilla Bean (page 326) or Buttermilk (page 330) Ice Cream.

SPECIAL EQUIPMENT: PASTRY BLENDER (OPTIONAL), 9-INCH PIE PAN (WE PREFER A PYREX OR CERAMIC PIE PAN HERE), OR SIMILAR SIZE CASSEROLE OR BAKING PAN

topping

⅔ cup (2⅜ ounces/66 grams) rolled oats

⅔ cup (3¼ ounces/93 grams) packed
brown sugar

⅔ cup (4 ounces/113 grams) all-purpose
flour

½ teaspoon ground cinnamon

6 tablespoons (¾ stick/3 ounces/
85 grams) cold unsalted butter, cut
into ½-inch dice

fruit mixture

2 cups (9 ounces/255 grams) raspberries

2 cups (8 ounces/227 grams) blueberries

½ cup (3½ ounces/100 grams) sugar (if
your berries are very sweet, you may
want to use less)

2 tablespoons all-purpose flour

*Putting brown sugar oats topping
on individual ramekins of fruit
crisp in the Dahlia Workshop*

1. Preheat the oven to 350°F. To make the crisp topping, combine the oats, brown sugar, flour, and cinnamon in a bowl. Add the diced butter to the dry ingredients and blend with a pastry blender or the tips of your fingers until crumbly. Set aside.

2. In another bowl, toss the berries with the sugar and flour, using a rubber spatula. Pour the berries into a 9-inch pie pan. Cover the berries with the crisp topping. Set the filled pie pan on a baking sheet to catch any juices, then place in the oven and bake for 40 to 45 minutes, until the topping is golden brown and the juices are bubbling, rotating the pan halfway through the baking time.

3. Remove the pan from the oven and cool briefly on a wire rack. Serve the crisp while still warm.

red haven peach blueberry crisp with cornmeal crumble

Red Haven peaches are my favorite crop out of Washington orchard country. Sometimes we even use a refractometer to measure their degrees Brix, or sweetness, and there's a race every year at the farmers' markets to have the sweetest peach in Washington, picked at the perfect time. It's important to remember that peaches do not get sweeter once they're picked, so you have one shot to get it right. When the blueberries are at their tartest, this is a perfect flavor combination.

Serve the crisp while still warm in wide shallow soup bowls with scoops of Vanilla Bean (page 326) or Buttermilk (page 330) Ice Cream.

Instead of blueberries, you could use raspberries, blackberries, or pitted cherries.

Because of the fuzzy skins, you may prefer to peel the peaches before they are sliced (see "How to Peel a Peach," page 219). If you are using nectarines, they don't need to be peeled.

If you made vanilla bean sugar (page 64), use it for the ½ cup sugar in the recipe instead of using a vanilla bean. Or, if you don't have a vanilla bean, you can omit it; the crisp will still be delicious.

SPECIAL EQUIPMENT: 9-INCH PIE PAN (WE PREFER A PYREX OR CERAMIC PIE PAN HERE), OR SIMILAR SIZE CASSEROLE OR BAKING PAN

5 medium (1¾ pounds/794 grams) peaches, peeled if you prefer, or nectarines

2 cups (8 ounces/227 grams) blueberries

½ cup (3½ ounces/100 grams) sugar

3 tablespoons (1½ ounces/40 grams) cold unsalted butter, cut into ⅛-inch dice

1 teaspoon freshly squeezed lemon juice

1 vanilla bean

1 tablespoon all-purpose flour

1 tablespoon cornstarch

Cornmeal Crumble with Lemon Thyme (page 100) for a 9-inch crisp

1. Preheat the oven to 350°F.

2. Cut the peaches in half, remove the pits, and slice them ¼ inch thick. You should have about 4 cups sliced peaches.

3. Put the peaches, blueberries, sugar, butter, and lemon juice in a large bowl. Split the vanilla bean lengthwise and use a paring knife to scrape out the seeds. Add the vanilla bean scrapings to the bowl and reserve the pod for vanilla bean sugar (page 64). Sift the flour and cornstarch into the bowl (see "How to Sift," page 13) and gently combine all the ingredients using a rubber spatula.

4. Put the peach mixture into a 9-inch pie pan, then evenly distribute the crumble all over the top. Here and there, gently squeeze some of the crumble between your hands to make larger clumps. Put the pie plate on a baking sheet to catch any drips and place it in the oven. Bake until the fruit is cooked and bubbling and the topping is golden, 50 to 55 minutes, rotating the pan halfway through the baking time.

5. Remove the pan from the oven and cool briefly on a wire rack. Serve the crisp while still warm.

The easiest way to peel peaches is to blanch them briefly. Cut a small X in the bottom of each peach, fill a bowl with ice water, and bring a saucepan of water to a boil. Add the peaches to the boiling water until the skins begin to pull away, about 30 seconds to 1 minute, depending on ripeness. Remove the peaches from the boiling water and immediately plunge them into the ice water for a few minutes. Remove the peaches from the ice water and peel them with a paring knife.

how to peel a peach

tarts that tempt

PASTRY TARTS AND THE APPLE DUMPLING

pear tarts with dreamy caramel sauce

Pear tarts have been on our menu from day one. The combination of rich caramel sauce, crisp pastry, and vanilla-scented pears is irresistible.

The most difficult part of this recipe is making the puff pastry. If you use store-bought puff pastry, you can serve this elegant company dessert to your guests with only a modest amount of effort (see "How to Bake Pear Tarts with Store-Bought Puff Pastry," page 224).

If you're really pressed for time, you could even buy a jar of good-quality caramel sauce instead of making your own. (We love Fran's; see Sources.)

You can use any ripe but firm pear, such as Anjou, Bosc, or Bartlett. If you are using pears that are larger than the size specified in the recipe, trim away a few pear slices from each pear half before you place it on the puff pastry square, or your puff may not rise as high. Be sure to leave a ½-inch border of puff around the pear.

You can use your puff squares straight from the freezer. They will thaw as you assemble the tarts.

The puff pastry squares can be made ahead and stored in the freezer. The pears can be poached ahead and stored, covered with their poaching liquid, in the refrigerator for a day or two. The almond cream can be made a few days ahead and stored, covered, in the refrigerator. You can bake the pear tarts early in the day and leave them at room temperature. Reheat them in a 375°F oven for 5 to 10 minutes before serving.

SPECIAL EQUIPMENT: MELON BALLER (OPTIONAL), ELECTRIC MIXER OR FOOD PROCESSOR

poached pears

3 small to medium (about 7 ounces each/21 ounces/595 grams) pears, ripe but firm

4 cups (32 ounces/907 grams) water

2 cups (13 ounces/375 grams) sugar

1 vanilla bean, split in half lengthwise

Six 4½-inch squares of "Worth the Effort" Puff Pastry (page 226), very cold or frozen, or six 4½-inch squares store-bought puff pastry, very cold or frozen

almond cream

3 tablespoons (2 ounces/57 grams) almond paste

2 tablespoons sugar

1½ tablespoons unsalted butter at room temperature, cut into ½-inch dice

1 large egg yolk

garnishes

Dreamy Caramel Sauce (page 69)

Sweetened Whipped Cream (page 193)

1. To poach the pears, peel the pears and cut them in half lengthwise. Trim out the stem and blossom end and remove the core using a melon baller or paring knife. Combine the water and sugar in a large saucepan. Add the vanilla bean and pears. To keep the pears submerged while they poach, put a piece of parchment or wax paper on the surface and weight it with a plate or small lid. Place the saucepan over high heat. When the liquid comes to a boil, turn the heat down to a simmer. The amount of time it will take to poach the pears depends on their ripeness, probably between 15 and 20 minutes after the pears come to a simmer. Test by poking a pear with the point of a small knife. As soon as the pears are tender but not mushy, remove the pan from the heat. Allow the pears to cool in the liquid.

2. Place the puff pastry squares on a parchment-lined baking sheet and set it in the freezer. Preheat the oven to 375°F. (Note: This oven temperature is for "Worth the Effort" Puff Pastry. If you are using store-bought puff pastry, see page 224 for notes on baking temperature and times.)

3. To make the almond cream, mix the almond paste and sugar using the paddle attachment of an electric mixer or in a food processor. The mixture will look crumbly. Beat in the butter, bit by bit. Add the egg yolk and mix until creamy and smooth. Set aside.

4. Remove the baking sheet of pastry squares from the freezer. Place about 2 teaspoons of almond cream in the center of each pastry square and flatten gently using your fingers or a small offset spatula. Remove the pears from the poaching liquid. (You can save the vanilla bean, dry it off,

top: Flattening the almond cream in the center of a puff pastry square

bottom: Fanning the sliced pear half over the almond cream

and use it to make vanilla bean sugar, page 64.) Dry the pears on a clean kitchen towel, then slice each pear half lengthwise into ¼-inch slices. Lift each sliced pear half with a spatula and place it over the almond cream, fanning it gently and being sure to leave a ½-inch border of puff pastry around the pears.

5. Slip another baking sheet underneath to double-pan and protect the bottoms of the tarts, then set the pan in the oven. Bake until the tarts are puffed and evenly golden brown, 50 to 55 minutes, rotating the baking sheet halfway through the baking time. (Note: This baking time and the double-panning method are for "Worth the Effort" Puff Pastry. For baking method and baking time for store-bought puff pastry, see below.)

6. Remove the pear tarts from the oven.

7. To serve the pear tarts, use a spatula to transfer a warm pear tart to each plate. Ladle about 3 tablespoons of caramel sauce over and around each tart and garnish with a mound of sweetened whipped cream.

How to Bake Pear Tarts with Store-Bought Puff Pastry

1. For the best texture and flavor with store-bought puff pastry, look for an all-butter brand, such as Dufour. All-butter store-bought puff pastry is more expensive, but the results are well worth it—the flavor and texture are closest to homemade.

2. Check the package for thawing instructions. If the dough is not ⅛ inch thick or close to that straight from the package (which it probably will be), roll it out to ⅛ inch thick. Then cut the puff pastry into the six 4½-inch squares (or squares very similar in size) called for in the recipe.

3. Puff pastry always bakes best when cold, so after cutting your puff pastry into squares, keep the squares chilled until you are ready to use them.

4. Assemble the pear tarts according to the directions in the recipe. For baking temperature and time, follow the baking instructions on the package. For store-bought puff pastry, you will not need to double pan.

5. We tested the pear tarts using two brands of supermarket puff pastry. Pepperidge Farm is easily available and inexpensive, but it is not made with butter. Dufour puff pastry, though more expensive, is made only with butter, flour, water, salt, and lemon juice, so the flavor and texture are much more like those of homemade puff.

6. A box of Dufour Classic Puff Pastry (14 ounces) contains one folded sheet of pastry about 10 inches × 13½ inches and ⅛ inch thick. According to the package instructions, thaw the sheet for 1 to 2 hours at room temperature or 2 to 3 hours in the refrigerator. Unwrap and unfold the sheet and place it on a lightly floured work counter. Cut the dough in half lengthwise into two 5 × 13½-inch strips, then cut each of the strips into 3 portions, each of which will produce six 4½ × 5-inch squares (not technically square, but close enough). If the dough has warmed up, chill the squares in the refrigerator for 30 minutes before proceeding. Then top the squares with almond cream and pears according to the recipe. Bake in a preheated 375°F oven (do not double-pan) until puffed and browned, about 40 minutes.

7. A box of Pepperidge Farm Puff Pastry (about a pound) contains 2 puff pastry sheets that are 9 inches square and ⅛ inch thick. Thaw the sheets according to the package instructions (40 minutes in the refrigerator) and unfold them. Cut each sheet into quarters, for a total of eight 4½-inch squares. You will need only six of these for the pear tart recipe. (You can save the other two in the freezer.) Top the squares with almond cream and pears according to the recipe. Bake in a preheated 400°F oven (do not double-pan) until puffed and browned, about 20 minutes.

"worth the effort" puff pastry

This is not classic puff pastry, because there's no butter block, but our recipe requires more folds, made with more precision, than rough puff pastry recipes. If you are intrigued by the project of making your own puff pastry from scratch, and you're willing to put in several hours over the course of two days, this is a recipe that will reward your efforts with beautifully crisp, buttery golden pastry that rises dramatically in the oven.

Precision is important in making puff pastry. Use a ruler to check your measurements and keep the dimensions as close as possible to those described in the recipe. Also, after you start making your "turns," the direction of rolling is critically important—always roll vertically, with the seam (or folded) sides to your right and left.

Keeping your puff pastry dough cold is crucial. If at any time while you are working the dough seems to be getting soft or warm, place it in the freezer for 10 minutes or the refrigerator for 20 minutes before continuing.

For puff pastry, we prefer the higher butterfat and lower moisture of a European-style butter, such as unsalted Plugra, but regular unsalted butter will also give you a good result.

This puff pastry requires an overnight rest in the refrigerator, so note that this is a two-day process and plan accordingly.

On the second day, after the overnight refrigerated rest, when you reach the step of forming a 10-inch square of puff pastry dough, you can freeze the dough and finish the recipe at another time (this is noted in the body of the recipe). If you have frozen your puff at this point, thaw it for at least 8 hours or overnight in the refrigerator before continuing with the recipe.

Or you can finish the recipe to the point of cutting squares, then wrap and freeze the puff pastry squares for later use. Puff pastry squares do not need to be thawed. Use them directly from the freezer.

Before starting this recipe, put the butter, diced into ½-inch bits, into the freezer for 30 minutes. You want the butter as cold as possible without being frozen solid.

SPECIAL EQUIPMENT: ELECTRIC MIXER, YARDSTICK OR LONG RULER, METAL BENCH KNIFE, PASTRY BRUSH. OPTIONAL BUT NICE TO HAVE: SPRAY BOTTLE, PASTRY WHEEL CUTTER

⅓ cup (2¾ ounces/80 grams) ice-cold water, plus a few more teaspoons as needed (see "How to Measure Ice-Cold Water for Pastry," page 159)

1 teaspoon distilled white or cider vinegar

1½ cups (8 ounces/227 grams) all-purpose flour

1½ cups (3 sticks/12 ounces/340 grams) very cold unsalted butter, preferably Plugra (see headnote), cut into ½-inch dice

2 teaspoons sugar

1½ teaspoons kosher salt

1. Combine the ice-cold water and the vinegar in a measuring cup or small container and set aside.

2. Combine the flour, butter, sugar, and salt in the bowl of an electric mixer fitted with the paddle. (You may want to hold a kitchen towel around the mixer before you start mixing, as the chunks of butter jump and sputter around and a few may fly out of the bowl.) Mix the dough on medium-low speed for 30 to 60 seconds or until the cubes of butter have lost their shape and are about three-quarters of their original size. The butter cubes will look smashed up, but you will still see biggish chunks of butter. (When in doubt, mix the butter less rather than more, as these chunks of butter will eventually become your puff pastry layers, so it is important not to crumb them down too much.)

3. Turn the mixer to low and add the water-vinegar mixture. Mix for about 15 seconds, just long enough to get the water evenly distributed but not worked in. The dough should not come together in the bowl, but when you squeeze the dough in your hand it will clump together. If the dough seems too dry, add another 1 or 2 teaspoons ice-cold water. While the dough is still in the bowl, work it with your hands for a minute to clump it together, then turn the dough onto a work surface. Gather the dough together with your hands and work it into a rough rectangular or square shape, using a metal bench knife to help you. (Your rough square or rectangle should be about 4 or 5 inches on each side.) Lightly flour your work surface, then roll the dough out to an 8 × 21-inch rectangle.

4. Use a knife or a metal bench knife to trim your rectangle to 7 × 20 inches with nice straight edges, saving all the scraps.

5. Use a dry pastry brush to brush off any excess flour, then give the surface of your rectangle a very light spray of water from a spray bottle or a few drops of cold water scattered from your fingers.

Take all the trimmings and arrange them over the top of the rectangle, pressing them to help them adhere.

6. Now you are ready to put your first turn in the dough, which will be a book fold. Turn the rectangle of dough so that it is horizontal to you. To make a book fold, pull the outer edges in to the center so they meet in the middle (leaving about a ¼-inch gap in the middle), giving the appearance of an open book, then fold "the book" closed, using the center seam as the point of folding (and the little gap will make folding possible). Use your rolling pin to press gently but firmly on the top of the "book" to seal. Now the dough should look like a closed book, with the "binding" on one side and the "pages" on the other. The rectangle of dough should now be approximately 7 × 5 inches.

7. Wrap the dough in plastic wrap and put it in the freezer for 30 minutes.

8. After chilling the dough in the freezer for 30 minutes, remove the plastic wrap and put the dough back on the lightly floured work surface, placing the seam sides (where you folded it, or the "pages" of your book) at your right and left and the short (5-inch) sides as your top and bottom. In other words, one of the short (5-inch) sides will be closest to your body. Using a rolling pin, roll in a vertical direction, from top to bottom. In other words, roll what used to be the 7-inch sides out to 20 inches. While you are rolling out the length, the shorter (5-inch) sides will expand naturally to about 6 inches (Don't worry about the exact width here; just be sure you get the 20-inch length.) While you are rolling the dough, keep preserving your straight sides by now and then pressing against them and straightening them with a metal bench knife.

9. When you have rolled the dough to a 6- or 7-inch × 20-inch rectangle, again brush off the excess flour and spray it very lightly with water, then turn the dough horizontal to you and give it a book fold (this is the second book fold). Again use your rolling pin to press gently but firmly to seal the block of dough. Then wrap the dough tightly in plastic wrap and allow to rest in the refrigerator for 1½ to 2 hours.

10. After the 1½- to 2-hour chill, place the dough back on a lightly floured work surface, again with the fold at your left, and roll the dough again in a vertical direction from top to bottom to a 20-inch length. Again brush off any excess flour and very lightly spray or sprinkle the dough with a few drops of water.

11. Turn the rectangle horizontally to you and this time make a "business letter fold" by folding the dough into thirds. In other words, fold in one short (7-inch) side toward the middle of the rectangle, then fold the other short side over and on top of it, just like you would fold a business letter. Use your rolling pin to press lightly on top of your block of dough to seal. Wrap the dough in plastic wrap and return it to the refrigerator to chill for 1½ to 2 more hours.

12. After the second 1½- to 2-hour chill, roll the dough back out again, with seam or folded sides at your right and left, rolling from top to bottom in the direction of the folded sides back out to a 20-inch length. Brush off any excess flour, spray the surface of the rectangle lightly with water, and fold the dough in half, pressing on it with the rolling pin lightly to seal. At this point, your dough should be approximately 7 × 10 inches. Wrap the dough tightly in plastic wrap and return it to the refrigerator to chill and rest overnight. (Note: Freezing is not resting—for this refrigerated overnight rest, do not put the puff pastry in the freezer.)

13. When you are ready to continue with the puff pastry the next day, remove the dough from the refrigerator, unwrap it, and place it on a lightly floured work surface with the seam (folded) sides on the right and left and, this time, the long (10-inch) sides of the dough at the top and bottom. Now, rolling in a vertical direction from top to bottom in the direction of the seam or folded sides, roll the dough out to a 20-inch length. You will now have a 10 × 20-inch rectangle. Brush off any excess flour, spray or sprinkle the dough very lightly with water, and fold the dough in half, which will give you a 10-inch square (or pretty close to that); then use the rolling pin to press gently on the square to seal. Wrap the dough in plastic wrap and place it in the freezer for 40 minutes, flipping the dough to the other side after 20 minutes so the block of dough is evenly super-chilled. (At this point, instead of leaving the dough in the freezer for 40 minutes, you can just leave the plastic-wrapped dough in the freezer to finish at a later time.)

14. When you are ready to roll and cut the dough, remove the 10-inch square of dough from the freezer. (Note: This means you can remove it from the freezer and work with it if it has been in the freezer for only 40 minutes. On the other hand, if the puff has been frozen longer at this point for the sake of convenience, you will have to thaw it for at least 8 hours or overnight in the refrigerator before continuing with the recipe. Before rolling and cutting dough that was frozen longer than 40 minutes and has now been thawed in the refrigerator, place it back in the freezer

for 30 minutes, flipping it to the other side after 15 minutes so that the dough is evenly super-chilled before continuing with the recipe.)

15. Place the chilled dough on the lightly floured work surface with the seam (or folded) sides left and right. Roll the dough in a vertical direction (in the direction of the seam or folded sides) out to 15 inches. (So, in other words, you're not rolling very far this time, just 5 more inches.) You will now have a rectangle that is 10 × 15 inches. Using a pastry wheel or a very sharp, thin knife, trim the dough to a 9 × 13½-inch rectangle. (In other words, trim approximately ¾ inch from each long side and trim approximately ½ inch from each short side.) Make clean, even cuts on all 4 sides of the dough, being sure not to pinch the layers while you cut the dough, because that will keep your puff from rising properly.

16. After you have trimmed the dough to a 9 × 13½-inch rectangle, cut the dough in half lengthwise to make two 4½ × 13½-inch rectangles, then cut each of the strips into 3 portions each, which will produce six 4½-inch squares. (You can place one of the strips in the refrigerator or freezer while the other is being portioned.)

17. When you have made your puff pastry squares, place them on a parchment-lined baking sheet, cover them tightly with plastic wrap, and place them in the freezer until you are ready to bake them. After the squares are frozen, you can stack them, wrap them in plastic, and place them in a sealable plastic bag in the freezer.

18. Puff pastry bakes best when very cold. Don't worry about thawing the dough if your pastry squares are frozen. The dough will thaw enough as you are assembling your tarts.

To make pear tarts, see the recipe on page 222.

apple dumplings with medjool date butter

These apple dumplings are like warm individual apple pies filled with date butter and fragrant with cinnamon. You can use any kind of apple in this recipe that is good for cooking. Our favorite is Granny Smith, because its high acidity level complements the sweet dates. Medjool dates are plump, moist, and especially rich in flavor.

Serve the dumplings warm. Scoops of Buttermilk (page 330), Vanilla Bean (page 326), or Streusel (page 327) Ice Cream are all fine companions to the flavors of apple, cinnamon, and date, but Jackie's Maple Syrup Ice Cream (page 333) may be best of all! Sweetened Whipped Cream (page 193) is another option. We doubt that anyone would complain if you add a drizzle of Dreamy Caramel Sauce (page 69) to the plate.

The All-Butter Pastry Dough can be made a day ahead and kept chilled. The date butter can be made a day or two ahead and kept chilled. The dumplings can be baked early in the day, kept at room temperature, and reheated in a 400°F oven for about 8 minutes or until warmed through before serving.

SPECIAL EQUIPMENT: FOOD PROCESSOR OR ELECTRIC MIXER, PASTRY BRUSH, MELON BALLER, LEAF-SHAPED COOKIE CUTTER (OPTIONAL)

date butter

10 Medjool or other dates (about 6 ounces/170 grams), pitted and chopped

6 tablespoons (¾ stick/3 ounces/ 85 grams) unsalted butter at room temperature

¼ cup (2 ounces/57 grams) packed brown sugar

1 teaspoon ground cinnamon

apple dumplings

All-Butter Pastry Dough (page 234), chilled for at least 1 hour

4 medium apples (about 7 ounces each/28 ounces/ 794 grams), peeled and halved lengthwise

1 large egg yolk

1 tablespoon heavy cream

¼ cup (2 ounces/57 grams) sugar

2 teaspoons ground cinnamon

1. To make the date butter, combine the dates, butter, brown sugar, and cinnamon in the bowl of a food processor or in an electric mixer with the paddle. Process until smooth. Transfer the date butter to a small bowl and refrigerate until somewhat firm.

2. To make the dumplings, preheat the oven to 400°F. Set out a small bowl of water and a pastry brush. Divide the pastry dough in half. On a lightly floured surface, roll out half the dough to a rough square shape about ⅛ inch thick. Trim the dough with a knife to make a 12-inch square, saving all the pastry trimmings for decorating the dumplings later. Cut the 12-inch square into quarters. You will have four 6-inch squares of dough. Repeat with the second half of the dough. You will now have eight 6-inch squares of dough. Keep the pastry squares chilled until you are ready to shape the dumplings.

3. Use a melon baller to remove the core of each apple half and create a little cavity. Fill the cavity of each apple half with a mound of the date butter. Put a dough square on the work surface and use a small knife to make a cut from each corner to about halfway to the center of the square. (These cuts will allow you to fold the dough up pinwheel fashion over the apple half later.) Place an apple half, core side down, on the center of the dough square. Brush the corners of the dough lightly with water. Fold the corners of the dough up over the apple on each pastry square in an alternating pinwheel fashion, pressing to seal. The apple is now completely sealed within the dough. Repeat with the remaining apples and dough squares.

NOTE: ANOTHER WAY TO FORM THE DUMPLINGS, WHICH THE DAHLIA WORKSHOP BAKERS NOW DO FOR THE SAKE OF SPEED, IS TO LEAVE EACH 6-INCH SQUARE WHOLE, WITHOUT THE "PINWHEEL" CUTS, PLACE THE APPLE DATE SIDE DOWN IN THE CENTER, THEN LIFT EACH OF THE 4 CORNERS OF THE PASTRY SQUARE UP AND OVER THE APPLE AND SEAL.

4. Place the dumplings on a parchment-lined baking sheet. Reroll the pastry trimmings and cut out 8 decorative leaf shapes using a small knife or a leaf-shaped cookie cutter. Place one leaf on each dumpling, fixing it on with a pastry brush dipped in a little water.

5. In a small bowl, beat the egg yolk lightly with the cream. Brush each dumpling with egg wash. In another small bowl, mix the sugar with the cinnamon. Sprinkle 1 or 2 teaspoons of cinnamon

sugar on each dumpling. Bake the dumplings in the oven for 20 to 25 minutes, or until the pastry is golden and the apples feel tender when pierced with a knife, rotating the pan halfway through the baking time. Remove the pan from the oven and cool briefly on a wire rack. Serve the dumplings warm with a scoop of ice cream or a dollop of whipped cream.

Using a small scoop to fill the cavity of an apple half with date butter

Using a knife to cut from each corner to about halfway to the center of a pastry square

Folding one of the corners of the pastry square up over the apple

Continuing to fold and seal the corners of the pastry square over the apple, pinwheel fashion

The apple is now enclosed in pastry. Affixing a decorative pastry leaf on top of the pastry-wrapped apple

Apple dumpling enclosed in pastry with pastry leaf decoration

Brushing the apple dumpling with egg wash

Sprinkling with cinnamon sugar

all-butter pastry dough

MAKES 8 PASTRY SQUARES FOR APPLE DUMPLINGS OR ENOUGH
DOUGH FOR 1 DOUBLE-CRUST CHOCOLATE PECAN TART

Making pastry dough in the food processor is fast and easy. The amount of water you'll need when making the dough, as for most pastry doughs, varies by the humidity in the air, the moisture in the flour, and other factors, so add the water carefully to find the exact amount needed for the dough to clump together in your hand. Also as for most pastry dough, if in doubt as to whether your dough is too dry, go ahead and add that extra tablespoon of water.

The flakiest pastry is made with very cold butter. Before you start the recipe, dice the butter and place it in the freezer for 30 minutes.

You can make the pastry dough ahead and keep it wrapped and refrigerated for a day or two, or you can keep the dough frozen for a few weeks. Thaw frozen dough by placing it in the refrigerator overnight.

See "About Pastry Doughs," page 158.

SPECIAL EQUIPMENT: FOOD PROCESSOR

2½ cups (12 ounces/345 grams) all-purpose flour

1 tablespoon sugar

1 teaspoon kosher salt

1 cup (2 sticks/8 ounces/230 grams)

unsalted butter, freezer cold (see headnote), cut into ½-inch dice

8 to 10 tablespoons (4 to 5 ounces/115 to 141 grams) ice-cold water or as needed (see "How to Measure Ice-Cold Water for Pastry," page 159)

1. Place the flour, sugar, and salt in the bowl of a food processor. Pulse a few times to mix. Add the cold butter all at once and pulse several times, until the butter and flour form crumbs slightly smaller than pea size. In a steady stream, gradually add 8 tablespoons (½ cup) of ice-cold water through the feed tube while pulsing. Remove the lid from the processor and see if you can form a clump by pressing some dough with your fingers. (Note: The dough will not form a ball in the processor, but you should be able to press the dough to form a clump.) If the dough seems too dry, add one more tablespoon water, pulse a few more times, and check the dough again. Add another tablespoon water if needed and pulse a few more times.

2. Take the lid off the processor, dump the dough out onto a work surface, and gather it together with your hands, forcing it into a flattened round. Wrap in plastic and chill in the refrigerator for about an hour or longer before rolling it out.

3. To make the apple dumplings, follow the directions in the recipe for making pastry squares.

4. To make the chocolate-glazed pecan tart, divide the dough into 2 unequal pieces, about two-thirds and one-third. Form each piece into a flattened round, wrap in plastic wrap, and chill for an hour or longer.

raspberries 'n' cream tart

Creamy vanilla pastry cream, gorgeous red berries, and a cornmeal short crust—this is the perfect tart to celebrate summer berries. Instead of raspberries, you can use blackberries, blueberries, or boysenberries. If you prefer to use strawberries, halve or quarter and lightly sugar them first.

If you are setting the tart out as a showpiece, fill the tart shell with the pastry cream, chill it for 30 to 60 minutes, then beautifully arrange the raspberries over the top, sieve a little powdered sugar over the berries, and set the tart on the table. But if you're not displaying the tart, it's easiest to slice it after the chilling time but without any berries on top. Plate the wedges of tart, decorate each wedge with berries and a dusting of powdered sugar, and serve.

If you prefer, you can make the Flaky but Tender Pastry Dough (page 183) for the tart shell.

The pastry cream must be made and chilled at least 3 hours ahead (or overnight), and the assembled tart needs to chill for 1½ hours before slicing, so plan accordingly.

Keep all the parts separate—the blind-baked tart shell at room temperature, the pastry cream covered and chilled, and the raspberries chilled. Then you'll be able to quickly fill the tart shell with pastry cream, chill it for 1½ hours, top with berries, and serve.

Vanilla Bean Pastry Cream (page 320), chilled for at least 3 hours

One 10-inch blind-baked and cooled cornmeal tart shell (page 238)

Three 6-ounce containers (18 ounces/ 510 grams) fresh raspberries

Powdered sugar as needed for sprinkling

1. Remove the bowl of pastry cream from the refrigerator and scrape it into the tart shell, using a rubber spatula to smooth the surface. For the cleanest slices, chill the pastry-cream-filled tart for about 1½ hours before slicing and serving.

2. When you are ready to serve the tart, arrange the raspberries decoratively over the surface. Unmold the tart from the tart pan (see "How to Unmold Cakes, Tarts, and Loaves," page 262). Sieve a little powdered sugar over the raspberries. Use a long serrated knife to cut the tart into wedges, using a sawing motion to cut through the edge of the pastry, then use an offset spatula to transfer each wedge to a dessert plate. Another way is to slice the tart and then decorate each slice with berries.

cornmeal tart dough

This tart dough calls for both cornmeal and almond meal. Use a medium-grind cornmeal, but not a stone-ground type (such as Bob's Red Mill), which has a coarse or rustic-looking grind. Almond meal is made of almonds ground as finely as flour. It is available at supermarkets and health food stores and online (see Sources).

A short dough of this type, in which the butter and sugar are creamed together, is best made in an electric mixer, not a food processor.

The dough must be refrigerated for at least 3 hours before being rolled, so plan accordingly.

See "About Pastry Doughs," page 158.

SPECIAL EQUIPMENT: ELECTRIC MIXER, 10-INCH REMOVABLE-BOTTOM TART PAN, DRIED BEANS FOR PIE WEIGHTS

1 cup (5¼ ounces/150 grams) all-purpose flour

⅓ cup (1½ ounces/40 grams) powdered sugar, sifted (measure first, then sift; see "How to Sift," page 13)

½ cup (1 stick/4 ounces/113 grams) unsalted butter, softened

¼ cup (1 ounce/30 grams) almond meal

¼ cup (1½ ounces/40 grams) medium-grind cornmeal

½ teaspoon kosher salt

3 large egg yolks

1 teaspoon pure vanilla extract

1. Into a bowl, sift the flour twice, then set aside (see "How to Sift," page 13).

2. In the bowl of an electric mixer with the paddle, combine the powdered sugar and the butter. Mix on medium-high speed for 3 to 4 minutes, until the mixture is pale and fluffy. Scrape down the bowl and paddle with a rubber spatula.

3. With the mixer on low speed, add the almond meal, cornmeal, and salt, mixing until combined. Add the egg yolks and vanilla extract and mix until combined.

4. With the mixer still on low speed, add the flour in 3 to 4 additions and mix just until combined. Do not overmix.

5. Gather the dough into a disk and wrap in plastic wrap. Refrigerate for at least 3 hours or overnight before using.

6. Preheat the oven to 325°F.

7. Remove the dough from the refrigerator and unwrap it. Place it on a lightly floured work surface and, using a lightly floured rolling pin, roll the dough out to a round 12 or 13 inches in diameter and ⅛ inch thick. This dough is not as flexible as some pastry doughs, and the pastry round may break if you try to fold it before transferring it. One way to transfer the dough is to slip both hands under the round of dough with your fingers splayed and quickly transfer it to the tart pan. The safest way to transfer the dough (and avoid tearing it) is to use a 10- or 12-inch round cake cardboard (see page 26) or a piece of sturdy cardboard cut to about this size. Slide the dough onto the cardboard, then slide it off on top of the tart pan. (But if the dough starts tearing as you transfer it, you can just pat it together to seal any cracks as you are patting the dough into the tart pan.)

8. Ease the dough gently into the pan. Don't stretch the dough or it will shrink when baked. Gently press the dough that forms the sides of the shell in and down and flush against the sides of the tart pan. Trim the dough to a ¼- to ½-inch overhang. Go around the top of the pan, using your thumb to press the dough against the metal rim of the pan to cut off the excess dough. Use a thumb and index finger (thumb against pastry inside the pan and index finger along the outside of the pan, rotating the pan as you go) to press gently all along the top edge of the rim and into the grooves along the sides of the tart pan to make sure the pastry crust is nice and straight and comes to the top of the pan. Chill the pastry-lined pan for 15 to 30 minutes before baking.

9. To blind-bake the tart shell, line the pastry shell with a square of parchment paper (make sure it is large enough that you will be able to grasp the corners and pull it out later), then fill it with dried beans. Put the tart shell in the oven and bake for 40 minutes. After 40 minutes, remove the tart pan from the oven and lift up a corner of the paper to look at the dough on the bottom of the pan, which should look lighter in color and matte (not shiny) when it is cooked enough. If the dough on the bottom of the pan looks uncooked, return the pan to the oven and continue to bake for a little longer.

10. When the bottom dough is cooked, remove the pan from the oven and grab the corners of the paper to lift out the paper and beans. Return the tart pan to the oven and bake until the edge of the tart is golden brown and the bottom is cooked through and only lightly browned, 6 to 8 minutes more. (Note: If you overbrown the crust for the cornmeal tart dough, you will lose the delicate short crust texture.) Remove the pan from the oven and allow to cool completely at room temperature before filling the tart shell.

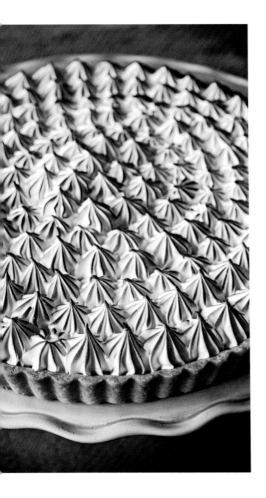

tangy lemon meringue tart

Soft, creamy, butter-yellow lemon curd and browned rosettes of meringue are the elements of this classic tart. It's hard to improve on a classic, but our lemon curd is both voluptuous and surprisingly tart and tangy with plenty of lemon flavor. The tartness of the curd is balanced by the sweetness of the meringue.

The pastry bakers make small, individual lemon meringue tarts for the Dahlia Bakery, but at home one large tart is easier and you don't have to buy a quantity of little tart pans.

Because of the large amount of butter in our lemon curd, we recommend that you use a handheld propane torch to brown the meringue rather than putting the tart under the broiler. Propane torches are available online and at kitchenware and hardware stores (see Sources).

Fitting a small star tip (rather than a large one) onto your pastry bag of meringue will help you pace yourself to make small dollops of meringue that completely cover the top of your tart. The recipe makes enough meringue to cover the pie with small dollops, not large rosettes, so the finished tart will taste balanced and not overly sweet.

If you prefer not to make the meringue, or if you don't own and don't want to buy a propane torch, you can top the pie with Sweetened Whipped Cream (page 193) instead.

If you prefer, you can make the Flaky but Tender Pastry Dough (page 183) for the tart shell.

NOTE: THE LEMON CURD MUST BE CHILLED FOR AT LEAST 3 HOURS—OVERNIGHT IS BETTER—AND THE FINISHED TART SHOULD BE CHILLED FOR AN HOUR BEFORE SERVING, SO PLAN ACCORDINGLY.

SPECIAL EQUIPMENT: ELECTRIC MIXER, INSTANT-READ OR DIGITAL PROBE THERMOMETER, PIPING BAG WITH SMALL (¼-INCH) STAR TIP (OPTIONAL), SMALL HANDHELD PROPANE TORCH

Tangy Lemon Curd (page 242), chilled for at least 3 hours

One 10-inch blind-baked and cooled cornmeal tart shell (page 238)

meringue

4 large egg whites

¾ cup plus 1 tablespoon (6 ounces/ 175 grams) sugar

⅛ teaspoon salt

1. Remove the lemon curd from the refrigerator and fill the prepared tart shell, spreading the curd evenly with a rubber spatula. Unmold the tart from the pan (see "How to Unmold Cakes, Tarts, and Loaves," page 262) and set aside.

2. To make the meringue, put the egg whites, sugar, and salt in the bowl of an electric mixer. Fill a saucepan wide enough to hold the mixer bowl with 2 or 3 inches of water and bring the water to a simmer over medium-high heat. Remove the electric mixer bowl from the machine, place it over the saucepan (the bottom of the bowl should not be touching the water), and cook the egg whites, stirring constantly with a rubber spatula, until the egg whites smell cooked and the temperature is 160°F on an instant-read or digital probe thermometer.

3. Remove the mixer bowl from the water bath and place it in the machine with the whisk attachment. Whip on medium-high speed until the egg-white-sugar mixture is as thick as shaving cream and holds stiff peaks, 6 to 8 minutes (see "How to Whip Egg Whites," page 14).

4. Remove the meringue from the mixer and use a rubber spatula to fill a pastry bag fitted with a ¼-inch star tip. (Never fill a pastry bag more than two-thirds full.) Hold the bag upright and squeeze small dollops of meringue all over the surface of the tart, completely covering the lemon curd. (If you have completely covered the pie with dollops of meringue and you still have a little meringue left in the pastry bag, it's okay to throw it away; you don't have to use all the meringue.) Another way to cover the pie with meringue is to spread it evenly over the surface of the tart with an offset icing spatula, picking up the spatula here and there to make some little peaks.

top: Piping meringue . . .

middle: . . . to cover the surface of the tart

bottom: Using a handheld torch to brown the meringue

5. Light your propane torch and carefully brown the meringue, holding the torch so the flame is 1 or 2 inches from the surface of the meringue. Remember that you don't need to completely brown the meringue everywhere—you are just making attractive browned patches.

6. Chill the tart for 1 hour, then slice it into wedges and serve.

tangy lemon curd

The large amount of butter in our version of lemon curd makes it uniquely voluptuous. There's also plenty of lemon juice, which makes the curd pleasantly sweet-tart.

Since you need the zest from 5 lemons and 1 cup of fresh lemon juice, zest the lemons first, then juice them. Five lemons, unless they are large and juicy, may not yield 1 cup of juice, so, while you're at the store, pick up about 3 more lemons so you can make more juice if you need to. You won't need any zest from these additional lemons.

To strain the lemon curd, use a fine-mesh strainer, but you don't need mesh as fine as a chinoise. A fine-mesh strainer with a medium-large or large diameter is best so that you can work the thick curd through the strainer fairly quickly.

To make the smoothest, most voluptuous lemon curd, add the softened butter to the curd while pulsing it in a food processor. You could also use a blender or an immersion blender for this step.

NOTE: THE LEMON CURD MUST BE CHILLED FOR AT LEAST 3 HOURS OR OVERNIGHT BEFORE USING, SO PLAN ACCORDINGLY.

SPECIAL EQUIPMENT: INSTANT-READ OR DIGITAL PROBE THERMOMETER (OPTIONAL), FOOD PROCESSOR

5 lemons (8½ ounces/241 grams), plus 1 to 3 extra lemons if needed

4 large eggs

1 cup (7 ounces/200 grams) sugar

1 cup (2 sticks/8 ounces/227 grams) unsalted butter, cut into ½-inch dice and softened

1. Zest the lemons using a fine Microplane grater, being careful not to remove any of the pith, then juice them. You should have 1 cup lemon juice; if not, juice 1 to 3 more lemons, or as many as you need to get the 1 cup of juice (but don't zest these additional lemons).

2. Set up a saucepan with 2 or 3 inches of water and bring it to a simmer over medium-high heat. Choose a saucepan that will be large and wide enough to hold a metal bowl and function as a hot water bath. Also, place a fine-mesh strainer over another bowl and set that near the stove.

3. Place the lemon juice and zest in a small saucepan and bring to a boil over medium-high heat. As soon as the juice boils, remove the pot from the heat.

4. Meanwhile, put the eggs and sugar in the bowl that you have chosen to fit over your water bath and use a whisk to combine them well. Add a ladle (about ⅓ cup) of the hot juice mixture and whisk. After you have tempered (or warmed) the eggs, add the remaining hot lemon juice mixture to the bowl and whisk again to combine.

5. Place the bowl of lemon-egg mixture over the saucepan of simmering water. (The bottom of the bowl should not touch the simmering water.) Cook the lemon curd over the simmering water, adjusting the heat as needed to keep the water at a simmer and whisking constantly until the curd is thick, 10 to 15 minutes. When the curd is thick enough, the tines of the whisk will leave a distinct trail as you are whisking.

6. Immediately strain the curd through the fine-mesh strainer set over a bowl, forcing all the curd through the strainer using a rubber spatula or plastic pastry scraper. (The zest will be left behind in the sieve and should be discarded.) If you check the temperature of the curd with an instant-read thermometer, it should read 140° to 150°F. If the curd is still very hot after it has been strained, use a rubber spatula to stir it a few times to cool it down slightly so the curd is not scalding hot but is still warm enough to melt the butter in the next step.

7. Transfer the curd to the bowl of a food processor and start gradually adding the butter through the feed tube, a few tablespoons at a time, while pulsing. Allow the clump of butter to be incorporated into the curd before adding more.

8. When all the butter has been incorporated and the curd is smooth, transfer the curd to a bowl, place a piece of plastic wrap directly over the surface (so it doesn't form a skin), and refrigerate until cold, at least 3 hours; overnight is even better.

toasted pine nut marzipan tart

This buttery double-crust tart filled with handmade pine nut marzipan was created as the dessert for the "Dinner with Dale Chihuly" menu in my book *Tom's Big Dinners*, and I've been baking it ever since. I liked the idea of making my own marzipan in the food processor rather than buying it at the store, and it worked out perfectly.

Serve a wedge of this tart with a scoop of Vanilla Bean Ice Cream (page 326) or with a glass of Vin Santo. If fresh figs are in season, a few slices of fig would go nicely alongside. Leftover tart is great for breakfast the next day with your morning cuppa.

The dough needs to chill for an hour before being rolled, so plan accordingly.

You can make the dough a day or two ahead and keep it refrigerated. You can bake the tart early in the day and leave it at room temperature.

See "About Pastry Doughs," page 158.

SPECIAL EQUIPMENT: ELECTRIC MIXER, FOOD PROCESSOR, BOARD SCRAPER, 9-INCH REMOVABLE-BOTTOM TART PAN

soft tart dough

1⅔ cups (8 ounces/228 grams) all-purpose flour

¼ teaspoon baking powder

¼ teaspoon kosher salt

½ cup plus 1 tablespoon (4½ ounces/127 grams) unsalted butter, softened

½ cup (2⅛ ounces/59 grams) powdered sugar

1 large egg plus 1 large yolk, lightly beaten

pine nut marzipan

1 cup (4 ounces/113 grams) pine nuts, toasted (see "How to Toast and Chop Nuts," page 13)

½ cup (3⅝ ounces/104 grams) sugar

1 large egg, lightly beaten

4 tablespoons (½ stick/2 ounces/57 grams) unsalted butter, softened

to finish the tart

1 large egg yolk

1 tablespoon heavy cream

About 2 teaspoons sugar as needed for sprinkling

1. To make the tart dough, combine the flour, baking powder, and salt in a bowl and set the dry ingredients aside.

2. In the bowl of an electric mixer using the paddle attachment, cream the butter and sugar together. Gradually beat in the eggs. It's okay if the mixture looks broken. Add the dry ingredients to the butter-egg mixture and mix just until the dough comes together. Scrape the dough out onto a work surface and divide into one-third and two-third portions, forming each portion into a flattened round. Wrap the rounds in plastic wrap and chill for at least 1 hour.

3. To make the pine nut marzipan, combine the pine nuts and sugar in the bowl of a food processor and pulse until finely ground. Add the egg and process until smooth. Gradually add the butter, a small bit at a time, pulsing until each bit of butter is completely incorporated. When all the butter is incorporated, scrape the marzipan into a bowl.

4. Preheat the oven to 400°F.

5. Unwrap the larger round of dough and place it on a lightly floured work surface. Using a lightly floured rolling pin, roll the dough out to an 11- or 12-inch round about ⅛ inch thick. Use flour as needed to roll the dough and lift the dough occasionally with a board scraper as you are working to check that it's not sticking. Transfer the dough to the tart pan. It's easiest to do this by folding the dough into quarters. Pick up the folded dough and place it in the pan, with the pointed tip of the dough in the center of the pan, then unfold gently.

6. Ease the dough gently into the pan, patting it up against the sides. Trim the overhanging dough to about ¾ inch. The dough is a bit fragile. If it tears while you are lining the pan, use the dough trimmings to patch any holes. Using a rubber spatula or an offset icing spatula, spread the marzipan evenly over the bottom of the tart. Unwrap the smaller round of dough and roll it out to a 9-inch round. Transfer the round of dough to cover the marzipan. (Again, it's easiest to fold the dough into quarters to transfer it.) Use a small knife to trim the dough to fit inside the top of the tart.

7. In a small bowl, beat the egg yolk lightly with the heavy cream. Brush the ½ inch of overhanging dough with some of the egg wash, then fold the overhang up over the top of the tart, pressing gently with the tines of a fork to seal. Brush the entire top of the tart lightly with egg wash and sprinkle with sugar. Cut a few 1-inch slashes in the top of the tart for steam to

escape. Place the tart pan on a baking sheet and bake until golden, about 30 minutes. Remove from the oven and allow the tart to cool on a rack for 15 minutes before removing the rim of the pan (see "How to Unmold Cakes, Tarts, and Loaves," page 262).

8. Allow the tart to cool for at least 15 minutes more before slicing and serving. (You can leave the tart on the metal tart pan bottom, or you can slide it onto a 9-inch round cake cardboard.) Cut the tart into thin wedges and serve slightly warm or at room temperature.

garrett's chocolate tart

MAKES ONE **10**-INCH TART; SERVES **12**

This sublime chocolate tart has a very intense, deep, and pure chocolate flavor, even though it's made with half milk chocolate and half bittersweet chocolate—which might lead you to believe the chocolate flavor will be lighter than it actually is. The purpose of the milk chocolate is to provide sweetness since there's not much sugar in the filling, a typical strategy from pastry chef Garrett Melkonian's playbook.

Often, pastry chefs make a chocolate crust to encircle a chocolate tart, but Garrett prefers the contrast of our Flaky but Tender Pastry with the rich chocolate filling.

Offset the chocolate intensity of the tart by serving each slice with a spoonful of lightly sweetened crème fraîche or Sweetened Whipped Cream (page 193). If it's cherry season, a spoonful of Brachetto Cherries with Fresh Lime (page 301) alongside is a marvelous touch. Serve the rest of the bottle of Brachetto (Italian sparkling red wine) with the tart.

The filling is not really difficult to make as long as you pay attention to details such as the temperature of a few ingredients. Be sure your eggs are slightly warmer than room temperature. Warm the eggs in a bowl of very hot tap water for 5 minutes before breaking them. Also, the melted chocolate should not be too hot when you add it to the whipped eggs or it will take the air out of the batter.

Be sure to use top-quality chocolate for this tart, for the milk chocolate as well as the bittersweet (see "Our Favorite Chocolates," page 21).

This is more salt than you usually see in a chocolate filling, but we like the way salt works with chocolate. Kosher salt is coarser in texture than table salt, so if you are substituting table salt, cut the amount in half (see "Salt," page 22).

NOTE: IF THE BLIND-BAKED TART SHELL SHRANK SLIGHTLY, OR IF YOU ACHIEVED EXTRA VOLUME WHEN WHIPPING YOUR EGGS (THE VOLUME CAN VARY DUE TO THE FRESHNESS AND EXACT TEMPERATURE OF THE EGGS AND OTHER FACTORS), YOU MAY HAVE UP TO ½ CUP MORE FILLING THAN YOU CAN FIT INTO YOUR TART SHELL. IF SO, DISCARD THE EXCESS AND DON'T WORRY—YOUR TART WILL TURN OUT JUST FINE.

SPECIAL EQUIPMENT: ELECTRIC MIXER

6 ounces (170 grams) milk chocolate, chopped (about 1 cup; see "How to Chop Chocolate," page 12)

6 ounces (170 grams) bittersweet chocolate, chopped (about 1 cup)

¾ cup (1½ sticks/6 ounces/170 grams) unsalted butter, cut into 1-inch dice

4 large eggs, slightly warmer than room temperature (see headnote)

3 tablespoons (1½ ounces/42 grams) sugar

1 tablespoon pure vanilla extract

¾ teaspoon kosher salt

One 10-inch blind-baked and cooled Flaky but Tender Pastry Tart Shell (page 183)

1. Put both chocolates and the butter in a heatproof bowl that has been placed over a saucepan of simmering water over medium heat. (The bottom of the bowl should not touch the water.) Adjust the burner to keep the water barely at a simmer. Melt the chocolates and butter, stirring to combine with a rubber or silicone spatula.

2. When the chocolate-butter mixture is melted, remove the bowl from the saucepan and allow the chocolate to cool to room temperature, about 20 minutes. The chocolate mixture should still be liquid, but no longer warm to the touch. Meanwhile, preheat the oven to 400°F.

3. In the bowl of an electric mixer with the whisk attachment, combine the eggs, sugar, vanilla extract, and salt. Whip on high speed until the mixture is very thick and fluffy and has tripled in volume, 4 to 5 minutes.

4. Remove the bowl from the mixer. Add about a third of the egg mixture to the bowl that contains the chocolate mixture and fold it in to lighten the chocolate. Then add the chocolate mixture to the remaining egg mixture in the bowl from the electric mixer, folding everything together quickly and gently but thoroughly using a rubber spatula.

5. Scrape the filling into the prepared pastry shell. (This amount of filling should fill the pastry crust all the way to the top of the pastry edge but should not overflow the edge; see headnote.) Put the tart in the oven and bake for about 18 minutes, until the top is dull and matte (not shiny) and will jiggle only a little when you shake the pan.

6. Cool for at least 20 minutes at room temperature, then unmold from the tart pan (see "How to Unmold Cakes, Tarts, and Loaves," page 262).

7. Slice into wedges and serve the tart slightly warm or room temperature.

chocolate caramel pecan tart

This is one of the first recipes we put on the dessert menu when we opened the doors at the Dahlia Lounge more than twenty years ago, and it's still one of my favorites. The caramel pecan filling is baked inside a double-crust tart. Then, after the tart is unmolded, you turn it upside down so the flat side is up and cover it with a chocolate glaze, which makes it look like a chocolate torte or cake. But when you slice and serve the tart, what you get is the best-ever candy bar of chewy pecan caramel drenched with dark chocolate. Serve each wedge of tart with a spoonful of Sweetened Whipped Cream (page 193) or a scoop of Vanilla Bean Ice Cream (page 326).

When caramelizing the sugar, choose a saucepan deep enough to give the cream room to sputter and bubble up when it is poured into the hot sugar. A 3- or 4-quart heavy-bottomed saucepan, such as All-Clad, is ideal.

Tart leftovers hold well for a few days, wrapped in plastic wrap and left at room temperature.

Making this tart is time consuming, and is probably best done over two days. The All-Butter Pastry Dough has to chill for an hour or more before rolling. The tart, after baking, must cool for at least 4 hours before being glazed, or just let the tart rest at room temperature overnight. The glaze will also need a few hours to set.

SPECIAL EQUIPMENT: PASTRY SCRAPER, 10-INCH REMOVABLE-BOTTOM TART PAN, PASTRY BRUSH, CANDY OR DIGITAL PROBE THERMOMETER, 9-INCH ROUND CAKE CARDBOARD (OPTIONAL)

All-Butter Pastry Dough (page 234), divided into 2 unequal (about two-third and one-third) flattened rounds and chilled for 1 hour or more

1 cup plus 2 tablespoons (7½ ounces/ 210 grams) sugar

⅓ cup (2⅝ ounces/75 grams) water

1 cup (8 ounces/227 grams) heavy cream

⅓ cup (4 ounces/113 grams) honey

4 tablespoons (½ stick/2 ounces/ 60 grams) unsalted butter, cut into ½-inch dice

2 cups (8½ ounces/240 grams) toasted, cooled, and chopped pecans (see "How to Toast and Chop Nuts," page 13)

2 teaspoons pure vanilla extract

½ teaspoon kosher salt

Starch water (see page 159)

Chocolate Honey Glaze (page 255), cooled for 5 to 10 minutes but still warm and liquid

1. Unwrap the larger round of dough and place it on a lightly floured work surface. Using a rolling pin, roll the dough into a round about ⅛ inch thick and 12 or 13 inches in diameter. Use flour as needed to roll the dough and lift the dough occasionally using a plastic pastry scraper as you are working to check that the dough is not sticking to the work surface. Transfer the dough to the tart pan. It's easiest to transfer the dough by folding it into quarters. Pick up the folded dough and place it in the pan, with the pointed tip of the dough in the center of the pan, then unfold gently. Ease the dough gently into the pan, patting it up against the sides. Trim the overhanging dough to ¼ to ½ inch. Refrigerate the pastry-lined pan until you are ready to fill it.

2. Unwrap the smaller round of dough and place it on a lightly floured work surface. Roll the dough into a 10-inch round about ⅛ inch thick. Transfer the dough to a parchment-lined baking sheet or a large round cake cardboard (again, you can fold the dough into quarters to transfer it) and refrigerate it until you are ready to finish the tart shell.

3. Preheat the oven to 375°F.

4. In a heavy-bottomed saucepan over medium-low heat, combine the sugar and water (see "How to Caramelize Sugar," page 67). Stir the mixture with a small whisk until the sugar is completely dissolved, about 3 minutes. After the sugar is dissolved, remove the whisk, clean the sides of the pot of any sugar crystals using a clean wet pastry brush, then raise the heat to high and bring the mixture to a boil, *without stirring*, until the syrup turns a medium-dark golden brown, about 15 minutes. If you see the sugar caramelizing in only one section, gently tilt or rotate the pan to distribute the color evenly, but do not whisk. If you see sugar crystals forming on the sides of the pan, wipe them down with a clean wet pastry brush.

5. As soon as the sugar is caramelized to a medium-dark amber, remove the pan from the heat and add the cream. Be careful and stand back because the mixture will bubble and sputter. When the bubbling settles down, add the honey and butter. Return the pan to medium to medium-high heat and stir with a heatproof spoon until the mixture is smooth, then continue to cook (the heat should be high enough so that the mixture is bubbling steadily), stirring occasionally, until the caramel registers 238° to 240°F on a candy or digital probe thermometer, about 10 minutes. Remove the pan from the heat and add the pecans, vanilla extract, and salt, stirring to combine.

6. Remove the pastry-lined tart shell and the pastry round from the refrigerator. Pour the filling into the tart shell and use a rubber spatula to spread it evenly. Transfer the pastry round to the top

of the tart. (If you have folded it into quarters to transfer it, place it on top of the tart with the pointed tip of the dough in the center of the tart pan, then unfold it gently.) If necessary, use a small knife to trim the dough so that it fits inside the top of the tart. Brush the outer (overhanging) rim of the pastry with starch water, then fold the overhang up over the top of the tart, pressing gently with your fingers or a fork to seal. Using a small knife, cut a 1-inch steam vent in the top crust. Put the tart on a baking sheet and place it in the oven. Bake the tart until the pastry is cooked through, 50 to 55 minutes. When the tart is cooked, the top should be evenly golden brown.

7. Remove the pan from the oven and place the tart pan on a wire rack to cool for about an hour. Then remove the sides of the tart pan, invert it onto a 9-inch cardboard circle, and remove the metal bottom of the pan. What was the top of the tart is now the bottom, and the top of the tart is smooth and flat. (Using a round cake cardboard slightly smaller than the diameter of the 10-inch tart allows the chocolate glaze to run off when you glaze the tart.) If you don't have a round cake cardboard, invert the tart onto a large flat plate, remove the metal bottom of the tart pan, then slip the metal bottom of the tart pan back underneath so the (newly inverted) top of the tart is smooth and flat and the bottom of the tart is supported by the metal tart pan bottom.

8. Put the tart back on the wire rack and allow to cool until completely room temperature, about 3 more hours. (If you prefer, you can allow the tart to rest at room temperature overnight and glaze it the next day.)

top: Start pouring the chocolate honey glaze in the middle of the tart.

bottom: Continue pouring the glaze gradually and evenly, working outward in concentric circles until the glaze flows over the edge of the tart.

9. When you are ready to glaze the tart, place it on a rack set over a baking sheet. You can line the baking sheet with parchment or foil for easier cleanup.

10. To glaze the tart, start pouring in the middle and gradually and evenly pour the glaze, working outward in concentric circles, until the glaze flows over the edges of the tart. You can gently shake the baking sheet to get the glaze to flow evenly over the edges of the tart, or you can touch up the sides of the tart, if needed, with a small offset icing spatula.

11. Allow the tart to rest at room temperature for about 2 hours, until the glaze has set, before slicing and serving.

chocolate honey glaze

MAKES ABOUT 2 CUPS GLAZE; ENOUGH FOR 1 CHOCOLATE CARAMEL PECAN TART,
1 CHOCOLATE HEARTLAND BUNDT, OR 10 ÉCLAIRS

Here's a simple, shiny, dark chocolaty glaze that's not at all difficult to make.
Glazing a tart or cake is easier than icing it, but it still gives you a polished,
professional look.

6 ounces (170 grams) bittersweet
chocolate, chopped (about 1 cup; see
"How to Chop Chocolate," page 12)

½ cup (1 stick/4 ounces/113 grams)
unsalted butter, cut into 1-inch dice

⅓ cup (3 ounces/90 grams) half-and-half

3 tablespoons (2 ounces 57 grams) honey

1 teaspoon pure vanilla extract

¼ teaspoon kosher salt

1. Put the chocolate and butter in a heatproof bowl that has been placed over a saucepan of gently
simmering water over medium heat. (The bottom of the bowl should not touch the water.) Adjust
the heat to keep the water barely at a simmer. Melt the chocolate, stirring to combine using a
rubber or silicone spatula, then remove the bowl from the heat.

2. Meanwhile, put the half-and-half into a small saucepan over medium-low heat just long
enough to make it feel slightly warm to the touch, then use a whisk to stir the half-and-half into
the melted chocolate mixture. Stir in the honey, vanilla extract, and salt. Allow the glaze to cool
for 5 to 10 minutes before pouring it over the cake or tart, but the glaze must still be warm and
liquid when you use it.

3. If you allowed your glaze to cool too much to pour, just place it back over the saucepan of
barely simmering water for a couple of minutes.

let them eat cake
CAKES AND CUPCAKES

double chocolate layer cake

Special occasions call out for a celebratory frosted layer cake. Frost this moist, fine-grained, dark chocolate cake with soft and creamy Fluffy Chocolate Sour Cream Frosting and you'll make every chocoholic's dreams come true.

The fact that the batter is made with oil that's emulsified into the eggs, similar to an old-fashioned mayonnaise cake, accounts for the cake's moistness and fine crumb.

For the best texture in a carefully emulsified and aerated cake batter like this one, pay attention to using room-temperature ingredients. Your eggs must be at room temperature or slightly warmer. Warm the eggs in a bowl of hot tap water for 3 or 4 minutes before breaking the shells. The buttermilk can be warmed up very slightly in a saucepan over low heat.

For the best flavor, use top-quality chocolate and cocoa (see "Our Favorite Chocolates," page 21).

SPECIAL EQUIPMENT: 9-INCH CAKE PAN, ELECTRIC MIXER, 9-INCH ROUND CAKE CARDBOARDS (OPTIONAL)

Softened butter as needed for the pan

1½ cups (8 ounces/230 grams) cake flour, plus 2 tablespoons for the pan

¼ cup plus 1 tablespoon (1½ ounces/45 grams) unsweetened cocoa powder, plus 2 tablespoons for the pan

¼ cup (2½ ounces/70 grams) finely chopped bittersweet chocolate (see "How to Chop Chocolate," page 12)

1 cup plus 1 tablespoon (7⅜ ounces/210 grams) granulated sugar, preferably superfine

½ teaspoon baking powder

½ teaspoon baking soda

½ teaspoon kosher salt

1 cup (8 ounces/230 grams) buttermilk at room temperature (see "How to Bring Ingredients to Room Temperature," page 12)

2 teaspoons pure vanilla extract

2 large eggs at room temperature or slightly warmer (see headnote)

⅓ cup (2½ ounces/70 grams) packed brown sugar

1 cup (7 ounces/200 grams) canola oil

Fluffy Chocolate Sour Cream Frosting (page 265), quantity for a 9-inch layer cake, or Vanilla Bean Buttercream (page 267), quantity for a 9-inch layer cake

1. Preheat the oven to 350°F. Butter the cake pan. Cut a 9-inch circle of parchment paper, place it on the bottom of the pan, and butter the paper. Whisk together 2 tablespoons of the flour and 2 tablespoons of the cocoa. Use this mixture to flour the pan, shaking out the excess. Chill the pan to set the coating while you are making the batter. (See "How to Prepare a Cake or Loaf Pan," page 261.)

2. Put the chocolate in a metal bowl and place it over a saucepan of hot, barely simmering water. (The bottom of the bowl should not touch the water.) Stir occasionally until the chocolate is melted. Remove the bowl from the saucepan and allow the chocolate to cool to slightly warmer than room temperature, about 5 minutes. When you add the chocolate to the cake batter later, the chocolate must still be liquid and slightly warm to the touch.

3. Sift together the remaining flour and cocoa powder, ½ cup of the granulated or superfine sugar, the baking powder, and the baking soda into a bowl (see "How to Sift," page 13). Sift twice more, then add the salt. Set the dry ingredients aside.

4. In a small bowl, combine the buttermilk and vanilla extract and set aside.

5. In the bowl of an electric mixer fitted with the whisk, combine the eggs, brown sugar, and remaining ½ cup plus 1 tablespoon granulated or superfine sugar and whip on medium-high speed until very pale and tripled in volume, 5 to 6 minutes. Using a rubber spatula, scrape down the bowl and the paddle.

6. Reduce the speed to medium and add ½ cup of the oil slowly and gradually, as if you were making mayonnaise. After the oil has been incorporated, add the slightly warm melted chocolate and mix to combine. (Note: If you allowed the chocolate to cool too much before adding it to the cake batter, return the bowl of chocolate to the hot water bath to rewarm it for a few minutes first.)

7. Then, still on medium speed, add the remaining ½ cup of oil slowly and gradually until incorporated into the batter. Scrape down the bowl and the paddle.

8. Turn the mixer to medium-low and add the buttermilk-vanilla mixture in a slow steady stream. When the buttermilk is incorporated, remove the bowl from the mixer and scrape the bowl and paddle down well using a rubber spatula. Remove the bowl from the machine.

Double Chocolate Layer Cake with Fluffy Chocolate Sour Cream Frosting and Buttery Layer Cake with Vanilla Bean Buttercream

9. Add the dry ingredients in 3 or 4 additions, folding with a rubber spatula or a balloon whisk (see "How to Fold with a Whisk," page 14). Do not overwork the batter.

10. Scrape the batter into the prepared pan and bake until a skewer comes out with a few moist crumbs and no batter, 50 to 55 minutes, rotating the pan halfway through the baking time.

11. Remove the pan from the oven and allow to cool on a wire rack for 5 to 10 minutes before unmolding the cake onto a 9-inch round cake cardboard. (If you don't have a cake cardboard, you can unmold onto a plate. See "How to Unmold Cakes, Tarts, and Loaves," page 262.)

12. Cool the cake to room temperature before splitting, filling, and frosting with Fluffy Chocolate Sour Cream Frosting or Vanilla Bean Buttercream (see "How to Split, Fill, and Frost a Layer Cake," page 269).

Coating a pan with butter and dusting with flour will help ensure that your finished cake slips out of the pan easily, without sticking. The coating also provides texture and color to the edges of your baked cake.

To prepare a cake pan, use soft butter to butter the pan all around the inside of the sides and the bottom. (If your butter is soft enough, you can use a brush, or you can just use your hands.) You don't need (or want) a thick layer of butter, but be sure to butter the pan well—it's better to be a bit too generous than too stingy—and be careful not to leave any uncovered spaces where the batter can stick to the pan.

To be completely sure your cake won't stick, it's best to use a parchment circle. For a 9-inch cake pan, cut a 9-inch parchment circle to fit inside the pan and place it on the bottom of the buttered pan, then butter the paper. (You can even find packs of precut parchment circles in some kitchenware stores and online; see Sources.)

To flour the pan, sprinkle the flour (or another dry ingredient as specified in the recipe, such as semolina or a mixture of flour and cocoa) into the pan, tilting and turning the pan to coat it evenly. Use more flour than you need so you can shake it around the pan, then tip it over the garbage can or compost pail and shake or tap out all the excess flour that isn't sticking to the butter in a thin, even layer.

After the pan has been coated, put it into the refrigerator to chill and set the coating while you assemble the cake batter. That way, when you pour your batter into the pan, the coating will stay in place.

For a Bundt pan, butter and flour the same way, being especially careful to butter really well around the tube. It's impossible to put a parchment circle in a Bundt pan, so it's best to buy one with a good nonstick coating, then butter and flour it.

For a loaf pan, butter and flour the pan in the same way. You could cut parchment to fit the bottom of a loaf pan, but generally we don't bother. Just be sure to butter the pan very well, then dust it with flour. Nonstick loaf pans are a good idea, but butter and flour them also.

how to prepare a cake or loaf pan

Professional bakers use round cake cardboards for unmolding. Cake cardboards can be purchased in some kitchenware stores and online (see Sources). When your cake or tart is unmolded onto a cardboard of the same diameter, you can easily move it around from place to place. You can put it on a decorative cake plate, and you won't see the cardboard. Cardboards are also useful if your cake is going to be frosted or glazed, because the cake can be moved to a clean cake plate without any drips or mess after you are done. But if you don't have cake cardboards you can unmold onto plates. To unmold a cake or a loaf of quick bread, you will need 2 round cake cardboards or 2 plates.

To unmold a cake, remove the pan from the oven and cool on a wire rack for about 10 minutes, then run a small knife between the perimeter of the cake and the pan. Place a cake board (or plate) over the cake pan and invert the pan. The cake should slide right out onto the cardboard. Peel off the parchment circle (from what used to be the bottom of the cake) and place another cake board (or plate) over the cake and invert again. Remove the top cake board (or plate) and the cake will be right side up. Then return the cake to the wire rack and cool completely to room temperature.

To unmold a quick bread from a loaf pan, use the same method, first cooling the loaf for 15 minutes, then running a small knife between the loaf and the pan before unmolding onto cardboards or plates. You will need to invert the pan once and invert it again to position the quick bread loaf right side up, just like a cake.

To unmold a Bundt pan, use the same method, but be sure to run the knife around the tube as well as around the rim of the pan. Also, a Bundt cake needs to be inverted only once, and the right side will be up, so you need only one cardboard or one plate.

To unmold a tart pan, place the tart pan on top of a large can or other cylinder and the removable rim will fall right off. Or you can remove the sides of the tart pan by pushing up on the bottom of the pan with your fingers and allowing the ring to fall away onto your arm, but do this only if the tart pan is cool so you don't burn your arm. You can leave the tart sitting on the metal bottom of the tart pan, or you can transfer the tart to a round cake cardboard or to a large flat plate.

If you want to transfer the tart off the metal bottom of the tart pan and the pan has cooled, you may find that butter has congealed between the tart and the metal bottom, causing the tart to stick to the pan. Just slide a long metal icing spatula between the metal pan bottom and the bottom of the tart shell to release it. Then slide the tart off the metal pan bottom and onto the cardboard or the plate.

buttery layer cake

MAKES ONE 9-INCH LAYER CAKE; SERVES 12 WHEN FILLED AND FROSTED

This is a cake with a delicate crumb and a beautifully light, airy texture. The butter and extra egg yolks add just the right amount of richness. You can cloak the cake with lush Vanilla Bean Buttercream (page 267) or Fluffy Chocolate Sour Cream Frosting (page 265).

Room-temperature ingredients are important for proper aeration and emulsification of the cake batter. Warm the eggs in a bowl of hot tap water before breaking them and be sure your butter is softened and your buttermilk is at room temperature not cold. If your kitchen is cold, you can even rinse your mixing bowls with warm water and dry them before using.

It's important to cream the butter and sugar really well. Be sure to start with softened butter, and when you are finished creaming, the sugar should have almost dissolved into the butter. You can certainly make this cake with regular granulated sugar, but superfine sugar works especially well here.

SPECIAL EQUIPMENT: 9-INCH CAKE PAN, ELECTRIC MIXER, 9-INCH ROUND CAKE CARDBOARDS (OPTIONAL)

¾ cup (1½ sticks/6 ounces/170 grams) softened unsalted butter, cut into several pieces, plus more for the pan

2 cups (9 ⅞ ounces/280 grams) cake flour, plus more for the pan

½ teaspoon baking soda

½ teaspoon baking powder

1½ teaspoons kosher salt

¾ cup (7 ounces/200 grams) buttermilk at room temperature

1 teaspoon pure vanilla extract

1½ cups (10 ounces/300 grams) sugar, preferably superfine

2 large eggs plus 2 large yolks at room temperature (see "How to Bring Ingredients to Room Temperature," page 12)

Vanilla Bean Buttercream (page 267), quantity for a 9-inch layer cake, or Fluffy Chocolate Sour Cream Frosting (page 265), quantity for a 9-inch layer cake

1. Preheat the oven to 325°F. Butter the pan. Cut a 9-inch round of parchment paper, place it in the bottom of the pan, then butter the paper. Flour the cake pan, shaking out the excess, then chill it to set the coating while you make the batter. (See "How to Prepare a Cake or Loaf Pan," page 261.)

2. Into a bowl, sift together the flour, baking powder, and baking soda. Sift twice more, then add the salt (see "How to Sift," page 13). Set the dry ingredients aside.

3. In a small bowl, combine the buttermilk and the vanilla extract and set aside.

4. Combine the butter and sugar in an electric mixer fitted with the paddle and cream on medium-high speed until pale, light, and fluffy, about 4 minutes, scraping down the bowl and paddle as needed. It is important to cream the butter and sugar together really well. If your butter was not thoroughly softened when you put it in the mixer bowl, start your 4-minute count from the time the butter is soft enough to smear easily.

5. Add one of the whole eggs while beating on medium speed. (Tip: Break your whole eggs into one ramekin or small bowl and your yolks into another. Then you can tip them into the mixer bowl as you need them.) Then turn the mixer to medium-high and beat for 30 seconds. Return the mixer to medium speed and add the second whole egg. Then turn the mixer to medium-high and beat for another 30 seconds.

6. Scrape down the bowl and paddle. Beat the batter on medium-high speed for 15 seconds. The batter should look very smooth. Add the yolks on medium speed, then turn the mixer to medium-high and beat for 20 seconds. The batter should be shiny and glossy. Scrape down the bowl and paddle. It's important to scrape the bowl and paddle thoroughly so you will be able to work the dry ingredients in as quickly as possible without a lot of scraping down of the bowl.

7. Remove the bowl from the mixer and, folding by hand using a rubber spatula, add the dry ingredients in 4 additions alternately with the vanilla buttermilk in 3 additions, beginning and ending with the dry ingredients. Work quickly and gently to fold everything together.

8. Scrape the batter into the prepared pan, smoothing the top with a rubber spatula. Place the pan in the oven and bake until done, about 1 hour and 8 to 10 minutes, rotating the pan about halfway through the baking time. The top of the cake should be golden brown and domed and a skewer inserted in the cake should come out free of batter but with a few crumbs clinging. Remove the pan from the oven and cool on a wire rack for about 10 minutes, then unmold onto a 9-inch round cake cardboard. (If you don't have a cake cardboard, you can unmold onto a plate. See "How to Unmold Cakes, Tarts, and Loaves," page 262.)

9. Allow the cake to cool completely before splitting, frosting, and filling (see "How to Split, Fill, and Frost a Layer Cake," page 269).

fluffy chocolate sour cream frosting

This fluffy, creamy chocolate frosting with the pleasant tang of sour cream is melt-in-your mouth delicious.

There's nothing difficult about making this frosting, but it's very important that the melted chocolate, butter, and sour cream all be at room temperature when you combine them. Melt the chocolate first, then remove it from the heat and set it aside to give it time to cool to room temperature. The butter should be soft and pliable, offering only a little resistance when pressed with a finger, but it should not be almost melting. The sour cream must be at room temperature when it is added to the butter-sugar mixture. You can let the sour cream sit out on the counter for a few hours to warm up, or you can carefully zap it for a few seconds at a time in the microwave, or you can put it in a small bowl placed in a larger bowl of hot tap water and stir it until it warms to room temperature.

Use quality chocolates, both bittersweet and milk chocolates (see "Our Favorite Chocolates," page 21).

There's just enough salt so that you taste it a bit in the finished frosting, which we think complements the flavor of chocolate. But be sure to use kosher salt or a sea salt of the same texture, coarseness, and weight as kosher salt. Do not substitute table salt in this quantity. If you substitute table salt, cut the amount in half (see "Salt," page 22).

This frosting should not be refrigerated before being used. Unlike buttercream, it can't be chilled firm and then beaten smooth again, because it will turn dull and grainy. The best strategy is to bake your cake or cupcakes first and allow them to cool to room temperature. Then, when you are ready to frost them, make the chocolate frosting. If you find that you're not quite ready to use it, just let it sit out at room temperature with a piece of plastic wrap on the surface.

SPECIAL EQUIPMENT: ELECTRIC MIXER

for frosting 12 cupcakes (makes about 2½ cups)

4 ounces (113 grams) bittersweet chocolate, chopped (about ¾ cup; see "How to Chop Chocolate," page 12)

2 ounces (60 grams) milk chocolate, chopped (about ⅓ cup plus 1 tablespoon)

½ cup (1 stick/4 ounces/113 grams) unsalted butter, softened, cut into 1-inch dice

½ cup (2 ounces/57 grams) powdered sugar, sifted (measure first, then sift; see "How to Sift," page 13)

½ cup (4 ounces/113 grams) sour cream at room temperature (see "How to Bring Ingredients to Room Temperature," page 12)

1 teaspoon pure vanilla extract

½ teaspoon kosher salt

for frosting a 9-inch layer cake (makes about 5 cups)

8 ounces (230 grams) bittersweet chocolate, chopped (about 1½ cups)

4 ounces (115 grams) milk chocolate, chopped (about ¾ cup)

1 cup (2 sticks/8 ounces/230 grams) unsalted butter, softened

1 cup (5¼ ounces/150 grams) powdered sugar, sifted (measure first, then sift)

1 cup (8 ounces/230 grams) sour cream at room temperature

2 teaspoons pure vanilla extract

¾ teaspoon kosher salt

1. Place both chocolates in a heatproof bowl that has been placed over a saucepan of simmering water over medium heat. (The bottom of the bowl should not touch the water.) Adjust the heat to keep the water barely at a simmer. Melt the chocolate, stirring occasionally with a rubber or silicone spatula. When the chocolate is melted, remove it from the heat and set it aside to cool to room temperature.

2. Put the butter and powdered sugar in the bowl of an electric mixer fitted with the paddle. Cream on medium-high speed for 5 full minutes, scraping down the sides of the bowl and the paddle a few times during the process. After 5 minutes, the mixture should look very pale and white. Scrape the bowl and paddle down again and turn the mixer to medium-low speed, then add the room-temperature sour cream. After the sour cream has been incorporated, scrape down the bowl and paddle again and add the (cooled) melted chocolate, vanilla extract, and salt. Turn the mixer up to medium-high speed and beat for 1 more minute.

3. The frosting is now ready to be used for your cake or cupcakes. (See "How to Split, Fill, and Frost a Layer Cake," page 269, or "How to Frost Cupcakes," page 282.)

vanilla bean buttercream

If you think you don't like buttercream, it may be because you've tasted only imposters made with powdered sugar and vegetable shortening. This is the real deal—voluptuously smooth, dotted with vanilla bean seeds, and tasting of real butter. Buttercream is not really difficult to make as long as you follow the instructions carefully.

Before starting the recipe, your butter must be pliable and soft, not too firm, but also not melting.

Superfine sugar is recommended for this recipe because it dissolves more quickly than regular granulated sugar.

Be sure your cakes or cupcakes have cooled completely to room temperature before frosting them with buttercream.

You can make the buttercream several hours ahead or even the day before and store it tightly covered in the refrigerator, and then beat until smooth (see "How to Store and How to Soften Buttercream," page 268).

SPECIAL EQUIPMENT: ELECTRIC MIXER, INSTANT-READ OR DIGITAL PROBE THERMOMETER (OPTIONAL)

for frosting 12 cupcakes (makes about 2½ cups)

1 vanilla bean, split in half lengthwise

2 large egg whites

½ cup (3½ ounces/100 grams) sugar, preferably superfine

1 cup (2 sticks/8 ounces/227 grams) unsalted butter, softened

2 teaspoons pure vanilla extract

¼ teaspoon kosher salt

for frosting a 9-inch layer cake (makes about 5 cups)

2 vanilla beans, split in half lengthwise

4 large egg whites

1 cup (7 ounces/200 grams) sugar, preferably, superfine

2 cups (4 sticks/1 pound/454 grams) unsalted butter, softened

1 tablespoon plus 1 teaspoon pure vanilla extract

½ teaspoon kosher salt

1. Use the tip of a paring knife to scrape the seeds from the vanilla bean. Reserve the scrapings to add to the buttercream later and save the pod to make vanilla bean sugar (page 64).

2. Place the egg whites and sugar in a bowl (it's easiest just to use the bowl of the electric mixer)

set over a pot of simmering water (the bottom of the bowl should not touch the water) and stir with a rubber spatula until the mixture begins to smell like cooked eggs, 8 to 10 minutes. The mixture should not be so hot that you can't put your finger in it, but it should be too hot to hold your finger in it for long. If you want to check the temperature with a thermometer, it should read 160°F.

3. Remove the bowl from the heat, place it in the electric mixer with the whisk attachment, and whip on medium-high speed until the egg white mixture is very thick and has cooled to room temperature (it should look as thick as shaving cream), 10 to 15 minutes. The egg white mixture will cool as it whips. Feel it with your finger at this point—it should feel like it is no longer warm enough to melt butter.

4. Turn the mixer to medium speed and add the butter gradually, about a tablespoon at a time, until all the butter is fully incorporated. When you get halfway through adding the butter, scrape down the bowl. Turn the mixer up to high speed and whip the buttercream for 1 minute.

5. Add the vanilla bean seeds, vanilla extract, and salt and whip for 30 seconds more. Scrape down the bowl again and be sure all the flavorings are well mixed in.

6. Use the buttercream immediately to frost cakes or cupcakes or, before you start to frost, make one of the flavor variations on pages 372 and 373.

7. If you are not using the buttercream immediately, see "How to Store and Soften Buttercream," page 273.

how to split, fill, and frost a layer cake

Cake cardboards (see Sources) are handy to have around when frosting a cake. You can easily move the cake back and forth from the cooling rack to the turntable and, as long as your cardboard is the same diameter as your 9-inch cake, you can frost right over the cardboard so no one can see it. If you don't have cake cardboards, you can cut 9-inch rounds from a piece of sturdy cardboard, or you can just use plates, or use the flat metal bottoms of removable-bottom tart pans.

SPECIAL EQUIPMENT: LONG SERRATED KNIFE, CAKE TURNTABLE (OPTIONAL BUT NICE TO HAVE), OFFSET AND STRAIGHT ICING SPATULAS, METAL BENCH KNIFE (OPTIONAL), 9-INCH ROUND CAKE CARDBOARDS (OPTIONAL BUT RECOMMENDED)

Double Chocolate Layer Cake (page 258), baked, unmolded, and cooled, or Buttery Layer Cake (page 263), baked, unmolded, and cooled

Fluffy Chocolate Sour Cream Frosting (page 265), quantity for layer cake, or Vanilla Bean Buttercream (page 267), quantity for layer cake

1. For the nicest-looking frosted cake, the top should be flat and even. One way to achieve this is to level the top of the cake by cutting off the domed part using a long serrated knife. Put the cooled cake back in the cake pan, domed side up, and use the knife to cut the cake along the top edge of the cake pan, first working your way around and then slicing toward the center. Remove the trimmed portion and discard—or snack on it for a baker's treat! Now unmold the cake onto a cake cardboard. The flat bottom of the cake will now be the top.

2. An easier way to achieve a flat top, and perfectly okay for the home baker, is to simply unmold the cooled cake onto the cake cardboard, inverting it only once so it's upside down and the flat (bottom) side is up. The domed side will be on the bottom, with the cake cardboard under it, and after the cake is frosted you won't notice that it isn't perfectly flat.

3. The next step is to use the serrated knife to divide the cake horizontally in half. To cut the cake, score all the way around with a large serrated knife, then start going deeper and deeper until the cake is cut horizontally into 2 layers. Each layer should be 1 inch tall. Remove the top layer and set it aside. An easy way to transfer the top layer is to slip a cake cardboard under it, or you can use the flat metal round of a removable-bottom tart pan.

4. Set the bottom layer of the cake, which is sitting on a cake cardboard, onto a cake turntable if you have one or onto a work surface if you do not.

5. Next, put about a quarter of the frosting on top of the first layer of the split cake. Use either an offset or a straight icing spatula to spread the filling, working from the center out. (Tip: When spreading frosting with your spatula, stay on top of the frosting at all times; if you don't roll your spatula into the cake, you won't get crumbs in your frosting.)

6. Then take the top layer (in other words, the layer with the nice flat top), put it on top of the frosting, and press gently.

7. Put half of the remaining frosting on top of the cake and spread with an offset spatula to cover the top, working from the center out.

8. Then run the frosting around the sides using the remaining frosting. (Tip: One technique is to put enough frosting along the length of the straight icing spatula so the frosting will touch both the base and the top of the cake at the same time.) Continue until the frosting completely covers the sides of the cake, rotating the cake turntable as you work. (If your cake is on a cake board, frost right over the board so it doesn't show.) Occasionally use an icing spatula to straighten and smooth the frosting that accumulates on the top rim of the cake.

9. When the sides are frosted and the top rim is smooth, you can use a metal bench knife to smooth the edges, holding the blade straight up and down and rotating the cake turntable as you work.

10. If you are using the chocolate frosting, you can make swirls on top using a small offset spatula or a straight icing spatula.

11. To transfer the cake from the turntable (or work surface) to a cake plate, slip a large spatula under the cake cardboard to lift the cake enough so you can get slide your fingers under it.

12. Leave the frosted cake at room temperature until you are ready to slice and serve.

Using a serrated knife, start scoring the cake, going all the way around.

Continue cutting the cake with the knife, going deeper and deeper . . .

. . . until the cake is cut horizontally into two layers.

Remove the top layer and set it aside.

Put a quarter of the buttercream on top and use an icing spatula to spread it, working from the inside out.

Put the top layer on top of the buttercream. A cardboard cake round is a good way to transfer the cake.

Put half of the remaining buttercream on top and spread with the icing spatula.

Run the remaining buttercream around the sides, rotating the cake turntable as you work.

Frost right over the cake cardboard that's underneath the cake so it doesn't show.

Use an icing spatula to smooth the sides.

Use a metal bench knife to smooth the edges.

Use an icing spatula to smooth the top.

"your favorite" buttercreams for cupcakes

This is as fun as going to a Coldstone Creamery and mixing your own ice cream flavor. The combinations are as endless as your imagination. My favorite way to flavor buttercream is to add ground espresso beans with a bit of crumbled almond roca. Oh, yeah! Here are a few more variations.

These recipes are intended for frosting cupcakes. If you want to make one of these flavored buttercreams for a 9-inch layer cake instead, make a batch of buttercream in the quantity for layer cake and double all the flavoring ingredients.

Before adding the flavors, the buttercream must be freshly made and soft. If it has been made ahead and chilled, see "How to Store and Soften Buttercream," page 273.

CHOCOLATE FLAKE BUTTERCREAM

Stracciatella is vanilla gelato streaked with little flakes of chocolate. This is like stracciatella buttercream!

Vanilla Bean Buttercream (page 267), quantity for 12 cupcakes, freshly made or softened

1 cup (3 ounces/90 grams) shaved bittersweet chocolate (see "How to Shave Chocolate," page 12)

¼ teaspoon kosher salt

Put the buttercream in a bowl and fold in the shaved chocolate and the salt using a rubber spatula.

CARAMEL CORN BUTTERCREAM

Buttery cupcakes with caramel corn buttercream will be a hit at any kid's birthday party, even for big kids!

You can pop the popcorn in an air popper, make microwave popcorn, or buy a bag of prepopped popcorn, but it's best to have popcorn that's low in salt and not too oily or buttery. If you don't want to make caramel sauce, you can use a top-quality jarred caramel sauce such as Fran's (see Sources). Note that the caramel sauce must be at room temperature to combine with the buttercream.

If you like, buy a box of caramel-coated popcorn snacks (such as Crackerjack) and decorate each frosted cupcake with a piece of popcorn.

SPECIAL EQUIPMENT: BLENDER OR
FOOD PROCESSOR

2 cups (5/8 ounce/198 grams)
    popped popcorn

Vanilla Bean Buttercream (page
    267), quantity for 12 cupcakes,
    freshly made or softened

1/2 cup (4 1/2 ounces/130 grams)
    Dreamy Caramel Sauce (page 69)
    at room temperature

1/4 teaspoon salt

Put the popcorn in a blender or food
processor and process until it is finely
ground. You should have about a cup of
finely ground popcorn. In a bowl,
combine the buttercream, popcorn
powder, caramel, and salt and vigorously
fold everything together using a rubber
spatula until well combined.

Buttercream stores well, so feel free to
double the batch and store it if you bake
cakes and cupcakes often.

Buttercream absorbs odors readily.
Before storing it in the refrigerator, transfer
the buttercream to an airtight container.
First cover the surface directly with a piece
of plastic wrap, then snap on the lid.

For longer storage, you can freeze
buttercream. To thaw, refrigerate the
buttercream overnight, then soften as
directed below.

To soften buttercream that has been
chilled, break it up into pieces and put it in
the bowl of an electric mixer, then beat,
using the paddle, until the buttercream is
smooth and creamy again. Another way to
soften cold buttercream is to put it in the
microwave for no more than 10 seconds at
a time on medium, then remove it from the
microwave and stir. Repeat as needed, but
do not microwave for more than 10 seconds
at a time.

how to store and soften buttercream

Buttery Cupcakes with Caramel Corn Buttercream (with caramel corn on top); Devil's Food Cupcakes with Chocolate Flake Buttercream (piped in a spiral); and Carrot Cupcakes with Brown Butter Cream Cheese Frosting (coated with decorative sugar)

carrot cupcakes with brown butter cream cheese frosting

MAKES **12** CUPCAKES

This is the most popular cupcake in the Dahlia Bakery—a nostalgic favorite made sophisticated with a touch of curry powder in the cake and brown butter in both the cake and the frosting.

Almond meal, also called *almond flour,* is made of finely ground almonds, ground as finely as flour. Almond meal is available at many supermarkets, health food stores, and online (see Sources).

You'll get the best emulsion when whisking the batter if both the brown butter and the egg whites are at room temperature.

The batter for the cupcakes needs to be refrigerated for 8 hours or overnight before being baked, so plan accordingly.

SPECIAL EQUIPMENT: PLASTIC DOUGH SCRAPER (OPTIONAL), MUFFIN PAN AND PAPER LINERS, 3-OUNCE ICE CREAM SCOOP (OPTIONAL)

14 tablespoons (1¾ sticks/7 ounces/ 200 grams) unsalted butter

1¼ cups (8¾ ounces/250 grams) packed brown sugar

1 cup (3½ ounces/100 grams) almond meal

¾ cup (3½ ounces/100 grams) cake flour

1¾ teaspoons baking powder

1 teaspoon ground ginger

¾ teaspoon Madras curry powder

¾ teaspoon ground cinnamon

8 large egg whites at room temperature (see "How to Bring Ingredients to Room Temperature," page 12)

¾ teaspoon kosher salt

1 cup (4 ounces/115 grams) finely shredded carrot (about 1 large carrot), grated on the small holes of the box grater

Brown Butter Cream Cheese Frosting (page 277)

1. Put the butter in a small saucepan and cook over medium heat, stirring often, until golden brown and aromatic, about 5 minutes. Remove the pan from the heat and transfer to a large bowl. Allow the brown butter to cool to room temperature.

Baker with cupcake tattoo

2. In another large bowl, sift together the brown sugar, almond meal, cake flour, baking powder, and spices. Use a rubber spatula or plastic dough scraper to push any lumps through the sifter (see "How to Sift," page 13).

3. Add the egg whites and salt to the dry ingredients and whisk until smooth. Put about a quarter of this batter into the bowl with the cooled brown butter and whisk until well combined. Then add the brown butter mixture back to the bowl of the remaining three-quarters of batter and whisk to combine. Using a rubber spatula, fold in the carrot.

4. Cover the bowl and refrigerate the batter for 8 hours or overnight.

5. When you are ready to bake the muffins, preheat the oven to 350°F. Line the wells of a muffin pan with paper liners and set aside.

6. Remove the batter from the refrigerator and scoop it into the prepared muffin pan, using a little less than ½ cup batter per cupcake and dividing the batter evenly among the wells of the muffin pan.

7. Bake for 25 minutes without opening the oven, until the tops of the cupcakes are nicely domed and evenly golden brown. After 25 minutes you can open the oven and check for doneness, baking a few minutes more if necessary, for a total baking time of 25 to 28 minutes.

8. Remove the pan from the oven and cool on a wire rack before removing the cupcakes.

9. Cool the cupcakes to room temperature before icing them with Brown Butter Cream Cheese Frosting (see "How to Frost Cupcakes," page 282).

brown butter cream cheese frosting

MAKES ABOUT 2½ CUPS; ENOUGH TO FROST 12 CUPCAKES

Children and adults alike delight in the pleasure of a delicately spiced carrot cupcake topped with a swirl of cream cheese frosting. The brown butter adds a warm richness.

Be sure the brown butter has cooled to room temperature before incorporating it into the frosting, but don't let it cool long enough to solidify.

There is more salt in this recipe than you usually see in a frosting because we like the punch of flavor it brings, but if you are substituting table salt for kosher salt, be sure to use less salt, about half.

You can make the frosting a few days ahead, cover, and refrigerate it. When you are ready to frost your cupcakes, put the chilled frosting in the bowl of an electric mixer and beat it with the paddle until smooth and softened.

SPECIAL EQUIPMENT: ELECTRIC MIXER

1 cup (2 sticks/8 ounces/227 grams) unsalted butter

1 pound (454 grams) cream cheese, softened

1 cup (4¾ ounces/135 grams) powdered sugar, sifted (measure first, then sift)

2 teaspoons pure vanilla extract

¾ teaspoon kosher salt

1. Put the butter in a small saucepan over medium heat and cook, stirring often, until golden brown and aromatic, 3 to 5 minutes after the butter melts. Pour the brown butter into a bowl and set it aside to cool completely to room temperature.

2. Put the cream cheese into the bowl of an electric mixer and add the powdered sugar, vanilla extract, and salt. Then, using the paddle attachment, beat the mixture for 2 minutes. Turn the speed down to medium-low and slowly drizzle in the brown butter. Continue beating for 1 more minute, then scrape down the paddle and bowl, and the frosting is ready to use.

devil's food cupcakes with chocolate flake buttercream

Devil's food is a classic American chocolate cake, though there's no exact definition of what it means. Generally devil's food is made with cocoa instead of chocolate (though we go over the top as usual and use both). The cocoa is often dissolved in boiling water, and usually there's some baking soda in the cake. Whether classic devil's food or not, we think these are just what everyone wants in a chocolate cupcake—chocolaty, moist, and light.

When making the batter, one of the most important steps is to slowly drizzle in the oil as if you were making a mayonnaise.

The bittersweet chocolate must be finely chopped because it is not melted but rather folded in at the end to give an extra depth of chocolate flavor to the cupcakes.

For the best flavor, use top-quality chocolate and cocoa powder (see "Our Favorite Chocolates," page 21).

For ultra-chocolaty cupcakes, frost them with Fluffy Chocolate Sour Cream Frosting (quantity for 12 cupcakes, page 265).

SPECIAL EQUIPMENT: MUFFIN PAN AND PAPER LINERS, ELECTRIC MIXER, 2½- OR 3-OUNCE ICE CREAM SCOOP (OPTIONAL)

½ cup (1¾ ounces/50 grams) cocoa powder

¾ cup (6¼ ounces/175 grams) boiling water

¼ cup (2 ounces/60 grams) sour cream

¾ teaspoon kosher salt

1½ cups (6½ ounces/184 grams) cake flour

2 teaspoons baking powder

½ teaspoon baking soda

2 large eggs at room temperature, separated (see "How to Bring Ingredients to Room Temperature," page 12)

⅓ cup (2 ounces/60 grams) packed brown sugar

¾ cup (6 ounces/170 grams) canola or other neutral-tasting oil

¼ cup (2 ounces/60 grams) granulated sugar, preferably superfine

⅔ cup (3½ ounces/100 grams) finely chopped bittersweet chocolate (see "How to Chop Chocolate," page 12)

2 teaspoons pure vanilla extract

Chocolate Flake Buttercream (page 272)

1. Preheat the oven to 350°F. Line a muffin pan with paper liners and set aside.

2. Put the cocoa powder in a bowl and pour the boiling water over it, whisking until you have a smooth paste. Add the sour cream and salt and whisk to combine. Set aside to cool to room temperature.

3. In a large bowl, sift together the cake flour, baking powder, and baking soda. Set aside.

4. Place the egg yolks in the bowl of an electric mixer with the whisk attachment. Add the brown sugar and begin mixing on medium-high speed. Drizzle in the oil in a slow, steady stream to emulsify the mixture as if you were making a mayonnaise. Remove the bowl from the mixer and set aside. (Note: Unless you don't mind whipping egg whites by hand, you will need to transfer the yolk-oil mixture to another bowl and wash the mixer bowl and the whisk attachment. Or, if you have an extra bowl for your electric mixer, you will have to wash only the whisk.)

5. Place the egg whites in the clean bowl of the electric mixer with the clean whisk attachment and, while whipping on medium-high speed, gradually add the granulated sugar, continuing to whip until soft peaks form. Set aside.

6. Add the cocoa mixture to the yolk-oil mixture and use a whisk (by hand) to combine. Pour this mixture into the bowl of dry ingredients and whisk by hand for 1 minute to aerate.

7. Fold in the whipped egg whites in 3 additions using a rubber spatula and taking care not to deflate the whites.

8. Fold in the chopped chocolate and vanilla extract.

9. As soon as you've finished the batter, fill the muffin pan and bake your muffins. Scoop the batter into the prepared muffin pan, using about ⅓ cup batter per cupcake and dividing the batter evenly among the wells of the pan.

10. Bake for 22 to 24 minutes, without opening the oven, until the tops are nicely domed with a few cracks on top and a skewer inserted in a cupcake comes out with a few moist crumbs clinging to it. Don't open the oven for at least the first 20 minutes to get the best rise from the cupcakes. After 20 minutes, you can check the cupcakes and bake for a few minutes longer as needed.

11. Remove the muffin pan from the oven and cool on a wire rack for 5 to 10 minutes, before removing the cupcakes from the pan. Continue to cool the cupcakes to room temperature before icing them with Chocolate Flake Buttercream (see "How to Frost Cupcakes," page 282).

buttery cupcakes with chocolate sour cream frosting

These light, fluffy, melt-in-your-mouth cupcakes are based on the same batter as our buttery layer cake. Instead of the chocolate sour cream frosting, try frosting these with caramel corn buttercream—perfect for a kid's birthday party!

As with the butter layer cake, room-temperature ingredients are important for a properly aerated and emulsified cake. Warm the eggs in a bowl of hot tap water for a few minutes before breaking them and be sure your butter is softened and your buttermilk is room temperature, not cold. If your mixer bowl is cold, warm it with warm water, then dry it.

SPECIAL EQUIPMENT: MUFFIN PAN AND PAPER LINERS, ELECTRIC MIXER, 2-OUNCE ICE CREAM SCOOP (OPTIONAL)

1½ cups (7½ ounces/215 grams) cake flour

½ teaspoon baking powder

¼ teaspoon baking soda

1 teaspoon kosher salt

½ cup (4¾ ounces/135 grams) buttermilk, at room temperature

1 teaspoon pure vanilla extract

9 tablespoons (4½ ounces/127 grams) unsalted butter, softened and cut into several pieces

1 cup (10 ounces/300 grams) sugar, preferably superfine

1 large egg plus 2 large yolks at room temperature (see "How to Bring Ingredients to Room Temperature," page 12)

Fluffy Chocolate Sour Cream Frosting (page 265, quantity for cupcakes)

1. Preheat the oven to 375°F. Line a muffin pan with paper liners and set aside.

2. Into a bowl, sift together the cake flour, baking powder, and baking soda. Sift twice more (see "How to Sift," page 13), then add the salt. Set the dry ingredients aside.

3. In a small bowl, combine the buttermilk and vanilla extract and set aside.

4. Combine the butter and sugar in an electric mixer fitted with the paddle and cream on medium-high speed until pale, light, and fluffy, about 4 minutes, scraping down the bowl and paddle as needed. It's important to cream the butter and sugar together really well. If your butter is not thoroughly softened when you put it in the mixer bowl, start your 4-minute count from the time the butter is soft enough to smear easily.

5. Add the whole egg while beating on medium speed, then turn the mixer to medium-high and beat for 30 seconds. Scrape down the bowl and paddle. Beat the batter on medium-high speed for 15 seconds. The batter should look very smooth. Add the yolks on medium speed, then turn the mixer to medium-high and beat for 20 seconds. The batter should be shiny and glossy. Scrape down the bowl and paddle. It's important to scrape the bowl and paddle thoroughly so that you can work the dry ingredients in as quickly as possible without a lot of scraping of the bowl.

6. Remove the bowl from the mixer and, folding by hand using a rubber spatula, add the dry ingredients in 4 additions alternately with the vanilla-buttermilk mixture in 3 additions, beginning and ending with the dry ingredients. Work quickly and gently to fold everything together.

7. Scoop the batter into the paper-lined muffin cups, using about ¼ cup batter per cupcake, dividing the batter evenly among the wells of the pan. (Note: There is just enough batter to make 12 cupcakes. Be sure to scrape every bit of batter out of the mixer bowl and off the paddle.)

8. Place the muffin pan in the oven and bake until the cupcakes are lightly browned, slightly domed, and cooked through, 20 to 25 minutes. For the best rise, don't open the door for the first 20 minutes, after which you can open the oven door and check the cupcakes to see if they need more time. A wooden skewer inserted into a cupcake should come out with a few crumbs clinging but no batter. Remove the muffin pan from the oven and cool on a wire rack for about 10 minutes before unmolding.

9. Cool to room temperature before frosting the cupcakes (see "How to Frost Cupcakes," page 282).

HOW TO FROST CUPCAKES

The Dahlia Workshop bakers decorate cupcakes by piping frosting or buttercream on top using either a regular or a disposable pastry bag. Disposable pastry bags (see Sources) are handy. When you are done piping, you can cut off and save the pastry tip, then just throw the bag away. Generally we use either a ¼-inch or ⁵⁄₁₆-inch plain tip or star tip or a petal tip for frosting cupcakes. If you're in the mood for doing a fancy, intricate piping job using small tips on your pastry bag, it's best to use the plain vanilla buttercream. If you're frosting with chocolate flake buttercream, use a pastry bag with a larger plain tip because the chocolate flakes can't get through a small tip.

Using the pastry bag, you can pipe little squirts or dollops of buttercream all over the top of the cupcake, or you can pipe in a circular motion or a spiral, covering the top of the cupcake. In either case, start piping from the outside rim of the cupcake and work your way to the middle.

Another idea, which looks polished and professional but is easier to do, is to use a small ice cream scoop to put a neat scoop of frosting or buttercream on top of a cupcake. Next, turn the cupcake upside down into a bowl of crystal sugar. By twisting and lightly pressing the cupcake into the sugar, you will smooth the buttercream evenly all over the top of the cupcake and coat the buttercream with sugar at the same time.

Piping buttercream on a cupcake using a petal tip (devil's food cupcake, vanilla buttercream)

Use a small ice cream scoop to put a neat scoop of buttercream on top of a cupcake (carrot cupcake, vanilla buttercream).

Turn the cupcake upside down into a bowl of decorative sugar.

By twisting and lightly pressing the cupcake into the sugar, you smooth the buttercream over the top of the cupcake and coat it with sugar at the same time.

The finished, decorated cupcake

To pipe dollops of buttercream on a cupcake, start working from the outside rim (devil's food cupcake, vanilla buttercream).

Work your way from the outside rim to the middle of the cupcake.

The finished, decorated cupcake

chocolate heartland bundt cake with chocolate honey glaze

This recipe for an ultra-moist darkly chocolate cake with a fine-textured crumb is a favorite of our Kentucky-born-and-raised pastry chef, Stacy Fortner. The secret ingredient is mashed potato. Serve each wedge of cake with a scoop of Vanilla Bean (page 326) or Stracciatella (page 328) Ice Cream.

As always, for the best flavor, use top-quality chocolate (see "Our Favorite Chocolates," page 21).

We don't often suggest tapping a cake pan on the counter as a way to settle the batter because it can let the air out of your cake, but in this case, since the batter is quite thick, a few sharp raps on the counter before you bake the cake will help you get rid of any air pockets.

When you glaze the cake, if it was unmolded onto a 9-inch round cake cardboard (which is slightly smaller than the cake's diameter), the excess glaze will run off rather than gather on the rim, giving a more professional appearance. If you don't have a cake cardboard, you can use a 9-inch metal round from a removable-bottom tart pan or go ahead and just use a plate to unmold the cake.

SPECIAL EQUIPMENT: POTATO RICER OR FOOD MILL, 10-INCH BUNDT PAN, ELECTRIC MIXER, 9-INCH ROUND CAKE CARDBOARDS (OPTIONAL)

8 ounces (227 grams) potatoes, preferably russet

1¾ cups (8½ ounces/285 grams) all-purpose flour, plus about 2 tablespoons for the pan

About 2 tablespoons unsweetened cocoa powder for the pan

½ cup (4 ounces/115 grams) unsalted butter, softened, plus more for the pan

2 teaspoons baking soda

¼ teaspoon kosher salt

½ teaspoon finely ground black pepper

6 ounces (170 grams) bittersweet chocolate, chopped (about 1 heaping cup; see "How to Chop Chocolate," page 12)

2 tablespoons honey

½ cup (4 ounces/115 grams) boiling water

¼ cup (2 ounces/60 grams) solid vegetable shortening (we use "trans-fat-free" shortening)

2 cups (14 ounces/400 grams) sugar

5 large eggs at room temperature (see "How to Bring Ingredients to Room Temperature," page 12)

1 tablespoon pure vanilla extract

½ cup (4 ounces/115 grams) cold water

Chocolate Honey Glaze (page 255), warm and liquid

1. Peel the potatoes and cut them into 1-inch chunks. Put the potatoes in a saucepan and cover them with cold water. Put the pan over high heat and bring to a simmer. Reduce the heat to maintain a simmer and cook until the potatoes are fork-tender but not mushy (8 to 10 minutes after the water comes to a simmer). Drain the potatoes well and let them sit in the strainer for about 5 minutes to steam off some liquid. Then put the potatoes through a ricer or a food mill fitted with the medium disk. You should have about 1 cup of riced potato (do not pack—discard any excess potato). Set the potato aside.

2. Preheat the oven to 350°F. Combine about 2 tablespoons flour and 2 tablespoons cocoa in a small bowl. Butter a 10-inch Bundt pan well and dust it with the cocoa-flour mixture, shaking out the excess. Place the prepared pan in the refrigerator to set the coating while you are making the batter. (See "How to Prepare a Cake or Loaf Pan," page 261.)

3. Sift the remaining flour and the baking soda into a bowl. Stir in the salt and pepper. Set the dry ingredients aside.

4. Combine the chocolate and honey in a bowl. Pour the boiling water on top and let it rest for 3 to 4 minutes. Whisk the chocolate, honey, and water together and set aside.

5. In the bowl of an electric mixer fitted with the paddle attachment, combine the remaining butter and the shortening and cream on medium-high speed until slightly pale, about 2 minutes. Scrape down the bowl using a rubber spatula. Add the sugar and continue to cream for 2 minutes. Add the eggs, one at a time, beating to incorporate each egg before adding the next. (Tip: Break the eggs into a bowl and add to the mixer one by one.) Then add the vanilla extract, scraping down the bowl as needed. Add the riced potato and incorporate it into the batter on medium speed. With the mixer still on medium, pour in the chocolate-honey mixture and mix slowly until fully incorporated. Scrape the batter down.

6. Add the dry ingredients in 3 additions on low speed, alternating the dry ingredients with the cold water and ending with the dry ingredients. You can turn the mixer on and off as needed as you do this. Don't overmix. When everything has been combined, turn off the mixer and scrape the bowl with a rubber spatula, going down to the bottom of the bowl to fold in any remaining

pockets of dry ingredients. The batter will be very thick, almost like a mousse, and may look broken, but that's okay.

7. Scrape the batter into the prepared Bundt pan and smooth the top. Tap the pan on the counter a few times to settle air pockets, then bake until the cake is cooked through, 65 to 70 minutes, rotating the pan halfway through the baking time. The top of the cake will look cracked and crusty and dark with some dark spots. A wooden skewer inserted into the cake should come out with a few crumbs clinging but no batter. (Because this is a thick batter baked in a deep pan, before taking the cake from the oven, check the cake in a few different places with the skewer, especially toward the inside of the cake, near the tube, and be sure to poke the skewer down about 3 inches to make sure there is no unbaked batter. If there is batter on your skewer, bake the cake a few more minutes.)

8. Remove the pan from the oven, transfer to a wire cooling rack, and allow the cake to cool for 10 to 15 minutes in the pan before unmolding. Unmold the cake (see "How to Unmold Cakes, Tarts, and Loaves," page 262) onto a 9-inch round cake cardboard or a plate and return it to the wire rack to cool to room temperature before glazing.

9. When you are ready to glaze the cake, place the wire rack with the cake on top of it on a baking sheet. You can line the baking sheet first with parchment or foil for easier cleanup. (Note: If you have unmolded the cake onto a plate, the glaze will pool on the plate rather than running off.) Pour the warm, liquid glaze slowly and evenly over the top crest of the cake, so the glaze flows evenly inside the hole and outside over the edges of the cake.

10. Allow the cake to rest at room temperature for about an hour to set the glaze, then slice and serve the cake. (If you don't mind a soft glaze, you can slice the cake after 30 minutes or so.)

For Fragrant Spiced Oranges in Bay Leaf Syrup, see page 305.

intense chocolate cake

In the eighties and nineties just about every restaurant had a molten chocolate cake or a "bête noire" or some other flourless chocolate cake on the menu. These days we get so many requests from our customers for gluten-free desserts that a flourless chocolate cake is right back in style. Unlike many "flourless" cakes, this one doesn't contain even a teaspoon of flour—which makes it truly gluten-free. This cake has a velvety texture somewhere between a chocolate truffle and a chocolate custard. Serve each slice with a drift of Sweetened Whipped Cream (page 193) or a spoonful of crème fraîche.

The cake batter is not difficult to make as long as you pay attention to details such as the temperature of a few ingredients. Be sure your eggs are slightly warmer than room temperature. Warm the eggs in a bowl of very hot tap water for 5 minutes before breaking them. Also, the melted chocolate should not be too hot when you add it to the whipped eggs or it will take the air out of the batter.

The cake bakes at a high temperature for a short period of time. One of the keys to success is to use very hot water in the water bath. When you set up a baking dish to function as a hot water bath, fill it with simmering water rather than hot tap water.

Also, the cake will continue to cook a little more after it is removed from the oven because it is left sitting in the water bath until it comes to room temperature.

Be sure to use top-quality chocolate, for the milk chocolate as well as the bittersweet (see "Our Favorite Chocolates," page 21). Kosher salt is coarser than table salt, so if you are substituting table salt, cut the amount to ½ teaspoon.

Note that, although mixing and baking the cake doesn't take long, you'll need to allow about 4 hours for the cake to rest at room temperature before serving, so plan accordingly and start the cake earlier in the day.

SPECIAL EQUIPMENT: 8-INCH CAKE PAN, ELECTRIC MIXER

Vegetable oil spray for the pan

6 ounces (170 grams) milk chocolate, chopped (about 1 cup; see "How to Chop Chocolate, page 12)

6 ounces (170 grams) bittersweet chocolate, chopped (about 1 cup)

¾ cup (1½ sticks/6 ounces/170 grams) unsalted butter, cut into 1-inch dice

4 large eggs, slightly warmer than room temperature (see headnote)

3 tablespoons (1½ ounces/38 grams) sugar

1 tablespoon pure vanilla extract

¾ teaspoon kosher salt

1. Spray the cake pan with vegetable oil spray. Cut a strip of parchment about 2 inches wide and about 16 inches long. Place the strip in the center of the bottom of the pan, press it up along both sides, and allow it to extend over the rim of the pan on both sides by an inch or two. Spray the paper. (This strip is extra insurance for unmolding the cake later, as you can tug on the strip of paper to pull the cake out of the pan if need be.) Then cut an 8-inch round of parchment paper, set it in the bottom of the pan (on top of the strip), and spray the paper. Set the prepared pan aside.

2. Put both chocolates and the butter in a heatproof bowl that has been placed over a saucepan of simmering water over medium heat. (The bottom of the bowl in the pan should not touch the water.) Adjust the heat to keep the water barely at a simmer. Melt the chocolates and butter, stirring to combine with a rubber or silicone spatula. When the chocolate-butter mixture is melted, remove the bowl from the heat and allow the chocolate to cool to room temperature, about 20 minutes. The chocolate mixture should still be liquid but no longer warm to the touch. Meanwhile, preheat the oven to 400°F.

3. In the bowl of an electric mixer with the whisk attachment, combine the eggs, sugar, vanilla, and salt. Whip on high speed until the mixture is very thick and fluffy and has tripled in volume, 4 to 5 minutes.

4. Remove the bowl from the mixer. Add about a third of the egg mixture to the bowl that contains the chocolate mixture and fold it in to lighten the chocolate. Then add the chocolate mixture to the remaining egg mixture in the bowl from the electric mixer, folding everything together quickly and gently but thoroughly using a rubber spatula.

5. Place a saucepan of water over high heat and bring it to a simmer. Scrape the filling into the prepared pan. Set the cake pan in a larger baking dish that can function as a water bath. Put the

baking dish into the oven, then pour enough of the simmering water into the baking dish to come halfway up the sides of the cake pan. (An easy way to transfer the simmering water to the baking dish is to first pour it into a large Pyrex liquid measuring cup.) Close the oven door and bake for 20 minutes. When the cake is done, the surface will be matte (not shiny), with a couple of dark spots starting to develop. When you shake the pan, the center should jiggle slightly.

6. Remove the baking dish from the oven and set it on a wire rack. Allow the cake (and the water) to cool to room temperature while sitting in the water bath, 45 to 60 minutes. Then remove the cake from the baking dish and place it (still in the cake pan) on the wire rack to rest at room temperature for 3 hours more before unmolding.

7. To unmold, put hot tap water back into the baking dish and place the cake pan in the hot water for a full minute. Remove the cake pan from the water bath, wiping it dry with a kitchen towel, then invert the cake onto a round cake cardboard or a plate. The cake should slip right out. If it doesn't slip out, tug gently on the extending ends of the parchment strip to ease the cake out of the pan. After the cake is unmolded, remove the parchment strip and peel off the parchment round. What was the bottom of the cake is now the top; don't invert the cake again. If you are not ready to slice and serve the cake now, you can leave the cake at room temperature for several more hours. The texture of the cake is best when served on the same day it is made.

8. When you are ready to slice and serve the cake, the best way is to use a knife dipped in hot water. Slice straight down and drag the knife out rather than lifting the blade, as if you were slicing a cheesecake.

cornmeal rosemary cake with lemon glaze

My father-in-law, Jim Cross, hosts an annual winter solstice supper, always anchored by a tremendous pot of fish stew. Thinking about Jim's Italian roots, I came up with this dessert as a perfect finish to his lovely feast. It's almost like this big, creamy, glossy, round, yellow disk of a cake represents the return of the sun all on its own.

The combination of cornmeal and mascarpone in the batter provides both texture and moisture in the finished cake, which is iced with a powdered sugar glaze flecked with rosemary leaves and lemon zest. Serve each wedge of cake with sliced fresh figs, a small bunch of grapes, or any of the fruit accompaniments on pages 301 to 305.

Because this cake is quite moist, you can make it a day ahead. After the cake is brushed with the syrup, allow it to cool completely, then wrap it tightly in plastic wrap and leave it at room temperature. A few hours before you're ready to serve the cake, make the fondant and glaze the cake.

SPECIAL EQUIPMENT: 9-INCH CAKE PAN, 9-INCH ROUND CAKE CARDBOARD (OPTIONAL)

cake

½ cup (1 stick/4 ounces/113 grams) unsalted butter, melted, plus more for the pan

1½ cups (7¾ ounces/220 grams) all-purpose flour

¾ cup (4 ounces/114 grams) medium-grind yellow cornmeal

1 tablespoon finely chopped fresh rosemary

1 tablespoon grated lemon zest

1 teaspoon baking powder

¼ teaspoon kosher salt

⅔ cup (4⅞ ounces/138 grams) mascarpone

4 large eggs

1⅓ cups (9⅓ ounces/264 grams) sugar

lemon syrup

½ cup (4¼ ounces/121 grams) freshly squeezed lemon juice

⅓ cup (2⅜ ounces/67 grams) sugar

lemon fondant

1 tablespoon fresh rosemary leaves

1½ cups (6⅛ ounces/175 grams) powdered sugar, sifted (see "How to Sift," page 13)

¼ cup (2⅜ ounces/68 grams) heavy cream

2 tablespoons freshly squeezed lemon juice

1 teaspoon grated lemon zest

1. Preheat the oven to 350°F. Butter a 9-inch cake pan, line it with a 9-inch round of parchment paper, and butter the paper.

2. In a bowl, combine the flour, cornmeal, rosemary, zest, baking powder, and salt.

3. In a large bowl, briefly whisk the mascarpone to loosen it. Add the eggs one at a time, whisking to combine. Add the sugar and whisk until smooth. Using a rubber spatula, fold the dry ingredients, in 2 batches, into the wet ingredients, mixing until smooth. Stir in the remaining butter.

4. Scrape the cake batter into the prepared pan and bake until a skewer comes out clean of batter but with a few crumbs clinging, about 40 minutes, rotating the pan halfway through the baking time.

5. While the cake is baking, make the lemon syrup. Combine the lemon juice and sugar in a small saucepan over medium heat and cook for a few minutes, stirring occasionally, until the sugar dissolves. Remove from the heat.

6. Allow the cake to cool in the pan on a wire rack for 5 minutes before unmolding. To unmold, run a small knife around the cake. Place a round cake cardboard or an inverted plate over the cake pan and, protecting your hands with a kitchen towel, invert the whole thing. The cake should slide right out onto the cardboard or the plate. Peel off the parchment paper, then place a 9-inch round cake cardboard or an inverted plate over the cake and again invert the whole thing. Remove the top cardboard or plate and the cake will be right side up (sitting on a cake cardboard if you used one).

7. With a wooden skewer, poke a few dozen holes all over the top of the cake. While the cake is still warm, brush the cake with the lemon syrup. Continue brushing for several minutes, giving the syrup time to sink into the cake, until you've used all or most of the syrup. Allow the cake to cool.

8. To make the lemon fondant, bring a small saucepan of water to a boil. Add the rosemary leaves and blanch them for 1 minute. Scoop out the rosemary leaves with a small sieve and drop them immediately into a small bowl of ice water. Drain and spread the rosemary leaves on a paper towel to dry. In a bowl, whisk the powdered sugar, cream, and lemon juice until smooth, then whisk in the blanched rosemary and the zest.

9. When the cake is completely cool, transfer it to a rack set over a baking sheet. (If your cake is not on a cake cardboard, use a wide spatula to transfer it.) Pour the fondant over the top of the cake and allow it to drip off the sides. You can gently tilt the cardboard circle or the wire rack back and forth to encourage the glaze to flow completely over the top of the cake.

10. While the glaze is still wet, transfer the cake to a cake plate. Allow the fondant to dry, an hour or more, before slicing and serving the cake. (Note: If you allow the glaze to dry before you transfer it, the glaze may crack a bit unless you are transferring it on a cake cardboard.)

rustic olive oil cake with honey syrup

The crunchy top crust and delectably moist, olive-oil-flavored crumb make this one of pastry chef Stacy Fortner's favorite cakes. For ultra-lusciousness, add a drizzle of citrus-scented honey syrup and a generous dollop of whipped cream to each slice. But if you don't feel like making the syrup, the cake is moist and delicious without it.

If you're not using the syrup, you can garnish the cake with Fresh Lime Brachetto Cherries (page 301) or Grappa-Soaked Berries with Lemon Zest (page 304).

To make the cake, use an extra virgin olive oil with a mellow, rounded flavor; it's not necessary to use the most expensive, precious bottle in your pantry. Since the cake calls for an entire cup of oil, it's best to avoid olive oils that are intensely flavored, grassy, or pungent.

Make the cake batter by hand with a bowl and a whisk. Don't be tempted to use your electric mixer here, because if you overaerate this cake it won't bake properly. Before making the cake, be sure to bring the eggs and milk to room temperature.

This is a cake that you don't want to underbake. If in doubt, it's better to bake it a few minutes too long rather than a few too little.

If you like, you can make the syrup ahead, store it covered in the refrigerator, and gently reheat to room temperature when you are ready to serve the cake.

Since this cake is so moist, leftovers last for a few days. Wrap only the cut edge of cake with plastic wrap to keep the crust of the cake as crisp as possible.

SPECIAL EQUIPMENT: 9-INCH CAKE PAN, 9-INCH ROUND CAKE CARDBOARDS (OPTIONAL)

cake

Vegetable oil spray as needed for the pan

2 cups (8⅝ ounces/243 grams) all-purpose flour, plus more for the pan

½ teaspoon baking powder

½ teaspoon baking soda

1 teaspoon kosher salt

1¼ cups (10 ounces/285 grams) whole milk at room temperature (see "How to Bring Ingredients to Room Temperature," page 12)

¼ cup (2 ounces/57 grams) Grand Marnier

¼ cup (2 ounces/57 grams) freshly squeezed orange juice

Grated zest of 1 lemon (about 1 tablespoon plus 1 teaspoon)

3 large eggs at room temperature

2 cups (13½ ounces/381 grams) sugar

1 cup (7½ ounces/213 grams) extra virgin olive oil

honey syrup

½ cup (7 ounces/196 grams) honey

½ cup (4½ ounces/127 grams) sugar

½ cup (4 ounces/113 grams) water

1 clove

1 strip of orange or lemon zest, about ½ × 4 inches, cut with a vegetable peeler

Sweetened Whipped Cream (page 193)

1. Preheat the oven to 375°F. Spray the cake pan with vegetable oil spray. Cut a 9-inch round of parchment paper and place it in the bottom of the pan, then spray the paper. Flour the pan, shaking out the excess. Set the cake pan aside.

2. In a bowl or onto a sheet of parchment, sift together the flour, baking powder, and baking soda (see "How to Sift," page 13). Stir in the salt. Set the dry ingredients aside.

3. In a small bowl, combine the milk, Grand Marnier, orange juice, and lemon zest. Set the wet ingredients aside.

4. Put the eggs and sugar in a large bowl and whisk by hand with a balloon whisk until well combined and smooth.

5. Gradually add the olive oil in a steady stream while whisking the egg mixture, as if you were making a mayonnaise. (Tip: Put the olive oil in a Pyrex liquid measuring cup first to make pouring easier. Also, you can make a cradle with a kitchen towel to hold your bowl steady as you whisk.)

6. After you have emulsified the oil into the egg mixture, start adding the dry ingredients in 3 additions, alternating with the wet ingredients in 2 additions, beginning and ending with dry. As you make each addition of dry and wet ingredients, whisk by hand just until the batter is smooth, without overbeating, before adding the next. Scrape down the bowl as needed.

7. Pour the batter into the prepared pan. Give the pan a couple of taps on the counter to settle any air bubbles in the batter.

8. Bake the cake until deep golden brown, slightly domed, and possibly cracked on top, about 70 minutes. A skewer should come out clean of batter but with a few moist crumbs.

9. Remove the pan from the oven and allow to cool on a wire rack for about 15 minutes. To unmold, run a small knife around the edges of the cake. Place a cake cardboard or a plate over the cake pan and invert the pan. The cake should slide right out onto the cardboard. Peel off the

parchment circle (from what used to be the bottom of the cake) and invert again. Remove the top board and the cake will be right side up. Allow the cake to cool on the wire rack until it is only slightly warm or at room temperature before slicing.

10. Meanwhile, while the cake is baking, make the syrup. Combine the honey, sugar, water, clove, and citrus zest in a small saucepan over medium-high heat. Bring to a simmer, stirring to dissolve the sugar and adjusting the heat as necessary to keep the liquid at a simmer. Simmer until reduced by almost half and as thick as a light syrup, 10 to 12 minutes. (You should have a little more than ¾ cup of syrup.) Remove the pan from the heat and pour the syrup into a container to cool to room temperature. Remove the clove and zest from the syrup and discard.

11. To serve, slice the cake and put the slices on plates. Drizzle each slice generously with honey syrup and dollop with the cream.

piedmontese hazelnut cake

When the big decade birthday comes along, or the big wedding anniversary, the dream place for Jackie and me always seems to be Italy. We've made at least half a dozen trips, to explore the wineries in the hills of Barbaresco and Barolo, to follow our noses to Alba for white truffles, ripe Tomme cheese, and gorgeous plums, stopping at our favorite restaurants, inns, and bed-and-breakfast places along the way. When we're lucky, we get a plate of impossibly small *plin* (ravioli in a delicate sage butter sauce). When we're really lucky, we end a meal with a slice of this regional Piedmontese cake, which has a rustic, crumbly texture and the sweet, deep fragrance of hazelnuts. This is a recipe I developed for my pasta house, Cuoco, to pay tribute to these memorable Italian cakes.

The flavor and aroma of this cake has everything to do with a long, slow toasting of the hazelnuts. Because hazelnuts are dense, they take longer to toast than many other nuts. We toast them at 350°F for about 18 to 20 minutes. Be sure the toasted hazelnuts are cool before you grind them. (See "How to Skin Hazelnuts," page 84.)

This is a European-style cake, so it's not as moist as an American cake. A slice of this cake calls out for a glass of Vin Santo or Moscato d'Asti. We like a spoonful of one of our fruit accompaniments (pages 301 to 305) alongside. In the morning or afternoon, a slice of hazelnut cake with an espresso is a treat.

SPECIAL EQUIPMENT: 9-INCH CAKE PAN, FOOD PROCESSOR, ELECTRIC MIXER, 9-INCH ROUND CAKE CARDBOARDS (OPTIONAL)

7 tablespoons (3½ ounces/100 grams) unsalted butter, softened, plus more for the pan

¼ cup (1¼ ounces/35 grams) semolina, plus more for the pan

2 cups (10½ ounces/300 grams) hazelnuts, toasted, skinned, and cooled (see headnote)

½ cup (2½ ounces/71 grams) cake flour

1 teaspoon baking powder

1 teaspoon kosher salt

1 cup (7 ounces/200 grams) packed brown sugar

3 large eggs at room temperature (see "How to Bring Ingredients to Room Temperature," page 12)

2 tablespoons pure vanilla extract

2 tablespoons olive oil

Powdered sugar as needed for sprinkling

1. Preheat the oven to 375°F. Butter a 9-inch cake pan. Cut a 9-inch round of parchment paper and place it in the bottom of the pan, then butter the paper. Dust the pan with semolina, shaking out the excess. Put the pan in the refrigerator to set the coating while you are making the batter. (See "How to Prepare a Cake or Loaf Pan," page 261.)

2. Put the hazelnuts in the bowl of a food processor and pulse until finely chopped. Remove the nuts from the processor and set aside.

3. In a small bowl, combine the cake flour, remaining semolina, the baking powder, and salt. Set the dry ingredients aside.

4. Put the remaining butter and the brown sugar in the bowl of an electric mixer with the paddle attachment and cream them together on medium speed for a few minutes.

5. Add the eggs one at a time, beating to incorporate each egg thoroughly before adding the next egg. Scrape down the bowl. Add the hazelnuts and beat briefly to combine.

6. Remove the bowl from the electric mixer and add the dry ingredients, gently folding everything together with a rubber spatula. Fold in the vanilla extract and olive oil, then scrape the batter into the prepared pan.

7. Bake the cake until the top is browned and a skewer inserted into the cake comes out with no batter but with a few moist crumbs clinging, 30 to 35 minutes. Remove the pan from the oven and allow to cool on a wire rack for about 15 minutes.

8. To unmold, run a small knife around the cake. Place a cake cardboard or a plate over the cake pan (if the top of the cake feels sticky, put a piece of parchment over the cake board first) and invert the pan. The cake should slide right out onto the cardboard. Peel off the parchment circle from what used to be the bottom of the cake, then place another cake board or plate over the cake and invert again. Remove the top cake board and the cake will be right side up. Allow the cake to cool on the wire rack. When the cake is completely cool, put some powdered sugar in a small sieve and sift the sugar generously over the top of the cake, then slice and serve.

9. This cake is also delicious served while it is still warm. If you are serving it warm, don't dust the whole top of the cake. Instead, dust each wedge of cake with powdered sugar right before you serve it.

brachetto cherries with fresh lime

This recipe was inspired by the Italian tradition of pouring wine or sparkling wine directly over a wineglass or dessert bowl filled with cherries, berries, sliced peaches, or other fruit. Serve a portion of cherries alongside wedges of a cake such as the hazelnut cake (page 298) or olive oil cake (page 295). Brachetto is good with chocolate, so also try a spoonful of these cherries alongside a serving of chocolate tart (page 248) or Intense Chocolate Cake (page 288).

Brachetto d'Acqui is an Italian sweet sparkling red wine, wonderful as a dessert wine. If you prefer, you could macerate the cherries in Moscato d'Asti. Either way, serve the rest of the bottle in glasses alongside the dessert.

The Brachetto cherries should be eaten within an hour of making them; they won't hold up well to longer storage. So if you're garnishing only three or four servings of cake, cut the recipe in half so you don't waste any cherries you can't eat.

Instead of using the cherries to garnish a cake or tart, you could serve them in glass bowls as a light dessert for 4 people, topping each portion with Vanilla Bean Mascarpone (page 63). Serve a couple Toasted Pine Nut Amaretti (page 139) on the side of each bowl.

Use a Microplane to grate the lime zest before you cut the lime in half to squeeze it for juice.

The cherries cure in sugar for 1½ hours and then macerate in the sparkling wine for at least another 30 minutes, so start the recipe about 2 hours before you plan to serve them.

SPECIAL EQUIPMENT: CHERRY PITTER (OPTIONAL BUT RECOMMENDED)

1¼ pounds (568 grams) sweet cherries, such as Bing or Lapin

⅓ cup (2⅓ ounces/65 grams) sugar

⅓ cup (2 ⅝ ounces/75 grams) Brachetto (Italian sparkling red wine)

1 tablespoon plus 1½ teaspoons freshly squeezed lime juice

Scant ½ teaspoon grated lime zest

¾ teaspoon pure vanilla extract

1. Remove the stems and pits of the cherries and place them in a bowl. (You should have about 4 cups pitted cherries.) Add the sugar, tossing well to combine, and place the bowl in the refrigerator until the sugar has dissolved and the cherries are giving off some juices, about 1½ hours. Stir the cherries occasionally to make sure the sugar dissolves.

2. Remove the cherries from the refrigerator and add the Brachetto, lime juice and zest, and vanilla extract. Allow the cherries to macerate (steep or soak in the liquid), refrigerated, for another 30 minutes and up to 1 hour before serving, but no longer than an hour.

3. Serve the cherries and some of their liquid alongside wedges of cake and serve with chilled glasses of Brachetto.

quick brandied bing cherries

During cherry season, my wife, Jackie, likes to use the Jubilee Cherries recipe from her favorite preserving cookbook, Helen Witty's *Fancy Pantry,* to put up plenty of jars for the winter months. But when the preserved cherries are gone, this quick dessert sauce does the trick.

Spoon the cherries and their syrup over a wedge of any plain, unfrosted cake. They're also delicious spooned over a scoop of Vanilla Bean (page 326) or Buttermilk (page 330) Ice Cream. You could also add one of these cherries to a Manhattan, instead of a maraschino.

You can make the brandied cherries up to a few weeks ahead and store them, covered, in the refrigerator. The flavor mellows and improves after a few days.

SPECIAL EQUIPMENT: CHERRY PITTER (OPTIONAL BUT RECOMMENDED)

⅔ cup (5 ounces/140 grams) sugar

½ cup (4 ounces/113 grams) water

1 vanilla bean, split in half lengthwise

1 pound (455 grams) Bing or other sweet cherries, stemmed and pitted, keeping the cherries whole

½ cup (4 ounces/110 grams) cognac or other good-quality brandy

Combine the sugar and ½ cup water in a heavy saucepan over medium-high heat. Use a paring knife to scrape the seeds from the vanilla bean and add both the seeds and the pod to the pot. Bring to a boil, stirring to dissolve the sugar. Add the cherries and ¼ cup of the cognac and simmer for 10 minutes. Remove from the heat and strain the cherries from the cooking liquid, reserving both the cherries and the liquid. Put the cherries and the vanilla bean pod in a heatproof bowl and return the liquid to the saucepan. Bring the liquid to a boil over medium-high heat and continue to boil until syrupy and reduced to ½ cup. Remove the pan from the heat and pour the hot syrup over the reserved cherries. Allow the brandied cherries to cool, then stir in the remaining ¼ cup cognac. You can set the bowl of cherries over a bowl of ice water to cool them more quickly if desired. Remove and discard the vanilla pod before serving. (Or rinse and dry the pod and save for vanilla bean sugar, page 64.)

grappa-soaked berries with lemon zest

You can use any sweet, ripe berries in season such as blueberries, raspberries, blackberries, or a combination of berries. It's especially nice to add some strawberries, hulled and cut into halves or quarters, because the juices of the cut strawberries mix well with the sugar and grappa. You can also add sweet cherries, pitted and either left whole or cut in half. Serve the berries within an hour of mixing them with the grappa.

Grappa is a clear, grape-based Italian brandy that is high in alcohol. A quality grappa will make the most delicious "soak" for the berries. We like to use the grappas from Clear Creek Distillery in Oregon or any Moscato-based grappa. Another alternative is to substitute a favorite liquor, like cognac or kirsch, or you can omit the alcohol and just serve sugared berries with a hint of lemon.

Use a Microplane grater to grate the lemon zest you need for the recipe before you cut the lemon in half to squeeze the juice.

4 cups (about 1 pound/500 grams) berries (see headnote)

3 tablespoons (1⅜ ounces/39 grams) grappa

1 tablespoon freshly squeezed lemon juice

3 tablespoons (1¼ ounces/37 grams) sugar

½ teaspoon grated lemon zest

1. Put the berries in a bowl. Drizzle with the grappa and lemon juice and sprinkle with the sugar and zest. Toss everything gently to combine. Cover the bowl with plastic wrap and allow the berries to sit, refrigerated, for 15 to 30 minutes before serving, but no longer than an hour.

2. Serve the berries and some of their liquid alongside wedges of Intense Chocolate Cake (page 288), Cornmeal Rosemary Cake with Lemon Glaze (page 291), Rustic Olive Oil Cake (page 295), or Piedmontese Hazelnut Cake (page 298).

fragrant spiced oranges in bay leaf syrup

MAKES 24 ORANGE SLICES; SERVES 8 AS AN ACCOMPANIMENT TO CAKE

Here's a fruit accompaniment for cakes and other desserts that's nice for the winter months. For an especially beautiful compote, use blood oranges instead of regular oranges, buying a few extra if the blood oranges are small.

If you can get fresh bay leaves, use them instead of dried. Steeping the bay leaves and spices in hot water before adding the sugar results in a stronger infusion.

The compote must chill for at least 2 hours before being served. You can make the compote a day ahead and store it, covered, in the refrigerator, but no more than that or the oranges will start to disintegrate.

4 (1¾ pounds/800 grams) oranges

⅔ cup (5 ounces/150 grams) water

4 bay leaves

4 cloves

1 cinnamon stick

1 cup (7 ounces/200 grams) sugar

1. Using a sharp knife, remove all the peel and pith from the oranges, leaving the orange flesh intact. Slice each orange crosswise into 6 slices, for a total of 24 orange slices. Place the slices in a heatproof bowl and set aside.

2. Put the water, bay leaves, cloves, and cinnamon in a small saucepan and bring to a boil. Remove the pan from the heat, cover, and allow to steep for about 10 minutes. Remove the cover from the pan, add the sugar, and return the mixture to a boil, stirring to dissolve the sugar. Remove the pan from the heat and pour the syrup over the orange slices. Put a piece of plastic wrap directly over the surface of the oranges and place the bowl in the refrigerator. Chill for at least 2 hours or until the oranges are cool and infused with the flavors of bay and spice.

3. To serve, place 2 or 3 orange slices alongside wedges of Intense Chocolate Cake (page 288), Cornmeal Rosemary Cake with Lemon Glaze (page 291), Rustic Olive Oil Cake (page 295), or Piedmontese Hazelnut Cake (page 298). Discard the bay leaves and spices and spoon a little of the syrup over the oranges on each plate.

creamy goodness
PUDDING, PASTRY CREAM, ÉCLAIRS

the best crème caramel in the world

Why? Because I say so, and I'm confident you'll feel the same as long as you don't commit the one cardinal sin with this recipe, which is overcooking past the set point to a curdle. When cooked exactly the way we tell you, there's nothing more luscious than this dessert. It makes you want to spread it all over your body. You can fool around with lots of different flavorings to add to your cream, but I like it best with just a fragrant vanilla bean.

A crisp sugar cookie (page 148) is the perfect crunchy foil for this creamy delicious dessert.

Caramel is best made in a good-quality heavy-bottomed pan (see "Pots and Pans," page 30). Caramelizing sugar isn't difficult, but it can be daunting the first time (see "How to Caramelize Sugar," page 67).

The crème caramels need several hours, or overnight, to chill before you can unmold them, so plan ahead.

You can put the caramelized sugar in the bottom of the ramekins several hours ahead of time and let them sit at room temperature until you are ready to make the custard. After the crème caramels are baked, you can store them in their ramekins, refrigerated, for 2 or 3 days. When they are completely cold, cover them with plastic wrap. Unmold right before serving.

SPECIAL EQUIPMENT: EIGHT 6-OUNCE OVENPROOF RAMEKINS

caramel

1 cup (7 ounces/200 grams) sugar

⅓ cup (3 ounces/85 grams) water

custard

4 cups (2 pounds plus 2 ounces/ 970 grams) heavy cream

1 cup (7 ounces/200 grams) sugar

1 vanilla bean, split in half lengthwise

10 large egg yolks

1. Preheat the oven to 300°F. Place eight 6-ounce ovenproof ramekins inside a baking pan (a roasting pan about 14 × 11 × 2 inches would be a good size, or you can split the ramekins between two smaller baking pans if you don't have a pan large enough to hold them all) and set this near the range.

2. To make the caramel, in a heavy-bottomed saucepan, combine the sugar and water. Stir over low heat until the sugar is completely dissolved. Raise the heat to high and cook without stirring until the sugar turns dark golden brown. You may need to swirl the pan gently to distribute the color evenly. Remove the pan from the heat and carefully pour a little caramel into each of the ramekins. There should be enough caramel in the pan to cover the bottom of each ramekin. Set the pan with the ramekins aside to cool while you make the custard.

3. To make the custard, in another saucepan, stir together the cream and sugar. Scrape the seeds from the vanilla bean and add both the scrapings and the pod to the cream mixture. Place the saucepan over medium-high heat, stirring to dissolve the sugar. In a bowl, lightly beat the egg yolks. Set a fine-mesh sieve over another bowl and keep it nearby. When the cream mixture is very hot, but still just below the boiling point, remove the pan from the heat. Whisk a small amount of the hot cream mixture into the egg yolks just to warm them. Then whisk the warmed yolks into the hot cream mixture, and as soon as the mixtures are well combined, strain the custard through the sieve, discarding the pod. (Or rinse and dry the pod and save it to make vanilla bean sugar, page 64.)

4. Fill the prepared ramekins in the baking pan with custard, dividing it evenly. Put the baking pan in the oven, then pour enough hot tap water around the ramekins to come about halfway up the sides. Loosely cover the baking pan with a piece of aluminum foil (you want steam to be able to escape) and bake for 50 to 60 minutes, until the custard is set. You can check by gently shaking a ramekin or by making a shallow cut with a small knife into the center of one of the custards. The custard may look soft, but it shouldn't be liquid inside. Carefully remove the baking pan from the oven and allow to cool. When the ramekins are cool enough to handle, remove them from the baking pan and set them in the refrigerator for several hours or overnight.

5. To serve the crème caramels, run a small knife around the edge of the custard. Invert a dessert plate over the top of the ramekin and, holding on tight, flip the whole thing over, giving the ramekin a sharp shake. The custard should slide right out onto the plate. Serve immediately.

vanilla bean crème brûlée

Dahlia Bakery crème brûlées are extra rich and delicious because they're made with egg yolks and heavy cream. The custard for our crème brûlée and crème caramel is exactly the same. The difference is that for the crème caramel, liquid caramel is poured into the ramekin before it is filled with custard and baked, whereas the crème brûlée is baked as a plain ramekin of custard that, after being chilled and right before being served, is given a topping of caramelized sugar.

To create the brittle, caramelized sugar crust on the top of each crème brûlée, you'll need a small kitchen torch, fueled by propane or butane, which you can purchase from hardware stores, kitchenware stores, or mail-order and online catalogs such as Sur La Table (see Sources).

The crème brûlées need to chill completely before being served, several hours or overnight, so plan accordingly.

You can make the crèmes up to 2 or 3 days ahead and store them, covered, in the refrigerator. When they are completely cold, cover them with plastic wrap. But don't caramelize the tops until right before you serve them.

Caramelizing the sugar with a handheld torch

SPECIAL EQUIPMENT: EIGHT 6-OUNCE OVENPROOF RAMEKINS, HANDHELD PROPANE KITCHEN TORCH

custards

4 cups (2 pounds plus 2 ounces/ 970 grams) heavy cream

1 cup (7 ounces/200 grams) sugar

1 vanilla bean, split in half lengthwise

10 large egg yolks

to caramelize the tops

About ½ cup sugar (about 3½ ounces/100 grams) as needed

1. Preheat the oven to 300°F. Place eight 6-ounce ovenproof ramekins inside a baking pan. (A roasting pan about 14 × 11 × 2 inches would be a good size.)

2. In a saucepan, stir together the cream and sugar. Scrape the seeds from the vanilla bean, using a paring knife, and add both the scrapings and the pod to the cream mixture. Place the saucepan over medium-high heat, stirring to dissolve the sugar. In a bowl, lightly beat the egg yolks. Set a fine-mesh sieve over another bowl and keep it nearby. When the cream mixture is very hot, but still just below the boiling point, remove the pan from the heat.

3. Whisk a small amount of the hot cream mixture into the egg yolks just to warm them. Then whisk the warmed yolks into the hot cream mixture and, as soon as the mixtures are well combined, strain the custard through the sieve, discarding the pod (or rinse, dry, and save to make vanilla bean sugar, page 64).

4. Fill the ramekins in the baking pan with custard, dividing it evenly. Put the baking pan in the oven, then pour enough hot tap water around the ramekins to come about halfway up the sides. Loosely cover the baking pan with a piece of aluminum foil (you want steam to be able to escape) and bake for 50 to 60 minutes, until the custard is set. You can check by gently shaking a ramekin or by making a shallow cut with a small knife into the center of one of the custards. The custard may look soft, but it shouldn't be liquid inside. Carefully remove the baking pan from the oven and allow to cool. When the ramekins are cool enough to handle, remove them from the baking pan and set them in the refrigerator for several hours or overnight.

5. When you are ready to serve the crèmes, remove them from the refrigerator. Sprinkle the top of a custard with about a tablespoon of sugar to make a thin, even coating. Use a propane torch to caramelize the sugar, which will melt and turn golden brown in less than a minute. Repeat until all the custards have been caramelized, allow the caramel to harden for a minute or two, and serve.

arborio rice pudding with cinnamon and vanilla

For the creamiest, dreamiest rice pudding, first cook Arborio rice slowly and gently in cinnamon-and-vanilla-scented milk, then fold in both a custard sauce (also called *crème anglaise*) and mounds of whipped cream.

For cooking the rice and making the crème anglaise, it's best to use good-quality heavy-bottomed saucepans (see "Pots and Pans," page 30).

Set a fine-mesh sieve over a bowl and place it near the stove so you can strain the crème anglaise as soon as it is thickened. You can serve the pudding immediately or chill it for a few hours before serving, but if you chill it much longer you will lose the special soft texture of the rice. (Note: After chilling and before serving, if the pudding seems too thick, you can stir in a splash of milk to loosen it a bit.)

Instead of the orange-juice-soaked currants or raisins, you can garnish the pudding with any of the fruit accompaniments on pages 301 to 305 or with fresh berries, sliced peaches, or figs.

SPECIAL EQUIPMENT: ELECTRIC MIXER (OPTIONAL)

crème anglaise

1 vanilla bean

½ cup (4 ounces/120 grams) heavy cream

¼ cup (2 ounces/60 grams) whole milk

2 tablespoons sugar

2 large egg yolks

cooked rice

4½ cups (39 ounces/1085 grams) whole milk

6 tablespoons (2⅜ ounces/68 grams) sugar

One 2-inch cinnamon stick

¾ cup (5½ ounces/160 grams) Arborio rice

¼ teaspoon kosher salt

to finish the pudding

⅓ cup (2¾ ounces/78 grams) heavy cream

½ teaspoon vanilla extract

garnish

½ cup (4¼ ounces/121 grams) freshly squeezed orange juice

⅓ cup (1½ ounces/42 grams) dried currants, raisins, or golden raisins

1. Split the vanilla bean in half lengthwise and scrape out the seeds with the tip of a paring knife, reserving both the scrapings and the pod.

2. To make the crème anglaise, combine the cream, milk, and sugar in a small saucepan. Place the saucepan over medium-high heat and scald (just below the boiling point until it begins to steam and small bubbles appear around the edge), stirring to dissolve the sugar. Meanwhile, put the egg yolks in a bowl, add the vanilla bean scrapings, and whisk until pale yellow. Gradually add a ladle of the scalded cream mixture to the yolks while whisking to combine and warm the yolks. Pour the tempered yolks into the saucepan and return to medium heat, stirring until the mixture is thick enough to coat the back of a spoon, which will take only 2 to 3 minutes for this small quantity of crème anglaise. Immediately pour the crème anglaise through a fine-mesh sieve into a bowl. Set the bowl inside a larger bowl of ice water and stir occasionally until cooled. Cover the bowl and refrigerate the crème anglaise while you are cooking the rice.

3. To cook the rice, combine the milk, sugar, vanilla bean pod, cinnamon stick, rice, and salt in a saucepan and bring to a boil over medium-high heat; then lower the heat so the mixture is at a gentle simmer. Continue to cook until the rice is soft and the mixture is very thick, 35 to 40 minutes, stirring and adjusting the heat as needed. As the milk cooks down you will need to stir more frequently to keep the mixture from sticking; stir constantly during the last 4 to 5 minutes of cooking.

4. When the rice mixture is soft and thick, transfer it to a bowl. Remove the vanilla pod and cinnamon stick and discard (or rinse and dry the pod and save it to make vanilla bean sugar, page 64). Place the bowl inside a larger bowl of ice water and stir occasionally until cool.

5. When the rice is cool, remove the bowl from the ice bath and stir in the chilled crème anglaise. To finish the pudding, put the ⅓ cup cream and the vanilla extract in the bowl of an electric mixer and whip to medium peaks. (If you don't have an electric mixer, you can whip the cream by hand using a whisk.) Fold the whipped cream into the pudding.

6. Meanwhile, put the orange juice in a small saucepan and bring to a simmer. Add the currants, cover the pan, and remove from the heat. Allow the currants to plump for about 30 minutes, then drain. Set the currants aside (refrigerated if you are not ready to serve the pudding).

7. Serve the rice pudding immediately or cover and chill for an hour or two before serving. For the best texture, don't chill the rice pudding much longer because the rice will eventually harden.

8. When you are ready to serve the rice pudding, spoon it into 6 dessert bowls, dividing it evenly. Top each serving of pudding with some of the currants and serve.

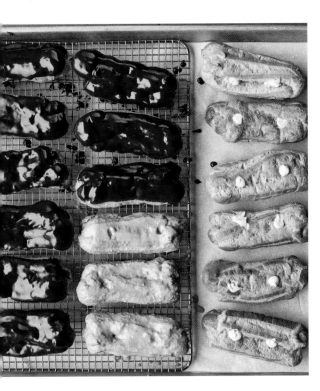

éclairs

There's always a row of éclairs, topped with shiny glazes and cradled in paper liners, anchoring the pastry case of the Dahlia Bakery. The morning bakers make them with just about every fruit and flavor under the sun. Here's a recipe with three of our favorite éclair filling and glaze combos: vanilla pastry cream filling with chocolate glaze, maple pastry cream filling with maple glaze, and lemon curd filling with royal icing glaze and lemon zest.

Make the pâte à choux when you are ready to pipe the éclairs, as it is best to pipe the dough immediately after it is made. Make any of the fillings at least 3 hours ahead or overnight to give them time to chill. Make any of the glazes shortly before you are ready to dip the éclair so they are still liquid.

When baking the éclairs, note that you preheat the oven to 425°F but turn it down to 400°F *before* you put the éclairs in the oven. After 20 minutes you turn the oven down again to 350°F to finish the baking.

It's very important not to open the oven door while the éclairs are baking; if you do, they will likely sink and not rise properly.

Many people fill éclairs by making holes in the bottom side, but we like to make the holes in the top side because, after the éclairs are glazed, the piping holes are sealed.

A small loaf pan is a good container for holding your glaze as you dip the éclairs as it is éclair shaped, or you can use a small, deep oval porcelain dish.

Éclairs taste best if you serve them shortly after they are filled and glazed, as soon as the glaze has set. You can refrigerate them if you must, but the pâte à choux will never be as crisp and fresh tasting after refrigeration.

The pastry creams or lemon curd must be made at least 3 hours ahead, and overnight is even better, so make them a day ahead and chill overnight. You can bake the éclairs several hours ahead and leave the unfilled shells at room temperature. They should be fine unless your kitchen is humid. If they do get soggy, and you need to recrisp them, put them on a baking sheet in a low (300°F) oven for 10 minutes or so. Remove from the oven and allow the éclairs to cool to room temperature. Then fill, glaze, and serve immediately.

SPECIAL EQUIPMENT: 2 PASTRY BAGS OR DISPOSABLE PASTRY BAGS (1 FOR THE PÂTE À CHOUX AND 1 FOR THE FILLING), ½-INCH OR ⅝-INCH PLAIN PASTRY TIP FOR PIPING ÉCLAIRS, METAL BENCH KNIFE (OPTIONAL), ¼-INCH PLAIN OR STAR TIP FOR PIPING THE FILLING, SMALL LOAF PAN OR SIMILAR CONTAINER FOR GLAZING ÉCLAIRS

Pâte à choux for éclairs, freshly made
   (page 319)

filling

Vanilla Bean Pastry Cream (page 320), quantity for éclairs, or Maple Pastry Cream (page 178), or Tangy Lemon Curd (page 242), each made ahead and chilled for at least 3 hours or overnight

glaze

Chocolate Honey Glaze (page 255), or Maple Sugar Glaze (page 323), or Royal Decorating Icing (page 151) plus 1 lemon, each freshly made

Piping vanilla pastry cream into an éclair

Glazing a pastry-cream-filled éclair with chocolate honey glaze

1. Preheat the oven to 425°F.

2. Fill a pastry bag fitted with a ⅝-inch plain tip with the pâte à choux. (Never fill a pastry bag more than two-thirds full.) Line a baking sheet with parchment paper. Press gently and steadily on the pastry bag to pipe 10 éclairs that are 5 inches long onto the baking sheet, setting them a couple inches apart. (For more tips, see "How to Pipe Éclairs," page 318.)

3. When all the éclairs are piped, turn the oven down to 400°F, put the pan in the oven, and bake for 20 minutes without opening the oven door. Then, still without opening the oven door, turn the oven down to 350°F and bake the éclairs for 15 more minutes. Then turn the oven off, but leave the éclairs in the turned-off oven for 20 minutes more. Remove the pan from the oven. The éclairs should be an even golden brown and should feel light when you lift one up.

4. Remove the éclairs from the baking sheet and place them on a wire rack to cool to room temperature before filling.

5. When you are ready to fill the éclairs, put the filling in a clean pastry bag fitted with a ¼-inch plain or star tip. Using the tip of a paring knife, make 2 slits (about ¼ inch in length) in the top side of an éclair, one near each end. Inserting the pastry tip first into one slit and then into the other, squeeze gently on the bag to fill the éclair. If necessary, clean off any excess drips of filling from the spots where you filled the éclairs using a clean finger. Continue filling the rest of the éclairs.

6. As each éclair is filled, place it on a parchment-lined baking sheet, top side up. Continue until all the éclairs are filled, using up all the filling. (If you have any filling left in the pastry bag when you are done, lift the éclairs to see if any feel light and fill those a little more.)

7. To glaze the éclairs, put your freshly made glaze in a container such as a clean loaf pan.

8. Pick up a filled éclair and dip it top side down into the container of glaze so that the glaze comes halfway up the sides of the éclair. You can rock the éclair gently from side to side to get it well coated in the glaze. Lift the éclair out of the glaze, then tilt the éclair at an angle to one end so excess glaze can drip off, then tilt the opposite angle so excess glaze can drip off on the other end.

Pipe the éclairs using a pastry bag fitted with a plain ½-inch or ⅝-inch tip and filled with pâte à choux. To fill a pastry bag, first insert your metal pastry tip into the opening at the tip of the pastry bag. Then fold the top of the bag outward to form a cuff. Use one hand to hold the bag underneath the cuff while you use a rubber spatula in the other hand to scrape the pâte à choux into the bag. Never fill a pastry bag more than two-thirds full or you won't be able to manipulate it. Unfold the cuff and use your hands on the outside of the bag to force all the filling downward while twisting the top of the bag closed. The filled bag should be taut and should not contain air pockets.

All 10 éclairs will fit on one baking sheet (if it's a commercial size, about 18 × 13 inches).

With the baking sheet set vertically to you (a short side of the pan is facing you), pipe 2 rows of 5 éclairs going down the long sides of the baking sheet, piping each éclair crosswise and staggering the éclairs slightly in the two rows.

To help you pipe the éclairs to the correct lengths, you can use a marking pen and a ruler to draw 5-inch lines where you want to place the éclairs on a sheet of parchment paper the size of the baking sheet. Then turn the paper over and place it on the baking sheet. You will be able to see the lines on the "wrong" side of the paper, but you won't get ink on your éclairs.

Another way to pipe straight 5-inch éclairs is to use the blade of a bench knife as a guide. The blade of your bench knife is probably 5 to 6 inches long. Some manufacturers stamp a handy measuring guide right on the blade's edge.

how to pipe éclairs

9. Place the éclair, top side up, on a wire rack and continue until all the éclairs are glazed. If you are filling the éclairs with lemon curd and glazing them with royal icing, as soon as the éclairs have all been dipped in the royal icing glaze, and while the glaze is still wet, grate some lemon zest over the top of each one using a lemon and a fine Microplane grater.

10. Allow the éclairs to rest on the wire rack until the glaze sets and hardens, 15 to 20 minutes. Serve immediately.

pâte à choux for éclairs

Pâte à choux is a unique dough that, after being piped into shapes, rises high in a hot oven, trapping steam inside each pastry, creating a cavity that can later be filled with pastry cream or other fillings. It's not difficult to make, but success depends on following the instructions carefully.

It's always best to use pâte à choux right away, while the dough is still warm.

SPECIAL EQUIPMENT: ELECTRIC MIXER

1 cup (8 ounces/235 grams) water

6 tablespoons (¾ stick/3 ounces/ 85 grams) unsalted butter, cut into several pieces

2 teaspoons sugar

½ teaspoon kosher salt

1 cup (4½ ounces/130 grams) all-purpose flour, sifted (measure first, then sift; see "How to Sift," page 13)

4 large eggs

1. Combine the water, butter, sugar, and salt in a saucepan over medium-high heat and bring to a boil, stirring occasionally. As soon as the mixture comes to a full boil, add the flour all at once and stir rapidly with a wooden spoon to combine everything into a paste. Lower the heat to medium and continue to cook for about 1 minute, stirring constantly, until the dough dries out and starts to form a ball and come away from the sides of the pot.

2. Remove the dough from the saucepan and immediately transfer it to the bowl of an electric mixer fitted with the paddle. Beat on medium speed for 1 or 2 minutes to allow the dough to give off steam and cool just slightly. Then, while beating on medium speed, add the eggs, one at a time, waiting for each egg to be fully incorporated before adding the next. When all the eggs are incorporated, beat on medium-high speed for about 1 minute more.

3. Transfer the dough to a pastry bag (never fill a pastry bag more than two-thirds full) and use immediately for piping éclairs.

vanilla bean pastry cream

A good-quality heavy-bottomed saucepan, such as All-Clad, works best for making pastry cream. To make the smaller amount (for the Banana Cream Pie), you'll need a small saucepan, 1 to 1½ quarts.

After you add the egg yolks, be sure to cook the pastry cream until it is quite thick, like a thick pudding. For an ultra-lush pastry cream, we finish with softened butter. Adding the butter using a food processor, instead of whisking it in by hand, makes this pastry cream silky smooth and shiny. Be sure your butter is room temperature and soft so it will incorporate quickly into the pastry cream.

Pastry cream must be chilled thoroughly before being used, at least 3 or 4 hours. You can make it a day ahead and chill it overnight.

SPECIAL EQUIPMENT: INSTANT-READ OR DIGITAL PROBE THERMOMETER (OPTIONAL), FOOD PROCESSOR

for banana cream pie

MAKES ABOUT 1 ¼ CUPS

½ vanilla bean

½ cup plus 2 tablespoons (5 ounces/ 142 grams) whole milk

½ cup (4 ounces/230 grams) heavy cream

6 tablespoons (2½ ounces/75 grams) sugar

2 tablespoons plus ½ teaspoon (¾ ounce/22½ grams) cornstarch

3 large egg yolks

3 tablespoons (1½ ounces/45 grams) unsalted butter, softened and cut into a few chunks

½ teaspoon pure vanilla extract

¼ teaspoon kosher salt

for raspberries 'n' cream tart and éclairs

MAKES ABOUT 2½ CUPS

1 vanilla bean

1¼ cups (10 ounces/285 grams) whole milk

1 cup (8 ounces/230 grams) heavy cream

¾ cup (5 ounces/150 grams) sugar

¼ cup plus 1 teaspoon (1½ ounces/ 45 grams) cornstarch

6 large egg yolks

6 tablespoons (¾ stick/3 ounces/ 90 grams) unsalted butter, softened

1 teaspoon pure vanilla extract

½ teaspoon kosher salt

1. Split the vanilla bean in half lengthwise and scrape out the seeds using the tip of a paring knife, reserving the vanilla bean scrapings. Place the scraped-out vanilla pod in a saucepan with the milk and cream and set aside.

2. Put the sugar and cornstarch in a bowl and use a whisk to combine. Add the egg yolks and the reserved vanilla bean scrapings and whisk vigorously until well combined and the color of the yolks pales slightly.

3. Meanwhile, scald the milk-cream mixture in the saucepan (bring it to just below boiling point until it steams and little bubbles appear around the edges) over medium-high heat. Remove the saucepan from the heat and temper the yolks by adding a few ladles of the hot milk-cream mixture to the sugar-yolk mixture, whisking to combine. Then scrape all the sugar-yolk mixture from the bowl into the saucepan and place the pan back on the stove over medium-high heat. Return the mixture to a boil while whisking constantly. (If at any time you think the pan is getting too hot and the pastry cream is in danger of scorching, lower the heat as needed or just move the pan on and off the heat, whisking steadily all the time. Note that for the smaller quantity of vanilla pastry cream you should reduce the heat to medium after you add the sugar-yolk mixture, because the smaller quantity will cook faster and may burn. Also, if you are using an electric coil burner, please see "How to Adjust for the Heat on an Electric Coil Burner," page 16.)

4. When the mixture comes to a boil, allow it to boil for about a minute while whisking constantly and vigorously. The pastry cream should be very thick, like a thick pudding. (If the pastry cream is not thick, continue to cook and whisk.) When the pastry cream is thick, remove the saucepan from the heat and transfer the pastry cream to a clean

Your pastry cream should be very thick, like a thick pudding.

bowl. Remove the vanilla bean pod (you can discard the pod or rinse it and use it for vanilla bean sugar, page 64). Stir the pastry cream with a rubber spatula for a few minutes to cool it down to between 140° and 150°F on an instant-read thermometer. (The pastry cream will no longer be scalding hot—you will be able to keep a finger in it—but it must still be warm enough to incorporate the butter, which is added in the next step.)

5. Transfer the pastry cream to the bowl of a food processor. Add the butter and pulse several times, until all the butter is incorporated and the pastry cream is smooth. Then add the vanilla extract and the salt and pulse to combine.

6. Transfer the pastry cream to a clean bowl and place it over a bowl of ice water. Stir occasionally until the pastry cream has cooled, then place a piece of plastic wrap directly over the surface (to prevent a skin from forming). Allow the pastry cream to chill completely before using it, 3 to 4 hours.

maple sugar glaze

This glaze carries a double wallop of pure maple flavor from both maple sugar and maple syrup. Try it on éclairs that have been filled with Maple Pastry Cream (page 178). When the glaze sets and hardens, the maple sugar will crystallize and give you a pleasant, slightly crunchy texture on top of the éclairs.

Maple sugar is available at well-stocked supermarkets such as Whole Foods, or you can order it online (see Sources). Made from the sap of maple trees, it's a treat that's worth tracking down. We prefer Grade B maple syrup because it's dark and flavorful.

⅔ cup (4 ounces/115 grams) maple sugar

¼ teaspoon kosher salt

1½ cups (6 ounces/170 grams) powdered sugar

⅓ cup (2¾ ounces/75 grams) heavy cream

3 tablespoons (1¾ ounces/50 grams) maple syrup

½ teaspoon pure vanilla extract

1. Put the maple sugar and salt in a large bowl, then sift the powdered sugar on top (see "How to Sift," page 13). Set aside.

2. Put the cream and maple syrup in a small saucepan and warm gently over medium heat. You don't want the cream mixture to boil, but to get just warm enough to dissolve the maple and powdered sugars. Stir in the vanilla extract, then pour the cream mixture over the sugars in the bowl, whisking to combine everything until smooth. (The maple sugar may not be completely smooth. That's okay; it will crystallize a bit more after you glaze the éclairs.)

3. Transfer the glaze to an appropriate container for dipping, such as a small loaf pan, and use immediately.

scooped

ICE CREAM AND ICE CREAM SANDWICHES

vanilla bean ice cream and two variations

MAKES ABOUT 1 QUART

Our forager, Peter, takes trips to Tahiti in the South Pacific and comes back with suitcases full of vanilla beans. When he brings them into the restaurants, he presents them in 5-pound stacks of dark brown beans, sticky and fragrant. This feels like being in a TV crime drama about an illicit drug deal until I get a whiff of that fabulous aroma.

This is plain ol' vanilla ice cream—not so plain for being flecked with vanilla bean seeds—and luscious whether eaten in a bowl with a spoon, served with caramel sauce (page 69), or scooped on top of just about any dessert. You can also make the vanilla ice cream base and turn it into either streusel or stracciatella ice cream (see the recipe variations).

The ice creams we produce for the restaurants and the Dahlia Bakery are made in a large professional ice cream maker that turns out a few gallons of ice cream in 15 minutes. But it's not at all difficult to make ice cream at home, and ice cream makers are available in all price ranges (see page 27).

Making vanilla bean ice cream in Dahlia Workshop using an industrial ice cream machine

Most of our ice creams are based on crème anglaise, a custard sauce made by cooking cream and milk carefully with egg yolks and sugar until thickened. For making crème anglaise, a good-quality heavy-bottomed saucepan is best (see "Pots and Pans," page 30).

The crème anglaise base must be chilled for at least a few hours before being churned into ice cream. Chilling the base overnight improves the texture. After being churned in your machine, the ice cream usually must be frozen for several more hours to be firm enough to serve, so plan accordingly.

SPECIAL EQUIPMENT: ICE CREAM MAKER

2 cups (16 ounces/480 grams) heavy
  cream

1 cup (8 ounces/230 grams) whole milk

⅔ cup (4¾ ounces/135 grams) sugar

1 vanilla bean

8 large egg yolks

½ teaspoon pure vanilla extract

1. To make the crème anglaise, place the cream, milk, and sugar in a saucepan. Split the vanilla bean lengthwise and scrape out the seeds using the tip of a paring knife. Reserve the scrapings and add the pod to the saucepan.

2. Place the saucepan over medium-high heat and scald (bring to just below the boiling point until it steams and small bubbles appear around the edges), stirring to dissolve the sugar. Remove the saucepan from the heat.

3. Meanwhile, put the egg yolks and vanilla bean seeds in a bowl and whisk until the yolks are pale yellow. Gradually add a ladle of scalded cream to the bowl of yolks while whisking to warm the yolks. Pour the warmed yolks into the saucepan with the cream mixture and return to medium heat, stirring until the custard is thick enough to coat the back of a spoon.

4. Immediately pour the custard through a fine-mesh strainer into a bowl. (Discard the vanilla pod or rinse, dry, and save for vanilla bean sugar, page 64.) Stir in the vanilla extract. Set the bowl of crème anglaise over a larger bowl of ice water. When cool, cover and refrigerate for at least a few hours or overnight.

5. Churn and freeze the chilled custard in an ice cream maker according to the manufacturer's instructions. (If you are making the streusel or stracciatella ice cream, follow the instructions in the variation.) Remove the ice cream to an airtight container. Cover and freeze several hours or overnight until firm before serving.

FOR STREUSEL ICE CREAM

Vanilla ice cream studded with bits of sweet crunchy streusel—try a scoop with a slice of apple pie!

Cinnamon Vanilla Streusel
(page 68)

Vanilla Bean Ice Cream
custard, chilled and ready to
pour into the ice cream
maker

1. Bake and cool the streusel before churning the ice cream. Preheat the oven to 325°F and place the streusel on a parchment-lined baking sheet, using your fingers to clump it together a bit here and there. Bake until evenly golden brown, about 15 minutes, stirring the streusel with a spatula about halfway through the baking time. Remove the pan from the oven and allow the streusel to cool to room temperature. The streusel will crisp as it cools.

2. When the streusel is cool, place the chilled custard in an ice cream maker to churn and freeze it according to the manufacturer's instructions. When the ice cream is mostly frozen and almost ready to be transferred out of the ice cream machine, gradually add the streusel while the ice cream is still spinning. (You may have to remove the lid, but many ice cream machines have an opening in the lid for mix-ins like chocolate chips, in which case you can add the streusel through the opening.) Turn the ice cream machine off and transfer the ice cream to an airtight container. Cover and freeze for several hours or overnight, until firm enough to serve.

FOR STRACCIATELLA ICE CREAM

By piping melted chocolate right into the spinning ice cream, you get flakes of chocolate that provide crunchy bursts of flavor against a background of pure vanilla.

SPECIAL EQUIPMENT: DISPOSABLE PASTRY BAG OR QUART-SIZE RESEALABLE PLASTIC BAG

1 Vanilla Bean Ice Cream custard, chilled and ready to pour into the ice cream maker

½ cup (3 ounces/85 grams) chopped bittersweet chocolate (see "How to Chop Chocolate," page 12)

1. Place the chilled custard in an ice cream maker to churn and freeze it according to the manufacturer's instructions. Put the chocolate in a heatproof bowl and bring a saucepan with a few inches of hot water to a simmer. When the ice cream is 5 to 10 minutes away from being frozen, set the bowl of chocolate over the barely simmering water (the bottom of the bowl must not touch the water), stirring occasionally until the chocolate is melted. Turn off the heat.

2. When the ice cream is mostly frozen and almost ready to be transferred out of the ice cream machine, but still spinning, transfer the chocolate to a disposable pastry bag and cut only a little off the tip of the bag so you have a very small hole (or put the melted chocolate in a quart-size

resealable plastic bag and cut a little bit off one corner of the bag so you can use it as a pastry bag). Hold your pastry bag over the ice cream machine while it is spinning (Note: you may have to remove the lid, but many ice cream machines have an opening in the lid for mix-ins like chocolate chips, in which case you can just use the opening) and pipe the melted chocolate in a thin, steady stream right into the spinning ice cream. Move your piping bag back and forth as far as the opening allows so the chocolate doesn't all clump up in one place. (But if you do get a few clumps, it's okay—no one will mind finding these extra treats in a scoop of ice cream!)

3. Turn the ice cream machine off and transfer the ice cream to an airtight container. Cover and freeze for several hours or overnight, until firm enough to serve.

buttermilk ice cream

Creamy, sweet, and tangy with a fresh, bright flavor, a scoop of buttermilk ice cream is perfect topping any fruit pie or fruit crisp. This is not a flavor you're likely to be able to buy at the store, so it's well worth making your own. You really have to taste this ice cream to appreciate the difference a cup and a half of buttermilk makes!

Crème anglaise, or classic custard sauce, is best made in a good-quality heavy-bottomed saucepan (see "Pots and Pans," page 30).

The ice cream base must be chilled for a few hours before being churned. Chilling the base overnight improves the texture. After being churned, the ice cream usually must be frozen for several hours to be firm enough to serve, so plan accordingly.

SPECIAL EQUIPMENT: ICE CREAM MAKER

1½ cups (12½ ounces/350 grams) buttermilk

1 teaspoon pure vanilla extract

½ teaspoon kosher salt

2 cups (16 ounces/470 grams) heavy cream

¼ cup (2 ounces/60 grams) sugar

¼ cup (3 ounces/90 grams) honey

8 large egg yolks

1. Put the buttermilk, vanilla extract, and salt in a large bowl. Place a strainer over the bowl. (You will use this setup after you make your crème anglaise.)

2. To make the crème anglaise, put the cream, sugar, and honey in a saucepan and scald (bring to just below the boiling point until it begins to steam and little bubbles appear around the edges), stirring to dissolve the sugar. Remove the saucepan from the heat.

3. Meanwhile, put the egg yolks in a bowl and whisk until the yolks are pale yellow. Gradually add a ladle of the scalded cream to the bowl of yolks while whisking to warm the yolks. Pour the warmed yolks into the saucepan with the cream mixture and return to medium heat, stirring until the custard is thick enough to coat the back of a spoon. Immediately pour the crème anglaise through the strainer into the buttermilk mixture. Set the bowl over a larger bowl of ice water and stir to combine. When cool, cover the bowl and refrigerate for a few hours or overnight.

4. Churn and freeze the chilled custard in an ice cream maker according to the manufacturer's instructions. Transfer the ice cream to an airtight container. Cover and freeze for several hours or overnight until firm before serving.

frozen chocolate custard

If you love chocolate ice cream, mark this page with a sticky note. The rich, deep chocolate flavor and smooth, silky texture of this frozen custard makes it one of the best recipes in the book.

As always, the flavor depends on using good-quality chocolate (see "Our Favorite Chocolates," page 21).

The custard base (crème anglaise) for the ice cream is best made in a good-quality heavy-bottomed pot (see "Pots and Pans," page 30).

The chocolate ice cream base needs to chill for at least a few hours before being frozen in the ice cream machine, but chill it overnight for the best texture. After being churned, the ice cream may need to be frozen for several hours or overnight until it is firm enough to serve, so plan accordingly.

SPECIAL EQUIPMENT: ICE CREAM MACHINE

6 ounces (about 1 cup/170 grams) bittersweet chocolate, roughly chopped (see "How to Chop Chocolate," page 12)

¼ cup (3 ounces/90 grams) honey

1½ cups (12 ounces/340 grams) whole milk

1 cup (8 ounces/230 grams) heavy cream

6 large egg yolks

½ cup (3½ ounces/100 grams) packed brown sugar

2 teaspoons unsweetened cocoa powder

1 tablespoon pure vanilla extract

½ teaspoon kosher salt

1. Place the chocolate and honey in a large bowl. Place a fine-mesh sieve over the bowl and set the bowl near the stove.

2. To make the crème anglaise, combine ¾ cup of the milk with the cream in a saucepan over medium-high heat and scald (bring to just below the boiling point until it begins to steam and little bubbles appear around the edges). Remove from the heat. Meanwhile, in another bowl, combine the egg yolks, brown sugar, and cocoa and use a whisk to whisk until slightly paler in color.

3. Temper the yolks by gradually adding a ladle of the scalded cream mixture to the bowl of yolks while whisking to warm the yolks. Pour the warmed yolk mixture into the saucepan with the cream mixture and return to medium heat, stirring constantly until the mixture is thick enough to coat a spoon. Immediately remove the pan from the heat and pour the crème anglaise through the sieve set over the bowl of chopped chocolate. Allow this to sit for 1 full minute to melt the chocolate, then use a rubber spatula to stir the mixture until smooth.

4. When the mixture is smooth, add the remaining ¾ cup of milk, the vanilla extract, and the salt and mix to combine well. Place the bowl of chocolate custard over a larger bowl of ice water and allow to cool, stirring occasionally with a rubber spatula. When the mixture is cool, cover the surface of the custard with plastic wrap and place it in the refrigerator to chill for at least 2 hours or, preferably, overnight.

5. Churn and freeze the chilled custard in an ice cream maker according to the manufacturer's instructions. Transfer the ice cream to an airtight container. Cover the ice cream and freeze until firm, a few hours or overnight, before serving.

jackie's maple syrup ice cream

My wife, Jackie, makes the easiest ice cream ever! No yolks to separate, no custard to cook—just cream, milk, and maple syrup. Try a scoop of this ice cream on the apple dumpling (page 231) or "Hot Buttered Rum" Apple Pie (page 199).

If you can find Grade B maple syrup, buy it. It's slightly less expensive, but darker and more flavorful than Grade A.

Because this ice cream is not based on a crème anglaise, you can churn it in your ice cream machine right away, as long as your milk and cream are cold when you mix the ingredients together.

SPECIAL EQUIPMENT: ICE CREAM MAKER

2 cups (1 pound plus 1 ounce/485 grams) cold heavy cream

¾ cup (6 ounces/180 grams) cold milk

1¼ cups (13 ounces/375 grams) pure maple syrup, preferably Grade B

½ teaspoon pure vanilla extract

¼ teaspoon kosher salt

1. Put the cream, milk, maple syrup, vanilla extract, and salt in a bowl and, using a whisk, mix lightly, just enough to combine everything well. Pour the mixture into your ice cream maker and freeze according to the manufacturer's instructions.

2. Transfer the ice cream to a container. Cover and freeze for a few hours or overnight, until the ice cream is firm.

oregon pinot noir raspberry sorbet

A recipe in Michele Scicolone's wonderful Italian dessert cookbook, *La Dolce Vita,* influenced me to make this sorbet. I like to use a good Pinot Noir from Oregon, preferably from the Willamette Valley. Adelsheim is one of my favorites, and there's no problem polishing off the rest of the bottle with dinner! Washington produces copious amounts of berries every summer, and we're always looking for ways to use the bounty. The wine gives this sorbet a gorgeous pink-red color and (because of the alcohol content) a smooth, creamy texture. This sorbet is equally delicious made with blackberries.

Chill the sorbet base until cold before churning it. After the sorbet has been churned, it must be frozen for several more hours to be firm enough to serve, so plan accordingly. It's best to use this sorbet within a few days, because after that the wine flavor begins to fade.

SPECIAL EQUIPMENT: FOOD MILL (OPTIONAL), ICE CREAM MAKER

2 pints (4 cups/18 ounces/510 grams) raspberries

1½ cups (10⅝ ounces/300 grams) sugar

1 cup (8 ounces/230 grams) Oregon Pinot Noir or other dry red wine

2 cups (16 ounces/460 grams) water

1. Combine the berries, sugar, wine, and water in a saucepan over medium-high heat. Bring to a boil, stirring occasionally to dissolve the sugar, then reduce the heat and simmer for 15 minutes.

2. Remove the pan from the heat and pass the mixture through a food mill, using the fine disk. Or use a rubber spatula to force the mixture through a sieve.

3. Chill completely, then freeze in an ice cream machine following the manufacturer's directions. Transfer the sorbet to an airtight container and freeze for several hours or overnight, until firm, before serving.

From bottom to top: Oregon Pinot Noir Raspberry Sorbet; Buttermilk Ice Cream; Frozen Chocolate Custard

Pizelle sandwiches filled with frozen chocolate custard and stracciatella ice cream

pizzelle

Pizzelle are Italian wafer cookies that are made from a batter baked on a special iron, which is similar to a small waffle iron. Some pizzella recipes contain anise extract and other flavorings, but we prefer to keep the flavor simple because we use the wafers to make ice cream sandwiches. If you eat pizzelle by themselves, you may think them a little too plain, but the beauty of the wafer is revealed when you press a couple together around a nice thick layer of ice cream. Using pizzelle instead of thicker cookies to make ice cream sandwiches means you get a crisp shell around the ice cream that's easy to bite through and allows the flavor of your homemade ice cream to shine. (See "How to Make Ice Cream Sandwiches," page 339.)

The exact number of wafers this recipe yields will depend on the size of a pizzella your particular iron makes. The nonstick coating on our iron (Chef's Choice) required it to be oiled lightly only the first time it was used. Read the instruction book for your iron before making pizzelle.

The batter must chill for a few hours or overnight before making the pizzelle, so plan accordingly.

SPECIAL EQUIPMENT: ELECTRIC MIXER, PIZZELLE IRON, ½-OUNCE SCOOP (OPTIONAL)

½ cup (2½ ounces/75 grams) all-purpose flour

¼ teaspoon ground cinnamon

¼ teaspoon baking powder

⅛ teaspoon kosher salt

1 large egg

1 large egg white

¼ cup (1¾ ounces/50 grams) sugar

2 teaspoons pure vanilla extract

2 tablespoons (¼ stick) butter, melted and slightly cooled

1. Sift the flour, cinnamon, and baking powder into a bowl or onto a sheet of parchment paper (see "How to Sift," page 13). Add the salt and set the dry ingredients aside.

2. In the bowl of an electric mixer fitted with the whisk, on medium-high speed, whip the egg and egg white, sugar, and vanilla extract together until slightly pale and thick, about 2 minutes.

3. Remove the bowl from the mixer and, using a rubber spatula, fold in the dry ingredients until well combined. Add the butter in 2 additions, folding it in with the rubber spatula.

4. Transfer the batter to a container, cover the surface of the batter with plastic wrap, and refrigerate for 2 to 3 hours or overnight.

5. When you are ready to continue, follow the manufacturer's instructions to heat the iron and cook the pizzelle. To make 4- to 4½-inch pizzelle on our iron, we used a ½-ounce scoop or 1 tablespoon of batter each.

6. Allow the pizzelle to cool completely to room temperature before making ice cream sandwiches. They will get crisper as they cool.

HOW TO MAKE ICE CREAM SANDWICHES

To make 6 ice cream sandwiches, you'll need about 3 cups of the ice cream flavor of your choice (about ½ cup ice cream per sandwich) and 12 pizzelle.

Pizzelle are fragile. To use them for ice cream sandwiches you must use ice cream that is somewhat soft. If your ice cream is too hard, soften it by placing it in the refrigerator for 15 minutes or more, checking it frequently to make sure it softens but doesn't melt.

Place 1 pizzella on the counter, patterned side down, and put a ½ cup scoop of soft ice cream on top (or you can use several smaller scoops). Gently flatten and spread the ice cream with the back of the ice cream scoop or an offset spatula to cover the surface of the wafer. Then sandwich everything together with another pizzella, patterned side up.

Wrap the sandwiches in plastic wrap and freeze until firm but not hard, 2 to 4 hours, depending on how soft your ice cream was. The pizzella ice cream sandwiches are best eaten the same day. If you freeze them overnight, the pizzelle will not be quite as crisp, but the sandwiches will still be delicious.

Don't prepare the ice cream sandwiches more than 1 day ahead or the pizzelle may get soggy. If the ice cream in your sandwiches is frozen too hard, you can temper them by placing them in the refrigerator for 5 minutes or more before serving.

You can use other cookies instead of pizzelle to make ice cream sandwiches—try the truffle cookies (page 133) with Stracciatella Ice Cream (page 328). (Of course, if the cookies have just been baked, let them cool completely before making ice cream sandwiches.) The truffle cookies are somewhat fragile, so if they are too soft to spread with ice cream, you can firm the cookies up in the freezer for 10 minutes or so first.

tomato soup and grilled cheese

tom's tasty tomato soup with brown butter croutons

When I was a kid and my mom made tomato soup, she would cut buttered toast into squares and float them on top of each bowl. My twist on Mom's toast is to make brown butter croutons, though when I'm really feeling feisty I go all the way and make grilled cheese croutons (page 346) to float on the soup.

To cut the bread for the brown butter croutons, take a 4-inch chunk of rustic bread (5 to 6 ounces) and cut off and discard the crusts using a serrated knife. Cut the bread into 4 slices, then cut the slices into 3/4- to 1-inch cubes.

SPECIAL EQUIPMENT: BLENDER

soup

1 tablespoon unsalted butter

1 tablespoon olive oil

1 medium onion, thinly sliced

3 garlic cloves, smashed with the side of a knife and peeled

5 cups canned whole tomatoes in juice

1 cup water

2/3 cup heavy cream

2 teaspoons kosher salt, plus more as needed

1/4 teaspoon freshly ground black pepper, plus more as needed

1/4 teaspoon crushed red pepper flakes

1/4 teaspoon celery seed

1/4 teaspoon dried oregano or 1/2 teaspoon finely chopped fresh oregano

1 tablespoon sugar

brown butter croutons

3 tablespoons unsalted butter

4 slices European-style rustic bread, crusts removed, cut into 3/4- to 1-inch cubes (30 to 36 cubes)

Kosher salt and freshly ground black pepper

1. Heat the butter and olive oil in a large saucepan and sauté the onion and garlic until the onion is translucent, about 5 minutes. Add the tomatoes, water, cream, salt, red pepper flakes, celery seed, oregano, and sugar. Bring to a boil, then lower the heat to a simmer and simmer for 15 minutes.

2. Remove from the heat and puree in batches in the container of a blender. Return the soup to the pot and reheat to a simmer, seasoning to taste with more salt and pepper.

3. Meanwhile, to make the brown butter croutons, preheat the oven to 350°F. Heat the butter in a small pan over medium heat and cook, stirring often, until the butter is golden brown and aromatic, about 3 minutes after the butter melts. Remove from the heat. Put the bread cubes in a bowl and pour the brown butter over them, tossing to coat. Season to taste with salt and pepper and toss again. Spread the bread cubes on a baking sheet and place it in the oven. Bake until the croutons are toasted and golden, about 20 minutes, stirring occasionally. Remove the pan from the oven.

4. Serve the soup hot, garnished with the croutons.

grilled cheese with bacon and avocado

For a soul-satisfying lunch, it's hard to think of anything that can beat a warm grilled cheese sandwich, toasted golden brown and oozing cheese—unless of course it's a warm grilled cheese sandwich with crisp slices of bacon and a layer of lush mashed avocado. My wife, Jackie, likes the avocado inside the sandwich, but I prefer to spread the cool avocado on top of the sandwich after it's been griddled.

Beecher's cheese, a local favorite, made every day in the Pike Place Market, has just opened a cheese-making facility and café at 20th Street and Broadway in Manhattan. My favorite Beecher's cheese is the Flagship Reserve truckle—a special version of the signature semihard cow's milk Flagship that is cloth-bound and open-air aged. (A truckle is a small wheel of cheese.)

Instead of Beecher's Flagship, you can substitute a white cheddar or regular cheddar cheese. Beecher's Flagship cheese is slightly crumbly, so it makes sense to grate it. If your cheese is firmer, you can, if you prefer, thinly slice it instead.

Dahlia Bakery cooks use our potato loaf for this sandwich. You can use any rustic bread as long as it doesn't have large holes; otherwise the cheese will seep through the holes and stick to the pan. The shape and size of your bread slices will depend on the size of your loaf, of course. Our bread slices were about 6 x 4 inches, and we used 12 ounces of cheese in all. If your slices of bread are smaller, you may need only 8 ounces of cheese to make 4 sandwiches.

8 thick-cut bacon slices

1 large ripe avocado

Kosher salt and freshly ground black pepper

A lemon or lime wedge

8 slices rustic bread, cut about ½ inch thick

4 to 6 tablespoons (½ to ¾ stick/2 to 3 ounces) butter, softened, as needed

8 to 12 ounces Beecher's Flagship or white cheddar or regular cheddar, grated, as needed

1. Cook the bacon in a skillet over medium-high heat until golden and crisp on both sides. Remove the bacon from the pan and drain on paper towels. Set aside.

2. Cut the avocado in half, remove the pit, and scoop out the avocado flesh. Put the avocado in a small bowl and mash with a fork. Season to taste with salt and pepper and a squirt of lemon or lime. Set aside.

3. Place the 8 bread slices on a work surface and generously spread one side of each slice of bread with some butter. Turn the bread over so the unbuttered sides are facing up. Top 4 slices of bread with grated cheese, covering the entire surface of the slice of bread and dividing the cheese evenly among the 4 slices. Spread the other 4 slices of bread with the mashed avocado, dividing it evenly, then top the avocado with 2 slices of bacon. Press a cheese-topped bread slice and an avocado-bacon-topped bread slice together, with the fillings on the insides and the buttered sides facing out. You will have 4 sandwiches.

4. Place 2 large sauté pans over medium heat and place 2 sandwiches in each pan. When the first side is golden brown, turn the sandwiches and brown the other side, about 3 minutes per side. If needed, add a little more butter to the pan while browning the sandwiches. When both sides are golden brown and the cheese is melted, remove the sandwiches from the pan, slice them in half on the diagonal, and serve hot.

variations

GRILLED CHEESE WITH HEIRLOOM TOMATO

Make grilled cheese sandwiches as in the master recipe, omitting the bacon, avocado, and lime or lemon wedge. After the 8 slices of bread are placed buttered side down on the work surface, divide the cheese evenly among all 8 slices. Place 1 or 2 slices of tomato (depending on size) on 4 of the slices of bread and season the tomato with salt and pepper, then press a cheese-and-tomato-topped bread slice and a cheese-topped bread slice together to make a sandwich, repeating to make 4 sandwiches. (The tomato will be in the middle of the sandwich with cheese on both sides of it.) Cook the sandwiches as directed in the master recipe. If your tomato slice is thick, you may need to lower the heat, put the lid on the pan, and cook for an extra few minutes to be sure the cheese is melted.

GRILLED CHEESE WITH BASIL PESTO

Make grilled cheese sandwiches as in the master recipe, omitting the bacon, the avocado, and the citrus and seasoning for the avocado. After the 8 slices of bread are placed buttered side down on the work surface, spread about 1 tablespoon pesto (page 347) on 4 slices of the bread. Pile the cheese on the other 4 slices of the bread. Then press a pesto-topped bread slice together with a cheese-topped bread slice to make a sandwich, repeating to make 4 sandwiches. Cook the sandwiches as directed in the master recipe.

GRILLED CHEESE CROUTONS FOR TOMATO SOUP

MAKES ENOUGH GARNISH FOR 6 SERVINGS OF TOMATO SOUP

Make 2 grilled cheese sandwiches following the technique in the master recipe and omitting the bacon, the avocado, and the citrus and seasoning for the avocado (in other words, make 2 plain grilled cheese sandwiches). Using a serrated knife or a chef's knife, cut each sandwich into thirds lengthwise and then into quarters crosswise to make 12 "croutons," for a yield of 24 croutons from the 2 sandwiches. Float the croutons on top of the bowls of tomato soup, dividing them evenly among the bowls.

basil pesto

This recipe makes more pesto than you'll need for grilled cheese sandwiches. Put the rest of the pesto in a small container with the surface covered directly with a piece of plastic wrap and save it for other uses, like saucing pasta or making salad dressing. Pesto also freezes well.

SPECIAL EQUIPMENT: FOOD PROCESSOR

3 cups loosely packed fresh basil leaves (about 2 ounces), washed and dried

2 tablespoons pine nuts, toasted (see "How to Toast and Chop Nuts," page 13)

½ teaspoon minced garlic

1 teaspoon freshly squeezed lemon juice

5 tablespoons extra virgin olive oil

3 tablespoons grated Parmesan cheese

About ½ teaspoon kosher salt

1. Process the basil, pine nuts, garlic, and lemon juice together in the bowl of a food processor until smooth. Slowly add the oil though the feed tube until well combined. Add the Parmesan and pulse a few times to mix, then season with salt to taste.

2. Transfer the pesto to a small container and keep tightly covered and refrigerated until needed.

grilled cheese with caramelized broccoli rabe and fontina

MAKES 4 SANDWICHES

No one has to tell me to eat my greens. I like to cook them just about every way, from sautéing up a pan of ruby chard with garlic and lemon to piling olive-oil-braised kale on a slow-roasted-pork sandwich. So it was a natural for me to throw some chopped broccoli rabe into a smokin' hot pan to get it wilted and a little caramelized, then to layer it between 2 slices of rustic bread with oozy, mellow fontina cheese. The slightly bitter greens spiced up with a few red pepper flakes balance the richness of the cheese. That's my kind of sandwich.

The Dahlia Bakery cooks use our potato loaf to make this sandwich. You can use any rustic bread as long as it doesn't have large holes; otherwise the cheese will seep through the holes and stick to the pan. The shape and size of your bread slices will depend on the size of your loaf, of course.

We love the full, rich flavor of Italian fontina, but if you prefer you can substitute another cheese that's good for melting, like cheddar or jack. The exact amount of cheese you will need depends on the size of the slices you get from your loaf of rustic bread.

1 bunch broccoli rabe (also called *rapini*), about 1 pound, washed and dried

About 5 tablespoons pure olive oil, as needed

½ medium yellow onion, thinly sliced

1 large garlic clove, thinly sliced

Kosher salt

¼ teaspoon crushed red pepper flakes

¼ cup balsamic vinegar

8 slices rustic bread, cut about ½ inch thick

4 to 6 tablespoons softened butter, as needed

8 to 12 ounces fontina cheese, grated (such as Fontina Val d'Aosta)

1. To make the caramelized broccoli rabe, trim off and discard the tough ends; then, using a chef's knife, slice up the broccoli rabe, moving from the leafy ends to the stem ends. You can slice up the leafy part of the broccoli rabe a bit more coarsely, but be sure to slice the stems very thinly so that they will be tender when cooked.

2. Place a very large sauté pan over high heat and get the pan hot. Add the olive oil, then toss in all the broccoli rabe. Stand back, because the oil may spit and splatter. Don't shake the pan or stir right away, because you want the broccoli rabe to caramelize a bit. After a minute or so, shake or stir the broccoli rabe. After a few more minutes, add the onion and garlic, adding a little more oil if needed. Shake the pan or stir until the onion is soft (but not brown), a few minutes more. Season to taste with salt, add the red pepper flakes, then add the balsamic vinegar and allow it to cook off. As soon as the balsamic vinegar cooks off, remove the pan from the heat. (The pan should have been hot enough that your broccoli rabe is fairly dry.) Check the seasoning and add more salt if needed. Spread the broccoli rabe on a baking sheet or a platter and set aside until cool enough to handle.

3. Place the 8 bread slices on a work surface and generously spread one side of each slice of bread with some butter. Turn the bread over so the unbuttered sides are facing up. Top each slice of bread with some of the grated cheese, covering the entire surface and dividing the cheese evenly among the slices. Then, for each slice of bread, cover the cheese with an even layer of the broccoli rabe, dividing it evenly among the 8 slices. Then press 2 slices of bread together, with the cheese and broccoli rabe on the inside and the buttered sides facing out. You will have 4 sandwiches.

4. Place 2 large sauté pans over medium heat and place 2 sandwiches in each pan. When the first side is golden brown, turn the sandwiches and brown the second side, about 3 minutes per side. If needed, add a little more butter to the pan while browning the sandwiches.

5. When both sides are golden brown and the cheese is melted, remove the sandwiches from the pan, slice them in half on the diagonal, and serve hot.

Clockwise from top: Blueberry Jam; Whole Strawberries in Syrup; Orange Marmalade; Peach-Vanilla Jam; Rhubarb Jelly

a bowl full of jelly

JAMS AND JELLIES

ABOUT JAMS AND JELLIES

Small jars of jams and jellies made from seasonal fruit are sold in the Dahlia Bakery year-round. The pastry bakers make refrigerator or freezer preserves rather than using traditional hot-water-bath canning methods, and our cookbook recipes follow suit. We like preserves with a fresh fruit flavor, and the longer cooking of a hot water bath would damage some of our delicate jams and jellies.

Because of the sugar content, most jams and jellies will last for about two months in the refrigerator and longer in the freezer. (The exception is the Whole Strawberries in Syrup, which should be refrigerated and used up within a week.) If you are planning to freeze your jam or jelly, first chill it in the refrigerator for at least 8 hours to allow it to set up, then freeze it.

Superfine sugar is preferred for all jams and jellies because it dissolves quickly, which lessens the chance of crystallization.

For success in making our jams and jellies, be sure to use the type of pectin specified in the recipe, and don't change the amount of sugar.

Our pastry bakers use apple pectin because of the delicate texture and clarity it adds to jams and jellies. Apple pectin is activated at 220°F, so when using it you must check the temperature of the simmering jelly with a candy or digital probe thermometer. A preserve made with apple pectin requires less sugar than preserves made with typical brands of supermarket pectin, which means more freedom to control the amount of sugar in the finished preserves.

The rhubarb jelly recipe calls for food-grade powdered apple pectin, which is a professional product, available online and specially formulated for jelly and jam making (see Sources). When we call for apple pectin, this is the product we are referring to; we are not suggesting you make homemade pectin from apple peels.

The peach jam calls for Pomona's Universal Pectin, which is available at some supermarkets, such as Whole Foods, and online. We like Pomona's because it doesn't require sugar to jell, which means you can use less sugar in your jam or jelly, and it doesn't require much cooking time. Since Pomona's Pectin is calcium activated, you'll find both a large packet of pectin powder and a small packet of calcium powder when you open the box. The directions on the Pomona's box tell you how to make "calcium water," but we don't use the calcium packet because the peaches already contain enough calcium to activate the pectin and adding the extra calcium makes the jam too thick and clumpy. So, when making our recipe for peach jam with Pomona's Universal Pectin, use only the pectin packet and ignore the calcium packet.

Citric acid, available as a granular white powder, is a mild natural acid that comes from citrus fruit. It increases the acidity of jams and jellies, helps prevent oxidation, and helps pectin gel. You can find citric acid (also called *sour salt*) at some supermarkets, sometimes in the bulk section or near the canning supplies, or online.

blueberry jam

This is the easiest jam recipe in this book, so start here if you've never made jams or jellies before. Blueberry jam is delicious spread on toast, biscuits, muffins, or scones or layered with yogurt and granola for a parfait (page 112). Try warming up some of this jam with a good splash of maple syrup, then pour it over pancakes.

We add Pinot Noir to the jam because we like the way the wine complements the flavor of berries. Instead of blueberries, you could substitute huckleberries.

Blueberries naturally contain plenty of pectin, so you can make jam without adding commercial pectin.

We prefer superfine sugar for all jams and jellies because it dissolves more quickly.

Store the jam in the refrigerator for up to 2 months or pack it into freezer containers with lids and, after the jam is set and chilled, freeze for longer storage.

SPECIAL EQUIPMENT: GLASS JARS WITH LIDS, SUCH AS 2 PINT JARS, OR OTHER CONTAINERS

3 cups (1 pound/454 grams) blueberries

½ cup (4 ounces/110 grams) water

½ cup (4 ounces/110 grams) Pinot Noir or other dry red wine

2 cups (1 pound/454 grams) sugar, preferably superfine

½ cup (5½ ounces/160 grams) light corn syrup

¼ cup (2 ounces/55 grams) freshly squeezed lemon juice

1 teaspoon pure vanilla extract

½ teaspoon citric acid (see "About Jams and Jellies," page 352)

¼ teaspoon grated lemon zest

1. Combine the berries, water, wine, and sugar in a pot and bring to a simmer over medium heat. Simmer until most of the berries pop but do not turn to mush, about 15 minutes, stirring occasionally with a rubber or silicone spatula. Add the corn syrup and lemon juice and cook for 1 minute more.

2. Remove the pot from the heat and add the vanilla, citric acid, and lemon zest. Ladle the jam into the jars. Place a piece of plastic wrap directly on the surface of the jam in each jar (to prevent a skin from forming) and allow the jam to cool to room temperature.

3. When the jam is at room temperature, remove the plastic wrap and screw the lids on the jars, then place the jars in the refrigerator until set, at least 8 hours.

peach-vanilla jam

This fragrant vanilla-scented jam is easy to make. You can use either peaches or nectarines; just be sure your fruit is delicious and ripe but not overly soft.

If your peaches have thin skins, you don't have to peel them, and you don't have to peel nectarines. If your peaches have very thick skins, you may want to peel them before chopping.

We use Pomona's Universal Pectin in this jam (but we don't use the calcium packet that's included in the pectin box). Pomona's Universal Pectin, which doesn't require sugar to jell, is available at well-stocked supermarkets such as Whole Foods, and also online.

It's best to use a heavy-bottomed saucepan for jam making (see "Pots and Pans," page 30).

Store the jam in the refrigerator for up to 2 months or pack it into freezer containers with lids and, after the jam is set and chilled, freeze for longer storage.

SPECIAL EQUIPMENT: GLASS JARS WITH LIDS, SUCH AS 2 PINT JARS, OR OTHER CONTAINERS

2½ pounds (about 6/1 kilogram/ 137 grams) peaches or nectarines, peeled or unpeeled (see "How to Peel a Peach," page 219)

1½ cups (10 ounces/283 grams) sugar, preferably superfine

½ cup (4½ ounces/125 grams) corn syrup

1 tablespoon plus 2 teaspoons freshly squeezed lemon juice

½ vanilla bean, split in half lengthwise

2 teaspoons Pomona's Universal Pectin (see "About Jams and Jellies," page 352)

1. Remove the peach flesh from the pits and roughly chop into about ¼- to ½-inch chunks using a chef's knife. (You should have about 7 cups chopped fruit.) Put the chopped peaches in a bowl with 1 cup of the sugar, the corn syrup, and the lemon juice.

2. Use the tip of a paring knife to scrape the seeds from the vanilla bean and add both the scrapings and the pod to the peaches. Stir to combine everything well.

3. Put the remaining ½ cup sugar and the pectin in a medium bowl and whisk to combine. Set aside.

4. Put the peach mixture in a large saucepan over medium-high heat and bring the liquid (peach juices, corn syrup, and dissolved sugar) to a boil. Then reduce the heat to a simmer and simmer for 15 minutes, adjusting the heat as needed and stirring occasionally. (There is no need to skim the foam even if you see some.)

5. Add about a cup of the hot peach mixture to the bowl of pectin-sugar mixture and whisk to form a paste. Scrape the paste back into the saucepan of peaches, return to a simmer, and simmer for 4 to 5 more minutes, stirring frequently.

6. Remove the jam from the heat and ladle it into jars, removing the vanilla pod. (You can save the vanilla bean, dry it off, and use it for vanilla bean sugar, page 64.) Place a piece of plastic wrap directly on the surface of the jam in each jar (to avoid forming a skin) and allow the jam to cool to room temperature. When the jam is at room temperature, remove the plastic wrap and screw the lids on the jars, then place the jam in the refrigerator until set, at least 8 hours.

orange marmalade

Citrus marmalade is my personal favorite preserve for slathering on biscuits, scones, or toast. That being said, marmalade is a fussy, time-consuming, and labor-intensive process. Before you get started, please note that the recipe requires a triple blanching of the julienned zest and 3 hours of slow simmering. But if you're up for it, this beautiful marmalade is well worth the trouble.

You can use any variety of orange, as long as it's juicy and flavorful. We often use Valencia, but, when available, we especially like Cara Cara, a navel orange grown in California that has a pink-orange peel, rosy flesh, and exceptionally sweet flavor. Plus the Cara Cara is seedless, so you won't have to pick out the seeds.

When you buy the oranges at the store, be sure to weigh them and buy exactly 1¼ pounds to make the marmalade. To make a successful marmalade, the weight of the sugar and corn syrup must equal the weight of the fruit. So, for the ratio of ingredients in this recipe to be correct, you must be careful to use 1¼ pounds of oranges for the julienned zest and pulp. To make tangerine marmalade, substitute 1¼ pounds of tangerines (about 6 tangerines—but be sure to weigh them) for the oranges.

In addition to the 1¼ pounds of oranges for julienned zest and pulp, buy 1 extra orange to yield the ½ teaspoon grated zest and the ¼ cup orange juice called for at the end of the recipe. Zest this additional orange first, then juice it.

Blanching is a crucial step because it makes the zests tender. We triple-blanch and change the water each time, which eliminates the bitterness. Traditional marmalades may leave in a little bitterness, but our version is sweet without being bitter.

Low heat and a long simmer make the julienned orange peel toothsome and tender, not tough. Also, keep the heat low so you don't caramelize the orange peel in the sugar syrup, which would ruin the taste and texture.

If you find it difficult to keep your burner at a low setting for the long, slow simmering time required in this recipe, you may want to buy a heat diffuser.

Use a good-quality heavy-bottomed pot to simmer the marmalade (see "Pots and Pans," page 30).

Store the marmalade in the refrigerator for up to 2 months or pack it into freezer containers with lids and, after the marmalade is set and chilled, freeze for longer storage.

SPECIAL EQUIPMENT: FOOD PROCESSOR, CANDY THERMOMETER OR DIGITAL PROBE THERMOMETER, GLASS JARS WITH LIDS, SUCH AS 2 PINT JARS, OR SIMILAR CONTAINERS

1¼ pounds (570 grams) oranges, about 3 depending on size (note: the weight of the oranges is important here, see headnote)

18¼ cups cold water

1 vanilla bean

1½ cups (10½ ounces/300 grams) sugar, preferably superfine

¾ cup plus 2 tablespoons (9½ ounces/270 grams) light corn syrup

¼ cup (2 ounces/55 grams) freshly squeezed orange juice

¼ cup (2 ounces/55 grams) freshly squeezed lime juice

½ teaspoon grated orange zest

¾ teaspoon citric acid (see "About Jams and Jellies," page 352)

1. Using a sharp knife, slice off the very top and bottom of each orange. (The slice should be deep enough that you see a circle of flesh on the top and bottom of the orange.) Discard the tops and bottoms.

2. Make 2 lengthwise incisions in the skin of the orange, spaced evenly apart, and going in deep enough to reach the flesh without cutting into it. Then work your fingers along the groove of each cut and carefully pull the peel (along with all the white pith) away from the orange, doing your best to remove it in large pieces. (It will be easier to make nice even julienne from large pieces of peel than from a bunch of small scraps.)

3. After the oranges are peeled, roughly chop the orange flesh. The best way to do this (unless your oranges are seedless) is to slice the oranges crosswise first so you can pick out and discard any seeds, then chop. Set the chopped orange aside in the bowl of a food processor.

4. Slice the peels (with the pith attached) into a julienne as thin as possible (about ⅛ inch).

5. Place 6 cups of the cold water and the julienned peels in a pot over medium-high heat. Bring the water to a boil, then reduce the heat to a simmer and simmer for 10 minutes. Remove the pot from the heat and pour the contents through a sieve, reserving the peels and discarding the water.

6. Place the peels back in the pot with another 6 cups of cold water and repeat the process, simmering again for 10 minutes. Remove the pot from the heat and pour the contents through a sieve, reserving the peels and discarding the water.

7. Place the peels back in the pot for a third time with another 6 cups of cold water. This last blanching time, simmer the peels for 20 minutes. Remove the pot from the heat and pour the contents through a sieve, discarding the water and reserving the blanched peels. Place the blanched peels in a bowl.

8. Cut the vanilla bean in half lengthwise. Using the tip of a paring knife, scrape out all the seeds and add the scrapings to the chopped orange flesh in the bowl of a food processor. (You can save the pod for vanilla bean sugar, page 64.) Pulse 10 to 15 times, until you have an evenly chunky paste. Transfer the orange pulp to the bowl with the reserved blanched peels. When you combine the pulp and the peels, you should have 2½ cups (20 ounces/570 grams) fruit.

9. Place the sugar, corn syrup, and remaining ¼ cup of water in a heavy-bottomed saucepan over medium-high heat, stirring with a whisk to combine, and bring to a boil. Brush down the sides of the pan with a clean pastry brush dipped in water (to prevent crystallization) and boil the sugar mixture until it reads 240°F on a candy or digital probe thermometer.

10. Add the orange pulp and peels to the sugar mixture and reduce the heat to a very gentle simmer over low heat. (If you are using an electric coil burner, see "How to Adjust for the Heat on an Electric Coil Burner," page 16.) Simmer the marmalade for about 3 hours or until the peels are translucent and the marmalade is thick. Any liquid that remains will be syrupy, not watery.

11. During this 3-hour cooking time, the marmalade must not boil vigorously or the peels will become tough instead of tender and translucent. You are looking for a "one bubble" simmer. After the first hour of cooking, start skimming off any foam or debris that rises to the surface, using a large, wide spoon. But don't start skimming until you've simmered the marmalade for 1 hour, because it's not effective. After an hour, the foam solidifies and is easier to skim. Always be careful when skimming not to skim too much of the marmalade away (see "How to Skim Marmalades and Jellies," page 359).

12. After the 3 hours of simmering, when the marmalade is thick, remove the pot from the heat, transfer the marmalade to a bowl, and allow to cool to room temperature.

13. When the marmalade is completely cool, stir in the orange and lime juices, the orange zest, and the citric acid.

14. Ladle the marmalade into the jars (2 pint jars will not be completely full). Cover the jars with lids and refrigerate for at least 8 hours before serving.

HOW TO SKIM MARMALADES AND JELLIES

For the clearest, most beautiful result, certain preserves must be skimmed of the debris that rises to the surface while they are simmering. One trick is to swirl the pan first, which collects the debris into a circle in the center of the pan. Then use a big heatproof spoon to skim off the scum.

If you keep a pitcher of water near the stove, you can dip your spoon into the water and shake off the debris. Then when you skim again, you have a clean spoon.

Always be careful not to skim too much or too frequently. Don't skim with a ladle—you will lose too much of your precious jelly, jam, or marmalade.

A large, wide, shallow metal spoon is the best tool for this job.

Also, skim foam away only when directed to do so by the recipe. Many jams, for example, don't need to be skimmed even if you see a bit of foam. In other recipes, if you start skimming foam too early in the procedure, you will lose too much volume.

To remove the last bit of scum from your finished marmalade or jelly, turn off the heat and use the paper towel trick. Place a paper towel directly over the surface of the pot, leaving one corner sticking up. Grab the corner of the paper towel and peel it from the surface—the last of the foam will come right off with it.

whole strawberries in syrup

MAKES ABOUT 3 CUPS

When strawberries are at their summertime peak, try simmering them whole in a syrup made from their own juices until the berries are delicately soft but still hold their shape. For a very special brunch or breakfast, make Malted Buttermilk Biscuits (page 93) or Serious Biscuits (page 89) and serve each one with a pat of butter plus a couple whole berries and a drizzle of syrup. For a splendid strawberry sundae, ladle the strawberries and syrup over scoops of ice cream. Or gently reheat the strawberries and syrup as a topping for pancakes or French toast.

Use beautiful, perfectly sweet and fragrant berries that are small or medium in size but not overly soft or mushy. Don't use large strawberries for this recipe, as they will not cook properly.

This is not really a jelly or jam—therefore not something you can store for a long time—and the texture of the berries won't survive freezing and thawing. So it's best to refrigerate the strawberries in syrup and use them up within a week.

Superfine sugar is preferred for this recipe because it dissolves quickly.

Use a good-quality heavy-bottomed saucepan (see "Pots and Pans," page 30).

SPECIAL EQUIPMENT: CANDY THERMOMETER OR DIGITAL PROBE THERMOMETER, GLASS JARS WITH LIDS, SUCH AS 2 PINT JARS, OR SIMILAR CONTAINERS

4 cups (1 pound/454 grams) small or medium strawberries

1½ cups (12 ounces/340 grams) sugar, preferably superfine

½ cup (5½ ounces/160 grams) light corn syrup

¼ cup (2 ounces/57 grams) water

2 tablespoons freshly squeezed orange juice

2 tablespoons freshly squeezed lemon juice

½ teaspoon citric acid (see "About Jams and Jellies," page 352)

1. Stem and hull the strawberries. Set aside.

2. In a heavy-bottomed saucepan, combine the sugar, corn syrup, and water. Bring the mixture to a boil over medium-high heat and cook to a temperature of 240°F on a candy or digital probe thermometer, brushing down the sides of the pan occasionally with a clean pastry brush dipped in water.

3. Add the strawberries, turn the heat down to medium, and stir gently with a rubber spatula. (If using an electric coil burner, see "How to Adjust for the Heat on an Electric Coil Burner," page 16.) The liquid will be very thick and almost candylike at first but will thin out as the berries release their juices, and it will become easier to gently stir them. As the berries release their juices, the liquid will turn red.

If the berries become very soft and seem in danger of breaking when being stirred, lift the saucepan slightly and give it a gentle swirl a few times instead of stirring with the spatula. After you swirl the pot, you will need to brush down the sides again with a clean, wet pastry brush. Continue to gently cook the strawberries until they are soft but not falling apart and are almost covered by a clear red liquid (8 to 10 minutes of cooking time after the berries are added to the pot, but exact cooking time depends on their ripeness). Remove the pot from the heat.

4. Use a slotted spoon to carefully remove the berries from the pot and place them in glass jars, dividing them evenly.

5. Brush down the sides of the pot with a clean wet pastry brush and return the pot to medium-high heat. Bring the liquid back to a steady boil. Cook for 5 minutes at a steady boil, stirring frequently. Remove the pot from the heat and, using a large metal spoon or a fine-mesh skimmer, skim off any foam and debris that has risen to the surface (see "How to Skim Marmalades and Jellies," page 359). Then add the orange and lemon juices and the citric acid to the syrup in the pot, whisking to combine.

6. Ladle the syrup over the strawberries in the jars, dividing it equally. (The two glass pint jars will not be entirely full.) Place plastic wrap directly over the surface of the preserves in the jars and allow cool to room temperature. When the preserves are at room temperature, cover and refrigerate for up to 1 week.

rhubarb jelly

This beautiful preserve is composed of small, tender pieces of rhubarb suspended in a clear rose-colored jelly. Jelly recipes require more time and commitment than jam, but if you're up for the challenge, the result will reward you.

As for other jams and jellies, the weight of your fruit must be the same as the weight of your sugar, so be sure to check that, after trimming away the tough ends and dicing the stalks, you have 4 cups of diced rhubarb, which will equal the weight of the sugar.

The ingredient list for this jelly calls for food-grade powdered apple pectin. Although it takes effort to find apple pectin, we favor it here for better texture and clarity. Supermarket pectin won't give you a jelly that's sparkling clear and delicate. (For more information on apple pectin, see "About Jams and Jellies," page 352.)

When you work with apple pectin, you must bring the jam to 220°F for the pectin to set properly, so you'll need a digital probe or candy thermometer (see Sources).

The ratio of pectin to liquid is important, so be sure to measure the liquid you get after draining the sugared rhubarb and adjust the amount to be exactly 2 cups, as directed in the recipe.

We prefer superfine sugar for jams and jellies because it dissolves more quickly.

The sugared rhubarb needs to rest overnight, before continuing with the jelly, so plan accordingly.

Store the rhubarb jelly in the refrigerator for up to 2 months or pack it in freezer containers with lids and, after the jelly is set and chilled, freeze for longer storage.

SPECIAL EQUIPMENT: CANDY THERMOMETER OR DIGITAL PROBE THERMOMETER, GLASS JARS WITH LIDS, SUCH AS 2 PINT JARS, OR SIMILAR CONTAINERS

About 1½ pounds (680 grams) rhubarb, tough ends trimmed, to yield 4 cups diced rhubarb

2½ cups (1 pound plus 2 ounces/ 500 grams) sugar, preferably superfine

1 tablespoon plus 2 teaspoons powdered apple pectin (see Sources)

3 tablespoons (1½ ounces/43 grams) freshly squeezed lime juice

3 tablespoons (1½ ounces/43 grams) freshly squeezed orange juice

¾ teaspoon citric acid (see "About Jams and Jellies," page 352)

⅛ teaspoon grated orange zest

1. Cut the rhubarb into ½-inch dice (pay attention to the size of the dice and be sure they are not larger than ½ inch), then place it in a bowl. If you have more than 4 cups, set the excess aside for another use.

2. Add 2 cups of the sugar, mixing to coat the rhubarb evenly. Cover the bowl with plastic wrap and refrigerate overnight to allow time for the sugar to draw the liquid from the rhubarb. For the first 1 or 2 hours, every once in a while, take the rhubarb out of the refrigerator, uncover, and stir to get all the sugar dissolved into the rhubarb liquid. Then re-cover and return to the refrigerator.

3. When you are ready to continue the jelly, remove the plastic wrap from the bowl of rhubarb and stir gently to dissolve any remaining sugar. Then pour the rhubarb into a sieve set over a bowl to strain the liquid from the rhubarb, pressing gently on the rhubarb to extract as much liquid as possible. Measure the liquid. (Reserve the rhubarb separately.) You should have 2 cups of liquid. If you have less, add enough water to total 2 cups. If you have more than 2 cups liquid, get rid of the excess. (You can mix it with ice and seltzer for a refreshing "chef's treat!") Put the 2 cups of rhubarb liquid in a saucepan and bring to a boil over medium-high heat.

4. Meanwhile, in a clean dry bowl, use a whisk to mix the remaining ½ cup sugar with the pectin until well combined and no pockets of pectin remain. Add a ladle or two of the boiling liquid to the sugar-pectin mixture and whisk until smooth, then add this mixture back to the saucepan of boiling liquid and return the mixture to a boil, stirring gently. (Don't stir or whisk vigorously, because you don't want to get air bubbles into your jelly.)

5. Reduce the heat to a simmer (if using an electric coil burner, see "How to Adjust for the Heat on an Electric Coil Burner," page 16) and allow the liquid to steadily simmer, skimming as needed, until the temperature is 220°F on a candy or digital probe thermometer (see "How to Skim Marmalades and Jellies," page 359).

6. Remove the saucepan from the heat and stir in the lime and orange juices and the citric acid, then add the reserved rhubarb. Return the saucepan to high heat and return the mixture *just* to a boil. Immediately remove the saucepan from the heat and allow it to sit at room temperature with a piece of plastic wrap placed directly on the surface for at least 1 hour, until the jelly has cooled and thickened enough for the rhubarb to stay suspended in it rather than floating to the top. The rhubarb should be soft but should still have texture and should stay in distinct pieces.

7. When the jelly has cooled to this point, gently stir in the orange zest, evenly distributing both the zest and the diced rhubarb throughout the mixture.

8. Carefully ladle the jelly into glass jars (the jelly won't completely fill 2 pint jars) and place plastic wrap directly over the surface (to keep a skin from forming). Refrigerate the jars (with plastic wrap directly on the surface but without lids) until completely cold, preferably overnight. When the jelly is cold, remove the plastic wrap and cover the jars with lids.

Our Joints

"Deliciousness served with graciousness" is the axis of our company mission statement. Everything we do starts there and gets better. When we started in 1989 with the Dahlia Lounge, we never dreamed that twenty-some years later we would be running fifteen different, diverse, and successful businesses and employ 700 people, including many world-class artisans in their fields. Our customers demand sustainable food sourcing as organic and local as possible, and we give it to them. We even started our own twenty-acre farm to help fill the needs, but also to practice what we preach. Our teammates love to gather for the plant in spring and the weeding and harvest throughout the summer and fall, and party hearty at the annual Beastfeast, where my neighbor's lamb gets a free ride on my applewood rotisserie.

When you're in Seattle, stop by one of our joints and check us out. Here's a quick list of them and what we serve there. Or if you're not coming out our way, try our Rub with Love spices and sauces. (For contact information on the Tom Douglas restaurants and products, see Sources.)

DAHLIA LOUNGE AND DAHLIA BAKERY

This is where it all started. It tickles me that Dahlia has been called the quintessential Seattle restaurant. Dahlia is known for five-spice rotisserie duck, potstickers, and fresh Dungeness crab cakes. The Dahlia Bakery is located right next door.

Dahlia Lounge
2001 Fourth Avenue
Seattle, WA 98121
(206) 682-4142

Dahlia Bakery
2001 Fourth Avenue
Seattle, WA 98121
(206) 441-4540

ETTA'S

Located on the north end of the Pike Place Market, this is our fish house, featuring wild king salmon and Dungeness crab but without forgetting the burger and steak lovers. Etta's also serves a terrific brunch.

Etta's
2020 Western Avenue
Seattle, WA 98121
(206) 443-6000

PALACE KITCHEN

Fitted out with a woodburning grill, a large U-shaped bar, an open kitchen, and a rustic menu including wood-grilled chicken wings and one of the city's most popular burgers, Palace is the place for late-night dining.

Palace Kitchen
2030 Fifth Avenue
Seattle, WA 98121
(206) 448-2001

LOLA

Located next to the Hotel Andra, Lola's menu is Greek inspired with handmade pita, ouzo-splashed kebabs, and roast lamb. Lola channels the spirit of my wife, Jackie's, Greek heritage.

Lola
2000 Fourth Avenue
Seattle, WA 98121
(206) 441-1430

SERIOUS PIE VIRGINIA AND SERIOUS PIE WESTLAKE

The two Serious Pies were developed as a natural extension of our bread bakery. This is pizza with a bread baker's soul—my vision of a simple but "serious" pie with a blistered crust, light textured but with structure and bite, and exactly the right amount of pizza toppings.

Serious Pie Virginia
316 Virginia Street
Seattle, WA 98121
(206) 838-7388

Serious Pie Westlake
401 Westlake Avenue North
Seattle, WA 98109
(206) 436-0052

SERIOUS BISCUIT/DAHLIA WORKSHOP

In addition to Serious Pie Westlake, the building at Westlake and Harrison in South Lake Union houses Serious Biscuit, the place for hearty breakfast and lunch sandwiches on our fluffy buttermilk biscuits, as well as the Dahlia Workshop, the workspace for our bread and pastry bakers.

Serious Biscuit/Dahlia Workshop
401 Westlake Avenue North
Seattle, WA 98109
(206) 436-0052

SEATOWN

On the corner right next to Etta's, the view over Victor Steinbrueck Park gives this newish little joint the feel of an instant Seattle classic. Come here for English muffin breakfast sandwiches and pour-over coffee or a cocktail and a smoked fish plate. Seatown also features rotisserie plates from our adjoining to-go spot, the Rub with Love Shack.

The Rub with Love Shack sells Rub with Love seasoned rotisserie meats and poultry to go as well as sandwiches made from the meat and poultry. The entire line of Rub with Love products is available for sale here.

Seatown and Rub with Love Shack
2010 Western Avenue
Seattle, WA 98121
(206) 436-0390

CUOCO

Located in the Terry Building in South Lake Union, Cuoco (which means "cook" in Italian) is a romantic pasta house where the focus is on the fresh pasta-making station located front and center when you walk in the door.

Cuoco
310 Terry Avenue North
Seattle, WA 98109
(206) 971-0710

BRAVE HORSE TAVERN

Also in the Terry Building, this big bustling tavern boasts shuffleboards, communal tables, juicy tavern burgers, wood-fired pretzels, and twenty-five beer taps.

Brave Horse Tavern
310 Terry Avenue North
Seattle, WA 98109
(206) 971-0717

TING MOMO

This Tibetan home cooking is close to my heart. My longtime Tibetan chef, Dekyi, lovingly reproduces the handcrafted dumplings of her homeland.

Ting Momo
Special Events and Catering
(206) 448-2001

ALL-CLAD METALCRAFTERS

For quality pots and pans. Widely sold in kitchenware stores and online stores.
800-255-2523
www.allclad.com

AMAZON.COM

For commercial-weight rimmed baking sheets (half sheet pans), parchment paper sheets, parchment cake circles, tulip papers, cardboard cake rounds, disposable plastic pastry bags, tabletop deep fryers, digital probe thermometers, citric acid, Pomona Universal Pectin, maple sugar, vanilla beans, and many more items, including tools, baking pans, electrical equipment, and ingredients, as well as Amazon's Tom Douglas by Pinzon line of knives, spatulas, and other kitchen tools.
www.amazon.com

BEECHER'S CHEESE

For Beecher's Flagship and other fine artisan cheeses.
Seattle store: 206-956-1964
New York store: 212-466-3340
www.beechershandmadecheese.com

BOB'S RED MILL

For cornmeal, almond meal, steel-cut oats, large-chip unsweetened coconut (called "coconut flakes"), and many flours and grains. Widely sold at supermarkets.
www.bobsredmill.com

CHUKAR CHERRIES

For Northwest dried cherries.
800-624-9544
www.chukar.com

FRAN'S

For caramel sauce (if you don't want to make your own), plus amazing chocolates and candies. Try the gray and smoked salt caramels!
800-422-3726
www.franschocolates.com

GUITTARD CHOCOLATE

For bittersweet, milk, and white chocolates sold in convenient meltable wafers, as well as cocoa.
650-697-4424
www.guittard.com

KING ARTHUR FLOUR

For all-purpose, whole wheat, bread, cake, almond, and pastry flours; maple sugar; chocolate chunks; bittersweet and unsweetened chocolate wafers (convenient for melting); bittersweet, milk, chocolate, and white chocolate bars; cocoa powder; large-chip unsweetened coconut (called "coconut flakes"); colored sugars; baking pans; ice cream scoops for muffins and cupcakes; pizzelle irons; metal bench knives and pastry blenders; probe thermometers; kitchen scales; disposable plastic pastry bags; tulip papers; parchment paper; rolling pins; silicone rolling mats; and more.
800-827-6836
www.kingarthurflour.com

KITCHEN AID

For electric stand mixers. Widely sold at kitchenware stores and online stores.

800-541-6390

www.kitchenaid.com

L'EPICERIE

For powdered apple pectin.

www.lepicerie.com

POMONA UNIVERSAL PECTIN

For Pomona Universal Pectin. Also available at supermarkets such as Whole Foods.

www.pomonapectin.com

SCHARFFEN BERGER

For bittersweet chocolate bars, slabs, and chunks, unsweetened chocolate, and cocoa powder.

800-930-4528

www.scharffenberger.com

SUR LA TABLE

For commercial-weight rimmed baking sheets; all types of baking pans; quality pots and pans; electrical equipment such as stand mixers, deep fryers, ice cream makers, and food processors; mixing bowls; rolling pins; silicone mats; timers; thermometers; kitchen scales; propane torches; knives; measuring cups and spoons; hand tools; round cake cardboards; and more.

800-243-0852

www.surlatable.com

THEO CHOCOLATE

For organic, fair trade chocolate produced in Seattle "from bean to bar."

(206) 632-5100

www.theochocolate.com

TOM DOUGLAS.COM

For information about the Tom Douglas restaurants and the Dahlia Bakery, Tom Douglas cookbooks, and Rub with Love products.

www.tomdouglas.com

VALRHONA CHOCOLATE

For bittersweet and white chocolates and cocoa powder.

www.valrhona-chocolate.com

WHOLE FOODS

For a variety of quality chocolates, Pomona Universal Pectin, maple sugar, King Arthur flour, Bob's Red Mill, Dufour all-butter puff pastry.

www.wholefoodsmarkets.com

WILLIAMS-SONOMA

For commercial-weight rimmed baking sheets; all types of baking pans; quality pots and pans; electrical equipment such as stand mixers, food processors, ice cream makers, and deep fryers; knives; measuring cups and spoons; mixing bowls; rolling pins; silicone mats; timers; thermometers; kitchen scales; propane torches; and more.

800-541-1262

www.williams-sonoma.com

Acknowledgments

The three dozen or so pastry bakers, bread bakers, and retail staff that show up at the Dahlia Workshop (production bakery) and Dahlia Bakery (retail bakery) every day—crazy early—to shape bread, roll pastry through the dough sheeter, load baking sheets into convection ovens, decorate cookies with icing-loaded pastry bags, fill pie shells with coconut pastry cream, box up layer cakes, chat with the customers, and ring up sales, are the heroes of this book. You'll find their portraits on pages vi to vii. I owe all of them my heartfelt thanks.

In particular, Gwen LeBlanc, bakery production chef, and Stacy Fortner, pastry chef, aided us with much invaluable advice and assistance on the English muffin, pastry, and dessert recipes. Molly Melkonian, Dahlia Bakery manager, shared her cake decorating expertise. Etta's/Seatown chef, Adrienne Lasko, worked with us on some of the savory recipes.

To those who did the heavy lifting of transforming my notion of writing a Dahlia Bakery cookbook into a solid reality, I thank my longtime associate and coauthor Shelley Lance for developing, writing, and testing recipes, as well as the ridiculously talented pastry chef Garrett Melkonian for working on a whopping chunk of the recipe development. For the nuts and bolts of recipe testing, thanks go to Julie Hartley and Beth Minker.

For multiple flights from SFO to Sea-Tac airport over the course of an almost month-long photo shoot resulting in hundreds of mouthwatering photos, I thank photographer Ed Anderson, as well as the photographer's assistant and my friend and former employee, Sarah Flotard.

There would be no cookbook without my agent, Judith Riven, who answers all my phone calls, and the hardworking team at William Morrow, including Cassie Jones, Jessica McGrady,

Liate Stehlik, Lynn Grady, Tavia Kowalchuk, Megan Swartz, Shawn Nicholls, Lorie Pagnozzi, Lorie Young, and Karen Lumley.

Thanks also go to tireless PR queen Carrie Bachman. Throughout the cookbook process, my highly efficient personal assistant, Jessica Moore, kept everything sorted out and all of us on the right track.

As always, I would not be writing cookbooks and gallivanting around the country promoting them if I didn't have my ace team here in Seattle running the businesses and minding both the store and the stove. My everlasting thanks go to my wife, Jackie Cross; partner, Eric Tanaka; and CEO, Pamela Hinckley, who lead that team.

There have been many Dahlia bakers, bread chefs, and pastry chefs over the years, and I thank each of them for the colorful history and tasty generosity in contributing to this book.

Cheers,

Tom Douglas

index

Note: Page references in *italics* indicate photographs of recipes.

Learn how to cook—try new recipes, learn from your mistakes,
be fearless, and above all have fun!

—JULIA CHILD